SACRED Harmony,

or a choice Collection of

Psalms and Hymns.

Set to Music

in two and three Parts, for

the Voice, Harpsichord & Organ.

Praise him in his holiness Praise him in his greatness

Let all things that hath breath, Praise the Lord

SACRED HARMONY

or a choice Collection of

Psalms and Hymns

Set to Music
in two and three Parts for
the Voice, Harpsichord & Organ

Published by
John Wesley

SACRED HARMONY

or a choice Collection of

Psalms and Hymns

Set to Music
in two and three Parts for
the Voice, Harpsichord & Organ

Published by
John Wesley

A Facsimile Edition
with
Introduction and Critical Notes
by
S T Kimbrough, Jr. *(General Editor & Texts)*
Carlton R. Young *(Music Editor)*
Charles A. Green *(Assistant Editor)*

A Facsimile of the First Edition
London, n.p., 1780

The Charles Wesley Society Series

RESOURCE *Publications* • Eugene, Oregon

SACRED HARMONY
or a choice Collection of Psalms and Hymns, Set to Music in two and three Parts for the Voice, Harpsichord & Organ

Copyright © 2020 S T Kimbrough, Jr. and Carlton R. Young. All rights reserved. Except for brief quotations in critical publications or reviews, no part of this book may be reproduced in any manner without prior written permission from the publisher. Write: Permissions, Wipf and Stock Publishers, 199 W. 8th Ave., Suite 3, Eugene, OR 97401.

Resource Publications
An Imprint of Wipf and Stock Publishers
199 W. 8th Ave., Suite 3
Eugene, OR 97401

www.wipfandstock.com

PAPERBACK ISBN: 978-1-5326-9689-3
HARDCOVER ISBN: 978-1-5326-9690-9
EBOOK ISBN: 978-1-5326-9691-6

Manufactured in the U.S.A. 01/07/20

Facsimile Reprint Number 10

The Charles Wesley Society
General Editor and texts, S T Kimbrough, Jr.
Music Editor, Carlton R. Young
Assistant Editor, Charles A. Green

The Charles Wesley Society Series
Facsimile Editions with Critical Notes

John Wesley's First Tune Book: A Collection of Tunes Set to Music, As they are commonly Sung at the Foundery, 1742

John Wesley's Second Tune Book: Select Hymns: with Tunes Annext: Designed chiefly for the Use of the People Called Methodists

John Wesley's Third Tune Book: Sacred Harmony or a Choice Collection of Hymns and Tunes Set to Music in two and three Parts for the Voice, Harpsichord and Organ

Contents of the Facsimile Reprint of *Sacred Harmony* 1780

Acknowledgments	7
Technical Matters	9
List of Abbreviations	11
Introduction	13
John Wesley's Three Tune Books	13
Printings of *Sacred Harmony*	14
Provenance of the Philadelphia Copy of *SH* 1780	16
Contents	16
Flaws in *SH* 1780	17
The Hymn Texts	19
The Music of *SH* 1780	45
The Hymn Tunes	51
Facsimile Reprint of *SH* 1780	1
Index (of Tunes)	2
Hymns 1–348	8
Index (of First Lines)	350
Appendix A: Flyleaf with John Wesley's Autograph and Date	431
Appendix B: John Wesley's Notes in *SH* 1780	433
Appendix C: Index of First Lines in *SH* 1780 with Comparisons to *FC* 1742 and *SH* 1761	435
Appendix D: Examples of the Tune SACRAMENT in *HS* 1754, *SH* 1761, and *SH* 1780	439
Appendix E: Cover of 1789 edition	441
Appendix F: Cover and Preface of 1822 edition	442
Selected Bibliography	445

---

[1] The page numbers in the right hand column refer to the consecutive pagination of this volume, except for the page numbers of the facsimile itself which are retained from the January-1780 printing.

Acknowledgments

The Charles Wesley Society expresses deep appreciation to Old St. George's United Methodist Church, Philadelphia, PA, for permission to reprint the copy of *Sacred Harmony* 1780 with John Wesley's autograph and personal notes from its archives, and particularly to Ms. Donna Miller for her assistance in this matter. In addition, the Society expresses its gratitude to Abingdon Press for permission to reprint tune commentaries previously printed in volume 7 of *The Works of John Wesley*. Finally, the editors are grateful for the aid of Timothy Binkley, archivist, The Bridwell Library, Perkins School of Theology, Southern Methodist University, Dallas, TX, and to Martin V. Clarke, Lecturer in Music, The Open University, Kents Hill, UK.

Technical Matters

1. *Musically unscored texts*

Not all of the texts are musically scored in *SH* 1780. When a hymn text appears only as a text block, generally it is in the same meter as the immediately preceding musically scored text and is therefore understood to be sung to that tune.

2. *John Wesley's editing of hymns*

There are instances in which John Wesley has drawn a line through a repeated section or lines of a hymn indicating he prefers the tune without the repetition of the deleted section. He also makes notations throughout the volume where he has decided on a tune different from the one printed for a text. Hence, he writes the name of the new tune choice in the margin or on the score and often draws a line through the printed tune name. Sometimes he indicates that an entire hymn should be deleted by placing a delete sign in the margin or by drawing a straight line through the entire hymn. Occasionally he also notes that a hymn should be inserted in a different place in the volume, e.g., on page 264, Hymn 105, he has written the note "After Bradford" p. 255.

There are occasional spelling corrections by John Wesley, e.g., p. 334, Hymn 126, where he corrects the misspelling of the tune name: "Chesunt" = "Cheshunt".

3. *Incorrect Binding of Pages*

There is an incorrect double binding of pages 341–344. Hence, after page 344 appears the second time, there follows the correct consecutive pagination to the end of the volume.

4. *Pagination*

There are three numbers of importance: the number for each text, the number for each hymn tune, and the consecutive page numbers for the entire volume at the center bottom of each page.

5. *Three additional errors*

a. On page 48 the hymn text beginning "Come thou high and lofty Lord" is numbered Hymn 26.
b. On page 50 the tune HOTHAM beginning with the hymn text beginning "Jesu lover of my soul" is also numbered Hymn 26.
c. The tune name YORKSHIRE is omitted on page 78 where the tune is printed. Hence, it is written in by hand.

List of Abbreviations

AM = *Arminian Magazine*.
CPH 1737 = *A Collection of Psalms and Hymns*. Charlestown: Timothy, 1737.
CPH 1738 = *A Collection of Psalms and Hymns*. London: [Bowyer for Hutton], 1738.
CPH 1741 = *A Collection of Psalms and Hymns*. London: Strahan, 1741.
CPH 1743 = *A Collection of Psalms and Hymns*, 2nd edition, enlarged. London: Strahan, 1743.
FC 1742 = *A Collection of Tunes, Set to Music, As they are commonly Sung at the Foundery*. London: A. Pearson, 1742.
FH 1746 = *Funeral Hymns*. [London: Strahan, 1746].
FH 1759 = *Funeral Hymns*. London [Strahan], 1759.
HAD 1746 = *Hymns for Ascension-Day*. Bristol: Farley, 1746.
HGEL 1742 = *Hymns on God's Everlasting Love*. London: Strahan, 1742.
HGF 1746 = *Hymns on the Great Festivals, and other Occasions*. London: for M. Cooper, 1746.
HIM 1758 = *Hymns of Intercession for all Mankind*. Bristol: Farley, 1758.
HLR 1746 = *Hymns for Our Lord's Resurrection*. London: Strahan, 1746.
HLS 1745 = *Hymns on the Lord's Supper*. Bristol: Farley, 1745.
HNYD 1750 = *Hymns for New Year's Day, 1750*. Bristol: Farley, [1749].
HOE 1750 [Pt. I] = *Hymns occasioned by the Earthquake, March 8, 1750* [Pt. I]. London: [Strahan], 1750.
HOE 1750 [Pt. II] = *Hymns occasioned by the Earthquake, March 8, 1750* [Pt. II]. London: [Strahan], 1750.
HOE, Pt. II (1756) = *Hymns occasioned by the Earthquake, March 8, 1750, Pt. II; to which are added an Hymn for the English in America, and another for the Year 1756*. 2nd edn. Bristol: Farley, 1756.
HS 1754 = Butts, Thomas, *Harmonia Sacra; or, a choice selection of Psalm and Hymn tunes*. London: n.p., ca. 1754.
HSP 1739 = *Hymns and Sacred Poems*. London: Strahan, 1739.
HSP 1740 = *Hymns and Sacred Poems*. London: Strahan, 1740.
HSP 1742 = *Hymns and Sacred Poems*. Bristol: Farley, 1742.
HSP 1749 [+ vol. & page number(s)] = *Hymns and Sacred Poems*, 2 vols. Bristol: Farley, 1749.
HTTP 1744 = *Hymns for Times of Trouble and Persecution*. [London: Strahan, 1744].
IH 1758 = *Hymns of Intercession for all Mankind*. Bristol: Farley, 1758.
JWW = *The Works of John Wesley*. Editors, Frank Baker, Richard P. Heitzenrater, Randy Maddox. Nashville: Abingdon, 1983. Originally published: Oxford: Clarendon Press: Oxford: New York: Oxford University, 1983.

PCWS [+ vol., year, & page number(s)] = *Proceedings of The Charles Wesley Society.*

PWHS [+ vol., year, & page number(s)] = *Proceedings of the Wesley Historical Society.*

RH 1747 = *Hymns for those that seek, and those that have Redemption in the Blood of Christ.* London: Strahan, 1747.

SH 1761 = Wesley, John, *Select Hymns with Tunes Annext: Designed Chiefly for the Use of the People Called Methodists.* London: n.p., 1761.

SH 1780 = Wesley, John, *Sacred Harmony.* London, n.p., 1780.

SM 1765, 1770, 1771 = *Sacred Melody,* the title given to the tune sections of the 1765, 1770, 1771 editions of *SH* 1761.

WH 1746 = *Whitsunday Hymns* (1746) (subtitle); original full title is *Hymns of Petition and Thanksgiving for the Promise of the Father.* Bristol: Farley, 1746.

Introduction

While Charles Wesley was a prolific writer of hymns, his brother John was on a constant quest for the best tunes to fit the texts of his brother, as well as the texts of scores of other authors. Strongly influenced by the singing tradition of the Moravians, which he first experienced on board ship during his voyage to America in 1735, he linked numerous tunes from continental Europe and Great Britain with English-language texts and textual translations. In addition, he and Charles favored a few meters of tunes that were essentially unknown in English-language hymnody but were well known in Germany and central Europe.

John Wesley's Three Tune Books

John published three collections of tunes beginning in 1742 with *A Collection of Tunes Set to Music, As they are commonly Sung at the Foundery*.[1] The second collection of tunes was published nineteen years later: *Select Hymns with Tunes Annext: Designed Chiefly for the Use of the People Called Methodists* (1761). It was a much-expanded, music-engraved volume when compared to the 1742 music type-set publication, and it included three sections: (1) the hymn texts in a block format numbered in sequence; (2) "The Gamut, or Scale of Music," a simple or abbreviated introduction to music theory; (3) the hymn tunes numbered in sequence generally with the first stanza interlined with the music.[2]

The third collection of tunes by John Wesley was titled *Sacred Harmony* (1780).[3] It was intended as a companion to the 1780 texts-only publication *A Collection of Hymns for the Use of the People Called Methodists*.[4] The full title of *SH* 1780 reveals immediately a major difference of this tune collection from the two published previously by John Wesley. It reads *Sacred Harmony, or a choice Collection of Psalms and Hymns Set to Music in two or three parts for the Voice, Harpsichord & Organ*. The previous tune collections were prepared only for monodic singing, i.e., music with only one melodic line, a single voice part. This was very much like an early baroque style with one singer and continuo ccompaniment. Early on, John Wesley expressed his preference for this style of

---

[1] See the facsimile reprint of this volume with critical notes by S T Kimbrough, Jr., and Carlton R. Young, published in 2011 by The Charles Wesley Society titled *John Wesley's First Tune Book: A Collection of Tunes Set to Music. As they are commonly Sung at the Foundery.*

[2] The tune sections of the 1765, 1770, and 1773 editions of *SH* 1761 were titled *Sacred Melody*, and were also published separately. For commentary on *Sacred Melody* see Martin V. Clarke, unpublished PhD dissertation, "John Wesley and Methodist Music in the Eighteenth Century: Principles and Practice." pp. 273–93.

[3] A copy of *SH* 1780 has been digitized by IMSLP/Petrucci Music Libary and is available online at http://hz.imslp.info/files/imglnks/usimg/7/77/IMSLP462314-PMLP750690-SacredHarmonyHymnal_wesley_1781.pdf.

[4] Carlton R. Young stresses that "In 1876 *Sacred Harmony* became the first Methodist tune collection to serve one hymnal when, beginning with the fifth edition of his 1780 *Collection*, Wesley put a tune name from *Sacred Harmony* over each text." Young, *Music of the Heart*, 79.

singing,[5] especially for congregations. However, by 1780 he had changed his view, perhaps influenced by the vocal and the choral styles of singing which George F. Handel popularized in his oratorios. In fact, on the cover of *SH* 1780 there is a printed example of a hymn to be sung in two parts. The present writers' view is it was essentially published for Methodists who increasingly sang harmonized/accompanied versions of the tunes in *SH* 1761, probably playing/singing them from Butts' *Harmonia Sacra, or A Choice Collection of Psalm and Hymn Tunes* (1754), which according to Baker and Beckerlegge, was sold at the Foundery until at least 1777.[6]

The only front matter in *SH* 1780 is an alphabetical index of tunes; however, many tune names are out of sequence. Immediately following this index begins the hymn sequence of #1 to #128. The volume concludes with an alphabetical index of the first lines of each hymn. This index also is flawed by numerous first lines being out of alphabetical sequence.

One of the things *SH* 1761 has in common with *SH* 1780 is that both publications often used a single tune for more than one text. Appendices at the conclusion of this volume indicate the texts and tunes that are common throughout the three collections of tunes and those that are peculiar to one or more collections.

Printings of SH 1780

According to Frank Baker's *Union Catalogue*[7] there were apparently five printings of *SH* 1780.[8] Baker states that it "was first published January 1780."[9] There is an existing copy with John Wesley's autograph with the date of Janu. 10, 1780 in his own hand, which is used for this facsimile reprint. Baker lists four additional printings which he labeled [A], [B], [C], and [D]. He suggests the date of 1780? for [A] whose engraver is "T. Bennet Sculp. Holborn Hill." No dates are suggested for [B], [C], and [D]. The engraver for [C] and [D] is "G. Maund sculpt/(FINIS)." No engraver is indicated for [B]. The Wesley-autographed edition and [A] and [B] all have the same pagination: i–vi and 2–349. [C] and [D]

---

[5] John Wesley expressed his preference for the use of only the melody line in his *Thoughts on the Power of Music*. "It is this counterpoint, it is harmony (so-called) which destroys the power of music. And if ever this should be banished from our composition, if ever we should return to the simplicity and melody of the ancients, then the effects of our music will be as surprising as any that were wrought by theirs, yea, perhaps they will be as much greater as modern instruments are more excellent than those of the ancients." *The Works of the Rev. John Wesley, A.M.* (1872) 13:473. Carlton R. Young notes, however, "For all his complaining about counterpoint, it is used in the anthems that [John] Wesley included in the 1788 edition of *Sacred Harmony*." *Music of the Heart*, 91.

[6] *Works* 7:739.

[7] Baker, *A Union Catalogue*, 164.

[8] The title of Wesley's *SH* 1780 is obviously dependent on the title of Butts' volume: *HS* 1754. The popularity and influence of *SH* 1780 is in part evidenced by the inclusion of the words "sacred harmony" in the titles of 76 tune collections from 1780 to 1820. See, Nicholas Temperley, "Source's Title contains 'sacred harmony'" in *Hymn Tune Index*, available online at: http://hymntune.library.uiuc.edu/SourceTitle.asp.

[9] Baker, *A Union Catalogue*, 164.

have the same pagination for the musically set pages (2–157) but vary in the opening pages i–iv [C] and i [D]. No prices are indicated for [A] and [B] but for [C] "Price two shillings and six pence" and for [D] "Price 4s. bound in Calf." Though Richard Green does not specifically date [C] and [D] ca. 1790, this would be a plausible date since [D] states that it was printed "for Whitfield." Green comments, "As Whitfield became Book-Steward in 1789, one of these, and probably the other, was not issued until after that date."[10]

The Wesley autographed printing of 1780 and [A], [B], [C], and [D] were probably published during John Wesley's lifetime. There are two later editions in the nineteenth century but they are not included in this study.

There has been considerable speculation regarding the year of the first printing of *SH* 1780. Richard Green surmised: "The most careful inquiry has led to the belief that it was not published until 1781."[11] He summarizes a number of date suggestions, even as early as 1761 by George Osborn, but appears to give credence to the date 1781 supported by William Sugden and C. D. Hardcastle, since seemingly the first announcement of *Sacred Harmony* appeared on the cover of the *Arminian Magazine* in 1781. Carlton R. Young has suggested that Nicholas Temperley has followed Green's proposal of the year 1781 as the most probable date of the first printing. Green's citation could not be verified by Timothy Binkley, Archivist, who searched the annual editions of *AM* held by the Bridwell Library of Southern Methodist University in Dallas, Texas.[12] Marvin V. Clarke suggests the original monthly issues may have had a soft cover bearing advertisements, which was considered unnecessary to include when binding issues together as an annual edition.[13]

Among the list of items located in various places in the USA that should be of interest to members of the Wesley Historical Society is the following statement in the 1937-issue of *PWHS*: "Philadelphia: . . . 'Sacred Harmony,' bound with autograph of John Wesley, Jan. 10, 1780."[14] Interestingly there is no mention of this citation or the autographed volume in Frank Baker's *Union Catalogue*, though he perhaps knew of it since he states specifically that it "was first published in January 1780." Nonetheless, he provides no exact evidence for this date.

In 1822 a carefully revised and corrected edition of 1789 printing[15] of *SH* 1780 was published by John Wesley's nephew, Charles Wesley, Jr., Esq. Organist to his Majesty: *Sacred Harmony, a set of Tunes Collected by the late Rev. John Wesley, For the Congregations in his Connexion*, 1822.[16]

---

[10] Green, *A Bibliography . . . of the Brothers Wesley*, 214.
[11] Green, *A Bibliography . . . of the Brothers Wesley*, 214.
[12] Email to Carlton R. Young, August 7, 2017.
[13] Email to Carlton R. Young, August 22, 2017).
[14] *PWHS*, 21 (1937): 92.
[15] For a digital copy of the 1789 printing see https://babel.hathitrust.org/cgi/pt?id=uiuc.7698936;view=1up;seq=19.
[16] Preface dated November 3, 1821.

Provenance of SH 1780

The copy used for this facsimile reprint is the one that bears the autograph of John Wesley and the date of Janu. 10, 1780 on an opening flyleaf. It is housed in the archives of Old St. George's United Methodist Church in Philadelphia, PA. The Charles Wesley Society expresses sincere gratitude to that church for the permission to use a copy of that volume for this facsimile reprint. Attached to the volume is also a document, which describes in some detail how this first printing of *SH* 1780 made its way to Philadelphia. The text of the document reads as follows:

> This book came into my possession about one year previous to my leaving England, which was in November 1793, under the following circumstances. When in that country I resided in London, Mr Charles Paramore printer was indebted to me a considerable amount, when he failed, being unable to pay me he gave me a number of Books among them was this one—being the manuscript (in Mr John Wesley's own hand writing) from which Mr Paramore the Elder printed the First Edition of Methodist Hymns [i.e. *A Collection of Hymns for the Use of the People Called Methodists,* 1780]. It has been in my possession over fifty-five years.
> Philadelphia 15 June 1848.   John Brown
>
> Along with the above I received a printed copy of the same (5th Edition) and "Sacred Harmony" with John Wesley's name written by himself in the first leaf with the date Jan 10th 1780.   John Brown

Contents

[A] and [B] have essentially the same format and pagination. After the title page, they begin with an index of tunes followed at the conclusion of the facsimile by an index of first lines. The former lists the page number on which the tune appears and the latter provides the page number and hymn number of the text. There is no metrical index. Generally, one stanza is interlined with the music unless the length of the tune requires the inclusion of a second stanza or the repetition of words or phrases. The remainder of the selected stanzas of a hymn appears in text blocks following the musical setting. Where possible John Wesley included the texts of entire hymns but occasionally he selected stanzas, particularly from longer hymn texts. Page numbers are in Arabic numerals and the hymn numbers in Roman numerals. Tune names appear on the upper left-hand side of the page above the first musical staff, treble clef, and key designation. There is a total of 120 tunes and 128 hymn texts in [A] and [B].

[C] and [D] are shorter versions of [A] and [B]. They were published in a much smaller size and with a different title page, which bears the same title as the earlier versions. After the title page, there is an index of tunes but no index of first lines. The order of the tunes varies slightly from [A] and [B]. [C] and [D] omit four tunes from [A] and [B] and add six new ones. Usually one stanza, and in some instances two, if required by the length of the tune, are interlined with the music. However, no text blocks of additional stanzas are included. Hence, this seems to have been an attempt to provide the tunes in the most economical space. The pages are numbered but unfortunately the tunes are not numbered and occasionally more than one tune appears on the same page. There are 122 tunes and 130 hymn texts in [C] and [D].

Flaws in SH 1780

The copy used for this facsimile reprint presents a significant problem. It includes no pages numbered 337, 338, 339, and 340. The numbering skips from 336 to 341. Hymn 126, "The voice of my beloved" begins on page 334 and covers three pages [334, 335, 336]. However, the tune stops abruptly before it ends at the bottom of page 336. Page 336 is followed by a page 341. It includes stanzas two and three of Hymn 126. Also, the tune for Hymn 126 is incomplete.

At the bottom of the page numbered 341 there is one stanza numbered Hymn 127. It is in the same meter as Hymn 126 and it may be assumed that John Wesley meant for it to be sung to the same tune as Hymn 126, since there is no additional tune for Hymn 127.

On the next page numbered 342 the tune for Hymn 128, "Before Jehovah's awful throne" begins. The tune for this hymn continues on pages 343 and 344 but ends abruptly without conclusion at the end of the page numbered 344.[17] The next page is numbered once again 341 and is a repetition of the previous page numbered 341. Again Hymn 128 begins on the following page that is numbered 342. This time Hymn 128 continues to its appropriate ending on page 349. One can but assume that this is a printer's binding mistake.

There appears to be more than one printing in the first twelve to sixteen months of the publication of *SH* 1780. The Philadelphia copy used for this publication unquestionably has an authentic autograph of John Wesley with the date Janu. 10, 1780 also in his hand. There is no engraver listed on the final page of this volume and no listing of the printer or date. The only date is that supplied by John Wesley.

In Frank Baker's *Union Catalogue* there are copies of *SH* 1780 listed in four categories: [A], [B], [C], [D]. [A] includes the engraver "T. Bennett Sculp. Holborn Hill" at the end. The Methodist Archives library at Drew University has two copies that list this engraver at the end. [B] lists no engraver. [C] & [D] list at the end "G: Maud sculpt. / (FINIS)." The editors of this volume suspect that the Philadelphia copy was a flawed first printing and during the same year or early 1781 there was a second printing, which would be Baker's [A]. This would mean that the flawed copy (Philadelphia) is not listed in Baker, but is mentioned in Green's bibliography.

---

[17] The tune for Hymn 127 is incomplete, as is the conclusion to Hymn 126.

The Texts of *Sacred Harmony* (1780)[1] in Alphabetical Order

"Ah lovely appearance of death" (Hymn LXXXII: 191–93; FUNERAL) by Charles Wesley was first published in *FH* 1746, 7–8, Hymn V with the title "On Sight of a Corpse" and six stanzas of eight lines. It appeared also in *HGF* 1746, 56–58, as Hymn XXII, with the title "Over the Corpse of a Believer" and six stanzas of eight lines. There are a few variants in the *HGF* 1746 version, though they were probably not made by Charles Wesley. *SH* 1780 includes the six stanzas as in *FH* 1746 with a few differences in punctuation.

"Ah tell us no more" (Hymn V: 8–9; SACRAMENT) by Charles Wesley was first published in *HLS* 1745, 78–80, Hymn XCII, with twelve stanzas of four lines. *SH* 1780 includes ten stanzas of the original (1–3, 5–7, 9–12).

"Ah woe is me constrain'd to dwell" (Hymn XLIX: 105–07; WEDNESBURY) by Charles Wesley was first published in *HTTP* 1744, 24–25, Hymn II, with twelve stanzas of four lines. *SH* 1780 includes stanzas 1–10 as in *HTTP* 1744 with the exceptions of some differences in punctuation. In addition, the original stanzas 1–10 are formatted as five stanzas of eight lines, omitting original stanzas 11 and 12.

"All glory and praise, To the antient of days" (Hymn I: 2; OLD GERMAN) by Charles Wesley was originally published in *HLS* 1745, 130–31, Hymn CLVI, with six stanzas of three lines. *SH* 1780 includes stanzas 1–4 and 6 as in *HLS* 1745 with the exception of some differences in punctuation and spelling (4:2, original "resign" = "risign" in *SH* 1780.

"All hail the true Elijah" (Hymn CXIX: 305–07; TRUE ELIJAH) by Charles Wesley was published in *HLR* 1746, 19–20, with the title "Hymn XVI. For Ascension-Day" and five stanzas of ten lines. *SH* 1780 includes all five stanzas as in *HLR* 1746 with some differences in punctuation and spelling (orig. 1:9, "rapt" = 1:9, "wrapt").

"All thanks to the Lamb, Who gives us to meet" (Hymn CXL: 282–83; NEW-CASTLE) by Charles Wesley was published in *HSP* 1749, 2:323–24, with the title [Hymns for Christian Friends.] "Hymn XLVIII" and seven stanzas of four lines. *SH* 1780 includes all seven stanzas with some differences in punctuation and spelling (3:1 & 2, *HSP* 1749 uses "thro'" while *SH* 1780 uses "through"). There are two lines with variants.

HSP 1749	*SH* 1780
4:3, He hindred our Flying, (His Goodness to shew)	He hinder'd our flying (His goodness to show)
7:4, And open thy Heaven, O Love, in my Heart.	And open thy heaven Of love in my heart.

---

[1] First lines in bold type indicate hymn texts that appear in *SH* 1780 and do not appear in John Wesley's other tune collections. First lines in italics indicate hymns that appear as block texts only in *SH* 1780. After each first line of a hymn in *SH* 1780 there follows in parentheses the hymn number, page number(s), and tune name.

"*All ye that pass by*" (Hymn IV: 6–7; PASSION) by Charles Wesley was published in *HSP* 1749, 1:87–88, with the title "XLII. Invitation to Sinners" and seven stanzas of six lines. *SH* 1780 includes six stanzas of *HSP* 1749: 1–3, 5–7. Stanza 3 in *SH* 1780 combines original stanzas 3 and 4. Original 3:3 "And low at his cross with astonishment fall" = "And lo, at his feet with astonishment fall" in *SH* 1780. Wesley completes stanza 3 with the last three lines of stanza 4.

> 3. He answer'd for all,
> O come at his call;
> And lo, at his feet with astonishment fall.
> [4.] Ye all may receive
> The peace he did leave
> Who made interecession, "My Father forgive."

There are some differences in punctuation.

"*Arise, my soul, arise, Thy Saviour's*" (Hymn LXXXVII: 206–10; WEST-STREET) by Charles Wesley was published in *HSP* 1739, 165–68, with the title "Hymn on the Titles of Christ" and fifteen stanzas of six lines. *SH* 1780 includes all fifteen stanzas as in *HSP* 1739 with some differences in punctuation and two variants: orig. 9:4, "Things in Heav'n, and Earth and Hell" = 9:4, "Things in earth, in heav'n and hell"; orig. 14:6, "Own'd thy Voice; Believ'd, and Lov'd!" = 14:6, "Own'd the voice, believ'd and lov'd."

"*Arm of the Lord, awake, awake*" (Hymn LXXVII: 176–78; ST LUKE'S) by Charles Wesley was published in *HSP* 1739, 222–23, with the title "Isa. li. 9, &c." and five stanzas of eight lines. *SH* 1780 includes the five stanzas as in *HSP* 1739 with some differences in punctuation and spelling (e.g., orig. 2:4, "died" = "dy'd"; orig. 3:3, "Favourites" = "Fav'rites"; orig. 5:1, "o're" = "o'er." There is one variant: orig. 5:3, "There sighing grief shall weep no more" = "There sighs and griefs shall be no more."

"*Away my unbelieving fear*" (Hymn CXXV: 330–33; LEOMINSTER) by Charles Wesley was published in *HSP* 1742, 138–39, with the title "Habakkuk 3. 17,18,19." and four stanzas of eight lines. *SH* 1780 includes all four stanzas as in *HSP* 1742 with some differences in punctuation and spelling (*HSP* 1742, 2:4, "elude" = *SH* 1780 2:4, "illude" [a change also made in the second edition of 1745]; *SH* 1780 prefers "although" for "altho'" and "dy'd" for "died" in *HSP* 1742). The stanzas of *SH* 1780 in block text are numbered 2 and 3 but should be numbered 3 and 4 since stanzas 1 and 2 are musically scored.

"*Away with our fears*" (Hymn VI: 10–11; DERBY) by Charles Wesley was published in *WH* 1746, 36, Hymn XXXII, with five stanzas of eight lines. *SH* 1780 includes eight stanzas of four lines each, omitting original stanza 4. There are the following variants:

WH 1746	SH 1780
1:2, Our troubles and fears	1:2, Our sorrows and fears
3:3, His comforts impart	5:3, His comfort impart (a change made in the 2nd edition of *WH* 1746 in 1747)
3:4, And set up his Kingdom of Love in the Heart.	5:4, And set up his kingdom of love in our heart.

"Away with our sorrow and fear!" (Hymn LXXXIII: 194–96; SION), by Charles Wesley was published in *FH* 1746, 11–12, Hymn VIII, with five stanzas of eight lines. *SH* 1780 includes the fives stanzas as in *FH* 1746 with some differences in punctuation and two variants: orig. 1:6, "And mount to our native abodes" = "And mount to our native abode"; orig. 1:8, "The palace of angels and gods" = "The palace of angels and God." Wesley follows the respective changes to "abode" in the 4th edition (1765) and to "God" in the 2nd edition (1746).

"Before Jehovah's awful throne" (Hymn CXXVIII: 342–49; THE 100 PSALM) by Isaac Watts was published in *The Psalms of David*, 256–57. It appeared in *CPH* 1737, 5–6, with the title: "Psalm 100" and four stanzas of four lines. *SH* 1780 includes all four stanzas as in *CPH* 1737 with some differences in punctuation. Wesley uses stanzas 2, 3, 5, and 6 of Watts' text. His adaptation of Watts' second stanza is as follows:

Watts	*CPH* 1737 / *SH* 1780
Stz. 2. Nations, attend before his Throne	1. Before Jehovah's awful throne
With solemn Fear, with sacred Joy;	Ye nations, bow with sacred joy
Know that the Lord is God alone;	Know that the Lord is God alone;
He can create, and he destroy.	He can create and he destroy.

"Being of Beings, God of love" (Hymn XLIII: 90–91; BRISTOL) by Charles Wesley was published in *HSP* 1739, 36–37, with the title "Grace after Meat" and five stanzas of four lines. *SH* 1780 includes all stanzas as in *HSP* 1739 with some differences in punctuation.

"Blow ye the trumpet, blow" (Hymn XCI: 219–21; TRUMPET) by Charles Wesley was published in *HNYD* 1750, 6–7, with the hymn number "III" and six stanzas of six lines. *SH* 1780 includes the six stanzas as in *HNYD* 1750.

"Brother in Christ and well-belov'd" (Hymn CXXVIII: 154–55; ISLINGTON, 52–53) by Charles Wesley first appeared in *HSP* 1740, 169–71, with the title "On the Admission of Any Person into the Society" and eight stanzas of four lines.

"Christ, our head gone up on high" (Hymn XXIX: 59; ASCENSION) probably by Charles Wesley was published in *HSP* 1740, 192–94, with the title "The Communion of Saints. Part III. John xvii.20, &c." and seven stanzas of eight lines. *SH* 1780 includes stanzas 1, 2, 5, and 7 as in *HSP* 1740 with some differences in punctuation and two misspellings (orig. 1:2 "Spirit" = "Spirt," and orig. 1:8 "ecchoed" = "echoed" respectively in *SH* 1780.)

"Christ the Lord is ris'n today" (Hymn XXI: 34–37; MACCABEES) by Charles Wesley was published in *HSP* 1739, 209–11, with the title "Hymn for Easter-Day" and eleven stanzas of four lines. *SH* 1780 includes stanzas 1–5 and 10 as in *HSP* 1739 with slight punctuation differences and the following variants: orig. 2:2, "Fought the fight the battle won" = "Fought the fight the battle's won"; orig. 4:3, "Dying once he all doth save" = "Once he died our souls to save." The change to 4:3 was made in the 4th edition (1743) and the 5th edition (1756).

"Clap your hands, ye people all" (Hymn XXIII: 41–43; COOKHAM) by Charles Wesley first appeared in *CPH* 1743, 77–78, with the title "Psalm XLVII" and thirteen stanzas of four lines. *SH* 1780 includes stanzas 1–13 as in *CPH* 1743 with some differences in punctuation and contractions within words. There are two misspellings in *SH* 1780: 3:1, "subde" = "subdue" and 12:1, "God keeps of the hostile lands" = "God keeps off the hostile lands."

"Come, and let us sweetly join" (Hymn XXVII: 53–55; LOVE FEAST) by Charles Wesley was first published in *HSP* 1740, 181–82, with the title "The Love-Feast. Part I" and four stanzas of eight lines. *SH* 1780 includes stanzas 1–4 as in *HSP* 1740 with some differences in punctuation and spelling (orig. 4:1, "Witnesses that Christ hath died" = "Witnesses that Christ hath dy'd").

"Come, desire of nations, come" (Hymn XX: 32–33; PARIS) by Charles Wesley was first published in *HOE* 1750, Part II, 23, Hymn 13, with six stanzas of four lines. *SH* 1780 includes all six stanzas as in *HOE* 1750, with the exception of some differences in punctuation.

"Come, Holy Spirit, heavenly dove" (Hymn XXXVIII: 80–81; CHIMES) by Isaac Watts first appeared in *Hymns and Spiritual Songs*, 159–60 (Book 2, no. 34), with the title "Breathing after the Holy Spirit; or, Fervency of Devotion desir'd" and five stanzas of four lines. John Wesley first included it in *CPH* 1738, 42–43, with the title "XXXIX. Breathing after the Holy Spirit." It appears also in *CPH* 1743, 44–45, with five stanzas of four lines. *SH* 1780 includes all stanzas as in *CPH* 1738 with the exception of some differences in punctuation.

"Come, let us anew" (Hymn VII: 12–13; NEW YEAR'S DAY) by Charles Wesley was originally published in *HNYD* 1750, 9, Hymn V, with three stanzas of eight lines. *SH* 1780 includes all three stanzas as in the first printing except for minor differences in punctuation and a misspelled word (2:8, "yiew" should be "view").

"Come, let us ascend" (Hymn XCIII: 225–27; BUILTH) by Charles Wesley was published in *HSP* 1749, 2:313–14, with the title "[Hymns for Christian Friends. Hymn XLI" and eight stanzas of six lines. *SH* 1780 includes the eight stanzas as in *HSP* 1749 with some differences in punctuation and spelling (orig. 5:2, "glorified" = 5:2, "glorify'd"; orig. 7:6, "beatified" = "beatify'd").

"Come, let us join our chearful songs" (Hymn XLVI: 98–99; CORNISH) by Isaac Watts was published in *Hymns and Spiritual Songs,* 46 (Book 1, no. 62), with the title "Christ Jesus, the Lamb of God, worshipped by all Creation, Rev. 5:11–13." It was published by John Wesley in *CPH* 1738, 34, Hymn XXX with the title "Christ Worship'd by All Creatures" and four stanzas of four lines. *SH* 1780 includes all stanzas as in *CPH* 1738 with the exception of some differences in punctuation and one variant: orig. 2:3, "Worthy the Lamb, our lips reply" = "Worthy the Lamb, our hearts reply." With the change of "lips" to "hearts" John Wesley follows a change made in *CPH* 1743, 136.

"**Come on my partners in distress**" (Hymn XCIV: 228–30; TRAVELLER) by Charles Wesley was published in *HSP* 1749, 2:29–31 with the title "XXII" and eight stanzas of six lines. *SH* 1780 includes the eight stanzas as in *HSP* 1749 with some differences in punctuation.

"*Come thou high and lofty Lord*" (Hymn XXVI: 48–49; FOUNDRY) probably by Charles Wesley was first published in *HSP* 1740, 182–83 with the title "The Love-Feast" Part II and four stanzas of eight lines. *SH* 1780 includes the four stanzas as in *HSP* 1740 with the exception of differences in punctuation and spelling (orig. 4:1, "compleat" = "complete" in *SH* 1780).

"*Come ye that love the Lord*" (Hymn XI: 17; BRENTFORD) by Isaac Watts, *Hymns and Spiritual Songs,* 2nd ed. (1709), 155–57 (Book 2, no. 30). John Wesley adapts the Watts text to eight stanzas, which he published in *CPH* 1737, omitting original stanzas 2, 9. *SH* 1780 includes six stanzas (1–5 and 8) as in *CPH* 1737 with some differences in punctuation. In Watts's 1709 edition the first line reads as follows: "Come, we that love the Lord."

"Eternal depth of love divine" (Hymn LXIV: 148–49; ANGLESEA) by Nikolaus Ludwig von Zinzendorf was published in the *Herrnhut Gesangbuch* 1735, 11–12 (No. 11). The hymn was translated by John Wesley and published in *HSP* 1739, 195–96, with the title "God with us. From the German" and four stanzas of eight lines. *SH* 1780 includes all stanzas as in *HSP* 1739 but formats them as eight stanzas of four lines. There are some differences in punctuation.

"Eternal power, whose high abode" (Hymn LXXI: 162–63; PALMI'S) by Isaac Watts was published in *Horae Lyricae* 159–60. It was published by John Wesley in *CPH* 1738, 45, Hymn XLII, titled "God Exalted Above All Praise" with five stanzas of four lines, omitting Watts' stanza 2. *SH* 1780 includes the five stanzas as in *CPH* 1738 with some differences in punctuation. Watts's stanza 3 becomes stanza 2 in John Wesley's version, but he edits significantly the opening line: Watts orig. 3:1, "The dazzling Beauties whilst he sings" = *SH* 1780, 2:1, "Thee while the first archangel sings." The rest of the stanza remains unchanged.

"Faint is my head, and sick my heart"[2] (Hymn CIX: 275–79; MOURNER'S) by George Herbert was published in his *The Temple. Sacred Poems and Private Ejaculations* 99–101, with the title "Home." John Wesley first published his adaptation of this thirteen-stanza text of Herbert in *HSP* 1739, 70–72, with the title "Home. From the Same" [i.e., Herbert] and thirteen stanzas of six lines. This poem illustrates one of John Wesley's most extensive adaptations of a poem of another author. *SH* 1780 includes the thirteen stanzas as in *HSP* 1739 with some differences in punctuation.

---

[2] See also *The Lord's Songs: a collection of composures in metre, such as have been most used in the late glorious revivals; Dr. Watts' psalms and hymns excepted* (1805), 241.

John Wesley's adaptation & rewrite[3] as it appears in *SH* 1780

Faint is my head, and sick my heart
   While thou dost ever, ever stay!
Fixt in my soul I feel thy dart,
   Groaning I feel it night and day:
Come, Lord, and shew thyself to me,
Or take, O take me up to thee?

Canst thou with-hold thy healing grace?
   So kind lavish of thy blood,
When swiftly trickling down thy face,
   For me the purple current flow'd!
Come, Lord, and shew thyself to me,
Or take, O take me up to thee?

When man was lost, love look'd about,
   To seek what help in earth or sky;
In vain: for none appear'd without;
   The help did in thy bosom lie!
Come, Lord, and shew thyself to me,
Or take, O take me up to thee?

There lay thy son: but left his rest
   Thraldom and mis'ry to remove
From those who glory once possest,
   But wantonly abus'd thy love.
Come, Lord, and shew thyself to me,
Or take, O take me up to thee?

He came—O my Redeemer dear!
   And canst thou after this *be strange?*
Nor yet within my heart appear?
   Can love like thine or *fail, or change?*
Come, Lord, and shew thyself to me,
Or take, O take me up to thee?

But if thou tarriest, why must I?
   My God, what is this world to me?
This world of woe—hence let them fly,
   The clouds that part my soul and thee,
Come, Lord, and shew thyself to me,
Or take, O take me up to thee?

Why should *this weary world* delight,
   Or sense th'immortal Spirit bind?
Why should frail beauty's charms invite,
   The trifling charms of woman-kind?
Come, Lord, and shew thyself to me,
Or take, O take me up to thee?

A sigh thou breath'st into my heart,
   And earthly joys I view with scorn:
Far from my soul, ye dreams depart,

George Herbert's poem "Home"

Come, Lord, my head doth burn, my heart is sick,
   While thou dost ever, ever stay!
Thy long deferrings wound me to the quick,
   My spirit gaspeth night and day.
     O show thyself to me,
     O take me up to thee!

How canst thou stay considering the pace
   The bloud did make, which thou didst waste?
When I beheld it trickling down thy face,
   I never saw thing make such hast,
     O show thyself to me,
     O take me up to thee!

When man was lost, thy pitie lookt about
   To see what help in th' earth or skie:
But there was none, at least no help without:
   The help did in thy bosom lie!
     O show thyself to me,
     O take me up to thee!

There lay thy sonne: and must he leave that nest,
   That hive of sweetnesse, to remove
Thraldome from those, who would not at a feast
   Leave one poore apple for thy love?
     O show thyself to me,
     O take me up to thee!

He did, he came: O my Redeemer deare,
   After all this canst thou be strange?
So many yeares baptiz'd, and not appeare?
   As if thy love could fail or change?
     O show thyself to me,
     O take me up to thee!

Yet if thou stayest still, why must I stay
   My God, what is this world to me,
This world of wo? hence all ye clouds away
   Away; I must get up and see.
     O show thyself to me,
     O take me up to thee!

What is this weary world; this meat and drink,
   That chains us by the teeth so fast?
What is this woman kinde, which I can wink
   Into a blacknesse and distaste?
     O show thyself to me,
     O take me up to thee!

With one small sigh thou gav'st me th' other day
   I blasted all the joyes about me:
And scouling on them as they pin'd away

---

[3] Words in italics indicate where Herbert's wording is generally retained by John Wesley. Wesley's adaptation also appeared in *SH* 1761, Hymn 117, page 116.

Nor mock me with your vain return?
Come, Lord, and shew thyself to me,
Or take, O take me up to thee?

Sorrow, and sin, and loss, and pain,
    Are all that here on earth we see;
Restless, we pant for ease in vain,
    In vain—till ease we find in thee.
Come, Lord, and shew thyself to me,
Or take, O take me up to thee?

Idly we talk of harvests here,
    Eternity our harvest is:
Grace brings the great sabbatic year,
    When ripen'd into glorious bliss.
Come, Lord, and shew thyself to me,
Or take, O take me up to thee?

O loose this frame, life's knot untie,
    That my free soul may use her wing;
Now pinion'd with mortality,
    A weak, entangled, wretched thing!
Come, Lord, and shew thyself to me,
Or take, O take me up to thee?

Why should I longer stay and groan?
    The most of me to heaven is fled:
My thoughts and joys are thither gone;
    To all below I now am dead.
Come, Lord, and shew thyself to me,
Or take, O take me up to thee?

Come, dearest Lord, my soul's desire,
    With eager pantings gasps for home:
Thee, Thee my restless hopes require;
    My flesh and Spirit bid thee come!
Come, Lord, and shew thyself to me,
Or take, O take me up to thee?

Now come again, said I, and flout me.
    O show thyself to me,
    O take me up to thee!

Nothing but drought, and dearth, but bush and break
    Which way so e'er I look, I see
Some may dream merrily, but when they wake,
    They dresse themselves and come to thee.
    O show thyself to me,
    O take me up to thee!

We talk of harvests, there are no such things,
    But when we leave our corn and hay:
There is no fruitful year, but that which brings
    The last and lov'd, though dreadful day.
    O show thyself to me,
    O take me up to thee!

O loose this frame, this knot of man untie!
    That my free soul may use her wing;
Which is now is pinion'd with mortalitie,
    As an intangled, hamper'd thing.
    O show thyself to me,
    O take me up to thee!

What have I left, that I should stay and groan?
    The most of me to heaven is fled:
My thoughts and joyes are all packt up and gone,
    And for their old acquaintance plead.
    O show thyself to me,
    O take me up to thee!

Come dearest Lord, passe not this holy season,
    My flesh and joyes are all packt up and gone,
And ev'n my verse, when by the ryme and reason
    The word is, Stay, sayes ever, Come.
    O show thyself to me,
    O take me up to thee!

"Father, how wide thy glories shine" (Hymn XLVIII: 102–104; ST PAUL'S) by Isaac Watts was published in *Horae Lyricae,* Book 1, 7–9, 1709, 18–19, nine stanzas of four lines. John Wesley published seven stanzas (four lines each) of the hymn in *CPH* 1738, 28, with the title "XXIV. God Glorious, and Sinners Saved." *SH* 1780 includes all seven stanzas as in *CPH* 1738, but formatted as three stanzas of eight lines (i.e., stanzas 1–6) and stanza 7 is combined with the four-line doxology from *HGL* 1742, 56, with the title "[Gloria Patri] VI." *SH* 1780 includes some differences in punctuation and spelling (orig. 1:1, "shines" = "shine"; and orig. 1:4, "thousand" = "thousands." *SH* 1780 includes stanzas 1 and 2 but with misspellings in stanza 1 which ruin the rhyme.

"Father, if justly still we claim" (Hymn LXIII: 145–47; ANGELS SONG) by Henry More was originally published in *Divine Dialogues, with Divine Hymns,* 504–06, with the title "An Hymn Upon the Descent of the Holy Ghost at the day of Pentecost." John Wesley adapted a hymn from More's text in fifteen stanzas of four lines, which were published in *HSP* 1739, 185–88, with the title "On the Descent of the Holy Ghost at Pentecost." The stanza beginning "Father, if justly still we claim" is the first line of stanza six of Wesley's adaptation. *SH* 1780 includes stanzas 6–15 with some differences in punctuation and one variant: orig. 13:1, "Like mighty wind, or torrent fierce" = 8:1, "Like mighty winds, or torrents fierce" (*SH* 1780).

"Father of lights, from whom proceeds" (Hymn C: 248–50; FRANKFORT) by Charles Wesley was published in *HSP* 1739, 85–86, with the title "A Prayer under Convictions" and eight stanzas of six lines. *SH* 1780 includes the eight stanzas as in *HSP* 1739 with some differences in punctuation, spelling (orig. 8:4, "Extasy" = 8:4, "extacy"), and the following variants: orig. 1:1, "Father of Light from whom proceeds" = 1:1, "Father of lights, from whom proceeds"; orig. 5:4, "A Heart to mourn, a Heart to pray" = 5:4, "An heart to mourn, an heart to pray."

"Father, Son, and Holy Ghost" (Hymn XCII: 222–24; DEDICATION) by Charles Wesley was published in *HLS* 1745, 129–130, Hymn CLV with six stanzas of six lines. *SH* 1780 includes four (1, 3, 4, and 6) of the six stanzas as they appear in *HLS* 1745 with some differences in punctuation.

"From whence these dire portents around" (Hymn XLI: 86–87; WENVO) by Samuel Wesley, Jr., was published in his *Poems on Several Occasions* (1736), 136–37, with the title "On the Passion of our Saviour." It also appeared the following year in *CPH* 1737, 44–45, Hymn VI titled "On the Crucifixion" with six stanzas of four lines. *SH* 1780 includes all six stanzas as in *CPH* 1737 with some differences in punctuation and spelling (orig. 4:1, "Streeming" = "streaming"; orig. 5:2, "born" = "borne").

"Glory be to God on high" (Hymn XII: 38–40; SALISBURY) by Charles Wesley was first published in *HSP* 1739, 128–29 and titled "Glory be to God on high, etc." with seven stanzas of four lines and is based on the "Gloria" in the service of Holy Communion in the BCP. *SH* 1780 includes all seven stanzas as in *HSP* 1739 with the addition of "Hallelujah" at the end of each line and some differences in punctuation.

"God of all grace and majesty" (Hymn XLV: 95–97; BROCHMER) by Charles Wesley first appeared in *HSP* 1749, 2:229–30, Hymn CLXVI with the title "For the Fear of God" and five stanzas of eight lines. *SH* 1780 includes all stanzas as in *HSP* 1749 with some differences in punctuation.

"God of all redeeming grace" (Hymn XXV: 46–48; FOUNDRY) by Charles Wesley was first published in *HLS* 1745, 117–18, Hymn CXXXIX, with four stanzas of four lines. *SH* 1780 includes all four stanzas as in *HLS* 1745, but formats them as two stanzas of eight lines.

"God of my life, whose gracious pow'r" (Hymn LXXIII: 166–67; WELLING) by Charles Wesley was published in *HSP* 1740, 149–151, with the title "At the Approach of Temptation" and fifteen stanzas of four lines. *SH* 1780 includes four stanzas of four lines (1–2, 14–15) as in *HSP* 1740, with the exception of some differences in punctuation.

"God of unexampled grace" (Hymn CXIV: 290–91; AMSTERDAM) by Charles Wesley was published in *HLS* 1745, 16–18, Hymn XXI, with nine stanzas of eight lines. *SH* 1780 includes only stanzas 1–3 as they appear in *HLS* 1745 with some differences in punctuation.

"Hail, Father, whose creating call" (Hymn XLVII: 100–101; BROOKS) by Samuel Wesley, Jr., was first published in *Weekly Miscellany,* 85 (July 27, 1734), 2, with the title "Hymn to God the Father." It was reprinted in his *Poems on Several Occasions* (1736), 1–3, with the title "An Hymn to God the Father" and six stanzas of four lines. It was published also in *CPH* 1737, 11–12, Hymn XI with the first-published title. *SH* 1780 includes all six stanzas as in *CPH* 1737 but as three stanzas of eight lines with some differences in punctuation and spelling (orig. 2:1, "inthron'd" = "enthron'd").

"Hail, holy, holy, holy Lord" (Hymn LIII: 115–17; TRINITY) by Samuel Wesley, Jr., was first published in *Weekly Miscellany,* 89 (August 24, 1734), 2, with the title "Hymn to the Trinity" and reprinted in *Poems on Several Occasions* (1736), 6–7, with the title "An Hymn to the Trinity, Three Persons and One God" and seven stanzas of four lines. It was also published in *CPH* 1737, 14, Hymn XIV, with the title "Hymn to the Trinity" and six stanzas, omitting original stanza 3. *SH* 1780 includes all stanzas as in *CPH* 1737, but formatted as three stanzas of eight lines with some differences of punctuation and spelling (orig. 3:4, "angelic" = "angelick") and one variant: orig. 2:2, "E'er time its round began" = "E'er time its course began." Samuel Wesley originally published "E'er time its race began."

"Hail the day that sees him rise" (Hymn XXVIII: 56–58; ASCENSION) was first published in *HSP* 1739, 211–13, with the title: "Hymn for Ascension-Day" and ten stanzas of four lines. *SH* 1780 includes all of the stanzas of *HSP* 1739 but as five stanzas of eight lines. There are some differences in punctuation and the following variants:

HSP 1739	*SH* 1780
3:3, Conqueror over Death and Sin	Conqueror o'er death, hell, and sin
6:1–3, Still for us his death he pleads;	Still for us he intercedes,
Prevalent, he intercedes;	Prevalent his death he pleads;
Near himself prepares our place,	Next himself prepares our place,
10:2, Partners of thy endless reign	Partners of thine endless reign

"Happy Magdalen, to whom" (Hymn XXX: 60–63; MAGDALEN) by Charles Wesley was first published in *HLR* 1746, 4–5, Hymn III, with seven stanzas of eight lines. The hymn also appears in *HGF* 1746, 23–26, Hymn 10. *SH* 1780 includes all seven stanzas as in *HLR* 1746 with the exception of some punctuation variations, e.g., the absence of a question mark at the end of 1:4, and a few spelling discrepancies (orig. 3:2, "Farther" = "Further"; orig. 4:2, "despair" = "dispair"; and orig. 6:4, "grace" = "graice").

"Happy soul, that safe from harms" (Hymn XXXI: 64–67; ARNE) by Charles Wesley was first published in *HSP* 1749, 2:151–52, Hymn IV, with the title "[Hymns for Those that Wait for Full Redemption.] Hymn IV, and ten stanzas of four lines. *SH* 1780 includes four stanzas of eight lines (1–2, 5–6, 7–8, and 9–10) as in *HSP* 1749 with the exception of some differences in punctuation. The entire original stanza 2 is musically scored twice and the first time through there is one variant: orig. 2:2, "Jesus takes his every care" = "Jesus marks his every care"; however, the second time through the original verb "takes" is used.

"Happy soul, thy days are ended" (Hymn LV: 122–23; EPWORTH) by Charles Wesley was published in *HSP* 1749, 2:75, with the title "[Desiring Death.] Hymn XII. For One Departing," with two stanzas of eight lines. *SH* 1780 includes both stanzas as in *HSP* 1749, but they are formatted as four stanzas of four lines.

"Happy the man who finds the grace" (Hymn LXI: 139–41; CAMBRIDGE) by Charles Wesley was first published in *RH* 1747, 25–26, Hymn XVIII with the title "Prov[erbs] iii. 13, &c. To: 'Sinners, obey the gospel-word'" (i.e., to Lampe's tune in *HGF* 1746) and nine stanzas of four lines. *SH* 1780 includes all nine stanzas as in *RH* 1747 with some differences in punctuation.

"He comes, he comes, the judge severe" (Hymn LXXVI: 174–75; JUDGMENT) by Charles Wesley was published in *IH* 1758, 30–31, with the title "Hymn XXXVII. The Same" [Thy Kingdom Come] and four stanzas of four lines. *SH* 1780 includes the four stanzas as in *IH* 1758 with some differences in punctuation.

"He dies! the heav'nly lover dies" (Hymn LXXVIII: 179–81; DRESDEN) by Isaac Watts was published in *Horae Lyricae* (1707), 80–81, with the title "Christ Dying, Rising, and Reigning" and six stanzas of four lines. *SH* 1780 includes all six stanzas as in *Horae Lyricae* but formats them as three stanzas of eight lines.

"Head of the Church triumphant" (Hymn CXX: 308–10; DYING STEPHEN) by Charles Wesley was published in *HTT* 1744, 2 ed. (1745), 68–69, with the title "V." in the section additional hymns "For the Year 1745" and four stanzas of eight lines. *SH* 1780 includes all four stanzas as in *HTT* 1744 (1745) with some differences in punctuation and one variant: orig. 3:8, "In thee we shall" = 3:8, "By thee we shall," a change made in *HGF* 1746.

"Holy Lamb, who thee receive" (Hymn XVII: 28–29; SAVANNAH) by Anna Dober (translated by John Wesley). The English translation first appeared in *HSP* 1740, 93–94, and titled "From the Same" [German]. Dober's hymn "Du heiliges Kind" appeared in the *Herrnhut Gesangbuch* (1737), 950–51. Of the original ten stanzas in German John Wesley translated stanzas one through seven and ten into English, i.e., eight stanzas of four lines. *SH* 1780 includes five stanzas (1–4 and 8) as in *HSP* 1740 with the exception of differences in punctuation and one misprint (orig. 2:1, "Jesu, see my pantin breast" = "Jesu, see my panting breast; orig. 2:2, "See, I pant, in thee to rest!" = "See I pant in the to rest" in *SH* 1780).

The Hymn Texts

"How sad our state by nature is" (Hymn XXXIII: 70–71; FETTER LANE) by Isaac Watts first appeared in his *Hymns and Spiritual Songs* (1709), 211–12 (Book 2, no. 90). John Wesley first published the hymn in *CPH* 1737, 52, with the title "XV. Faith in Christ" and six stanzas of four lines. See also *CPH* 1743, 30–31, with the same title. *SH* 1780 includes all stanzas as in *CPH* 1737 with the exception of some punctuation differences and the two variants: orig. 2:2, "Sounds from thy sacred word" = "Sounds from the sacred word"; orig. 4:4, "From crimes of deepest dye" = "From sins of deepest dye."

"I thirst, thou wounded Lamb of God" (Hymn LXV: 150–51; STOCKTON) is a cento of portions of four hymns that appeared in the *Herrnhut Gesangbuch* (1735) translated from the German by John Wesley. Stanzas 1–2 are by Zinzendorf from "Ach! mein verwundter Fürste," No. 1197. Stanzas 3–6 are by Johann Nitschmann from "Du blutiger Versöhner," No. 1201. Stanza 7 is also by Zinzendorf from "Der Gott von unserm Bunde." Stanza 8 is by Anna Nitschmann from "Mein König, deine Liebe," No. 1233 (See *John Wesley and the German Hymn,* 50, 146–48). John Wesley's translation was first published in *HSP* 1740, 74–76, with the title "From the German" and eight stanzas of four lines. Also in *HSS*, 1753. *SH* 1780 includes all eight stanzas as in *HSP* 1740 with some differences in punctuation.

"I'll praise my Maker while I've breath" (Hymn CXXII: 314–17; OLD 113th PSALM TUNE) by Isaac Watts was published in *The Psalms of David* (1719), 384–85, with the title "Psalm CXLVI. as the 113th Psalm. Praise to God for his Goodness and Truth."; in *CPH* 1737, 9–10, with the title [Hymn] "9. Psalm 146" and four stanzas of six lines. *SH* 1780 includes four stanzas (1, 3, 4, and 6) of Watts' original hymn as in *CPH* 1737 with some differences in punctuation and variants. Stanzas 2 and 3 of *SH* 1780 in block texts should be numbered 3 and 4, since stanzas 1 and 2 are musically scored.

Watts	*SH* 1780
1:1, I'll praise my Maker with my Breath	1:1, I'll praise my Maker while I've breath
3:3, And Earth and Seas and all their Train	2:3, And earth and heav'n[4] with all their train
4:1, The Lord hath Eyes to give the Blind	[3]:1, The Lord pours eye-sight on the blind
4:2, The Lord supports the sinking Mind	[3]:2, The Lord supports the fainting mind

There is a misprint in *CPH* 1737, 3:6, "And grants the prisoner sweat release," which was corrected to "sweet" in the *CPH* 1741 printing of the hymn. *SH* 1780 also prints "sweet."

"Infinite Pow'r, Eternal Lord" (Hymn XXXIX: 82–83; LEEDS) by Isaac Watts was published in *Horae Lyricae* (1709), 73–74. John Wesley published it in *CPH* 1738, 74–75, Hymn VII, with the title "The Comparison & Complaint," and stanzas 1–9 of the original, omitting stanza 10. *SH* 1780 includes the nine stanzas as in *CPH* 1738 with the exception of some differences in punctuation and spelling (orig. 5:3, "inslav'd" = "enslav'd"; orig. 7:4, "mold" = "mould.")

"Jesu, Lover of my soul" (Hymn XXVI: 50–52; HOTHAM) by Charles Wesley was first published in *HSP* 1740, 67–68, with the title "In Temptation" and five stanzas of eight lines. *SH* 1780 includes four stanzas (1–2, 4–5) as in *HSP* 1740 with some differences in punctuation.

"Jesu, my Lord attend" (Hymn XII: 18–19; LAMP'S) by Charles Wesley was first published in *RH* 1747, 1–2, Hymn I, with the title "Hymn I. To: 'Father our hearts we lift,'" (i.e., the tune of John Lampe to this text found in *HGF* 1746), and four stanzas of eight lines. *SH* 1780 includes three stanzas (orig. 1, 3 and 4) with two variants: orig. 3:1, "O then impute, impart" = "Come then, impute, impart" in *SH* 1780; orig. 3:6, "I long to testify" = "Grant me to testify" in *SH* 1780.

"Jesu, thou art my righteousness" (Hymn L: 108–109; SPITTLEFIELDS) by Charles Wesley was first published in *HSP* 1740, 95–96 with the title "Christ Our Righteousness" [1 Corinthians 1:30], and six stanzas of four lines. *SH* 1780 combines stanzas 1 and 4, 5 and 6 to form two stanzas of eight lines. The text of *SH* 1780 is essentially as in *HSP* 1740 with some differences in punctuation and two variants: orig. 4:3, "Sprinkle me ever in thy blood" = "Sprinkle me ever with thy blood; orig. 6:4, "And all my soul be love" = "And all my soul is love."

"Jesu, thy blood and righteousness" (Hymn LVII: 127–29; CANON) by Nickolaus Ludwig von Zinzendorf was translated from German by John Wesley and published in *HSP* 1740, 177–81 with the title "The Believer's Triumph. From the German" and twenty-four stanzas of four lines. Zinzendorf's hymn appeared in *Herrnhut Gesangbuch* 1735, 1136 (#1258, and added in *Anhänge* to the 1739 edition). *SH* 1780 includes ten stanzas (1–7, 11, 23–24) as in *HSP* 1740 with some differences in punctuation and spelling (orig. 6:3, "died" = "dy'd"; orig. 7:1, "pretious" = "precious"; and orig. 24:3 "glorious" = "plorious" [a misprint]; orig. 2:3, "Fully thro' these absolv'd I am" = "Fully absolv'd through these I am."

"Jesu, thy boundless love to me" (Hymn CI: 251–55; BRADFORD) is a translation by John Wesley of a hymn by Paul Gerhardt that appeared in the *Herrnhut Gesangbuch* (1737), 24–26, No. 23. Wesley's translation was published in *HSP* 1739, 156–59, with the title: "Living in Christ. From the German" and sixteen stanzas of six lines. *SH* 1780 includes all sixteen stanzas as in *HSP* 1739 with some differences in punctuation, spelling (orig. 16:6, "died" = 16:6, "dy'd"), and two variants. Orig. 3:4, "Where'er thy healing Beams arise" = "Where'er thy healing streams arise." Here John Wesley follows the change to streams made in the 4th (1743) and 5th (1756) editions. Orig. 8:5, "Nor may we ever parted be" = 8:5, "Nor ever may we parted be." Once again he follows the change made in the 4th and 5th editions.

---

[4] *CPH* 1737 uses Watts's phrase "And earth and seas and all their train" and *SH* 1780 changes to Watts 4:1,2.

"Jesus, come, thou hope of glory" (Hymn IX: 15; HAVANT) by Charles Wesley was published in *HSP* 1749, 2:155–56, with the title "[Hymns for Those that Wait for Full Redemption.] Hymn VIII, with nine stanzas of three lines. *SH* 1780 includes seven stanzas (1–3, 5–8) as in *HSP* 1749 with minor differences in punctuation. There is also one variant: orig. 6:5, "Mourn th' astonied Hosts above" = "Mourn th' astonish'd hosts above," which follows a change made in the sixth edition of 1771 and thereafter.

"Jesus drinks the bitter cup" (Hymn CXVI: 296–98; HAMILTON'S) by Charles Wesley was published in *HLS* 1745, 16–18, Hymn XXI. The first line, "Jesus drinks the bitter cup," is the first line of stanza four. The hymn begins "God of unexampled grace" and originally has nine stanzas of eight lines. *SH* 1780 includes six stanzas (4–9) as in *HLS* 1745 with some differences in punctuation and spelling (orig. 8:7, "Worship'd" = 5:7, "Worshipp'd"; orig. 9:8, "quires" = 6:8, "choirs").

"Jesus, in whom the Godhead's rays" (Hymn LXVI: 152–53; ATHLONE) probably by Charles Wesley was published in *HSP* 1740, 68–69, with the title [Matthew 1:21] "He shall save his people from their sins" and six stanzas of four lines. *SH* 1780 includes all six stanzas as in *HSP* 1740 with some differences in punctuation and one variant: orig. 3:1, "Save me from wrath, the plague expell" = "Save me from pride, the plague expel." "Pride" follows the change made in the 1743 edition of *HSP* 1740.

"Jesus, my love, my life, my peace" (Hymn CXXVII: 341; CHESHUNT) by Charles Wesley was published in *SH* 1762, 1:296, No. 936, and is based on the Song of Solomon 2:16, "My beloved is mine, and I am his." *SH* 1780 includes the original single stanza as a block text to be sung to CHESHUNT.

"Lamb of God, whose bleeding love" (Hymn CXVII: 299–301; CALVARY) by Charles Wesley was published in *HLS* 1745, 15, Hymn XX, with four stanzas of eight lines. *SH* 1780 includes all four stanzas as in *HLS* 1745 with some differences in punctuation, two printing errors (2:8 and 3:8, "And bids us go in peace" should be "And bid us go in peace" as in stanzas 1 and 4) and one variant: orig. 1:2, "We thus recall to mind" = 1:2, "We now recall to mind."

"Let heav'n and earth agree" (Hymn LXXXVI: 203–05; MISS EDWIN'S) by Charles Wesley was published in *HGEL* 1742, 31–33 with the title: "Hymn XI" and ten stanzas of six lines. *SH* 1780 includes all ten stanzas as in *HGEL* 1742 with some differences in punctuation and spelling (e.g., orig. 4:3, "musick" = "music"; orig. 8:5,6, "applied" and "justified" = "apply'd" and "justify'd"; orig. 9:5,6, "crucified" and "died" = "crucify'd" and "dy'd."

"Lo, God is here, let us adore" (Hymn XCIX: 245–47; MARIENBORN) by Gerhard Tersteegen was published in the *Herrnhut Gesangbuch* (1737), 515–16, No. 581, and was translated into English by John Wesley and published in *HSP* 1739, 188–89, with the title "Publick Worship. From the German" and six stanzas of six lines. *SH* 1780 includes all six stanzas as in *HSP*

1739 with some differences in punctuation, spelling (orig. 2:2, "quires" = 2:2, "choirs"), and two variants: orig. 1:5, "Who know his Pow'r, his Grace who prove" = 1:5, "Who feel his pow'r, his grace who prove"; orig. 2:4, "Heaven's Hosts their noblest Praises bring" = "Heaven's host their noblest praises bring."

"Lo! He comes with clouds descending" (Hymn LVI: 124–26; OLIVERS) by Charles Wesley was first published in *HIM* 1758, 32–33, with the title "Hymn XXXIX. The Same" [Thy Kingdom Come] and four stanzas of six lines. *SH* 1780 includes the four stanzas as in *HIM* 1758 with some differences in punctuation and spelling (e.g., 3:5, orig. "rapture" = "repture" most certainly a misprint).

"Lord, all I am is known to thee" (Hymn XXXV: 74–75; BEXLY) by Isaac Watts first appeared in *The Psalms of David* (1719), 369–72, with the title "Psalm CXXXIX, First Part. God is Everywhere." John Wesley included it in *CPH* 1738, 48–49 with the title "IV. Psalm CXXXIX, Part I." and five stanzas of four lines. *SH* 1780 includes all stanzas as in *CPH* 1738 with some differences in punctuation and spelling (2:3, orig. "publick" = "public"; 3:1 and 4:3, orig. "lye" = "lie").

"Lord and God of heavenly pow'rs" (Hymn XVIII: 30–31; PLYMOUTH) probably by Charles Wesley was first published in *HSP* 1739, 128, titled "Therefore with Angels, &c." (Preface to the Sanctus in Holy Communion according to the BCP) and three stanzas of four lines. The hymn appeared later in *HLS* 1745, Hymn CLXI. *SH* 1780 includes stanzas 1–3 as in *HLS* 1745 with the exception of punctuation differences and one spelling variant: 1:4, "chant" = "chaunt" in *SH* 1780.

"Lord, if thou the grace impart" (Hymn XIX: 31; PLYMOUTH) by Charles Wesley was published in *CPH* 1741, 2nd edition 1743, with the title "Psalm CXXXI" and five stanzas of four lines. *SH* 1780 includes all five stanzas as in *CPH* 1743 with some differences in punctuation.

"Love divine, all loves excelling" (Hymn CXVIII: 302–04; WESTMINSTER) by Charles Wesley was published in *RH* 1747, 11–12, with the title "Hymn IX. To: 'Jesus, shew us thy salvation,'" [i.e., the tune of John Lampe in *HGF* 1746 for that text], and four stanzas of eight lines. *SH* 1780 includes all four stanzas as in *RH* 1747 with some differences in punctuation.

"My God I am thine" (Hymn II: 3, OLD GERMAN) by Charles Wesley was published in *HSP* 1749, 2:219–20, with the title "[Hymns for Believers.] Hymn XVI," which originally included six stanzas of three lines. In *SH* 1780 all six stanzas of *HSP* 1749 were published with one variant: orig. 2:3, "My heart it doth dance to the sound of his name" = "And my heart doth rejoice at the sound of his Name."

"My soul before thee prostrate lies" (Hymn LXII: 142–44; PUDSEY) by Christian Friedrich Richter appeared in *Herrnhut Gesangbuch* (1735), 724–25, #804. The translation by John Wesley was first published in *CPH* 1737, 56–58, with the title "XX. From the German" and twelve stanzas. It was subsequently published in *HSP* 1739, 94–96, with the title "Hoping for Grace.

From the German" and eleven stanzas of four lines, omitting stanza 4 of *CPH* 1737. *SH* 1780 includes eleven stanzas as in *HSP* 1739 and two variants: orig. 8:1, "Still I do watch and labour still" = 7:1 (*SH* 1780) "Still will I watch and labour still." This change already appeared in *HSP* 1739.

"O for an heart to praise my God" (Hymn XXXVII: 78–79; YORKSHIRE) by Charles Wesley was published in *HSP* 1742, 30–31, with the title "Psalm li. 10. 'Make me a clean heart, O God, and renew a right spirit within me'" and eight stanzas of four lines. *SH* 1780 includes all eight stanzas as in *HSP* 1742 with the exception of some differences in punctuation, e.g., an exclamation mark appears only at the end of line one, whereas in the original one appears at the end of lines two and four.

"O God, my God, my all thou art" (Hymn LXXIV: 168–70; ITALIAN) by Daniel Israel Lopez Laguna was published in a volume he edited, *Espejo fiel de vidas que contiene los Psalmos de David* 1720, 116. John Wesley translated the hymn and published it in *CPH* 1738, 6–7, with the title "Psalm LXIII. From the Spanish," and ten stanzas of four lines and subsequently in *HSP* 1739, 196–98, with the title "God our Portion. From the Spanish," and ten stanzas of four lines. *SH* 1780 includes all ten stanzas as in *CPH* 1738 with some differences in punctuation and spelling (e.g., orig. 2:2, "desert" = "desart") and the following variants: *CPH* 1738, 2:4, "Thy all enliv'ning pow'r display" = "Thine all enliv'ning pow'r display"; 8:4, "I muse on all thy hands have wrought" = "I muse on all thine hands have wrought.

"O God of good th'unfathom'd sea" (Hymn CXXIII: 318–22; YORK) by Johann Scheffler and published in *Herrnhut Gesangbuch*, 1737, 537–38, No. 605, translated by John Wesley and published in *HSP* 1739, 159–61, with the title "God's Love to Mankind. From the same [i.e., from the German]," and eight stanzas of six lines. *SH* 1780 includes the eight stanzas in *HSP* 1739, however, the stanzas of block text are wrongly numbered 2 through 7, but should be numbered 3 through 8, since stanzas 1 and 2 are musically scored. The stanzas appear as in *HSP* 1739 with two variants:

HSP 1739,	*SH* 1780,
2:2, unsufferable	2:2, insufferable
7:3, Sov'reign of earth, air, hell, and sky	6:6, Sov'reign of earth, hell, air, and sky

"O God of our forefathers hear" (Hymn CVI: 266–68; NORWICH) by Charles Wesley was published in *HLS* 1745, 106, Hymn CXXV, with four stanzas of six lines. *SH* 1780 includes all four stanzas as in *HLS* 1745 with some differences in punctuation and spelling (orig. 3:1, "thro'" = "through"; orig. 3:4, "died" = "dy'd"; orig. 4:3, "shewn" = "shown"). There are two pronoun variants in orig. 1:3, "To thee thro' Jesus we draw near" = "To thee thro' Jesus I draw near"; orig. 1:5, "In whom thy smiling face we see" = "In whom thy smiling face I see." These changes may have been made in order to conform to the first-person pronoun in orig. 1:6, "In whom thou art well-pleased with me."

"O Jesu, source of calm repose" (Hymn CXXI: 311–13; CANTERBURY), by Johann Freylinghausen published in *Herrnhut Gesangbuch,* 1735, 32–33, #30, stanzas 1, 3–5, 8, 13; translated by John Wesley and first published in *CPH* 1737, 38–39, with the title "XL. From the German," and six stanzas of six lines. The hymn also was published in *HSP* 1739, 181–82, with the title "Christ *protecting and sanctifying. From the same*" [i.e., From the German] with some variants that are included in *SH* 1780. John Wesley corrects the error "Ere" in 2:2,3 to "E'er" in the sense of "before" in *SH* 1780.

CPH 1737	*HSP* 1739 & *SH* 1780
2:5, Did'st not disdain the Virgin's Womb	2:5, Didst not abhor the virgin's womb
5:3, No charms to thee but these are dear	5:3, No charms but these to thee are dear
5:6, But faith and heav'n-born peace are there	5:6, But faith and heav'n-born peace be there
6:5, But still t' adore and praise and love	6:5, But still t' adore, believe and love

"O Jesus, my hope" (Hymn III: 4–6; PASSION) by Charles Wesley was originally published in *HSP* 1749, 1:81–82, Hymn VI, with the title [Penitential Hymns] and six stanzas of six lines. *SH* 1780 includes stanzas 1–2, 5–6 as in *HSP* 1749 with the repetition of the last line in each stanza and some differences in spelling.

"O Lord, incline thy gracious ear" (Hymn XL: 84–85; MANCHESTER) by Charles Wesley was first published in *CPH* 1743, 7–8, with the title "Psalm V," and seven stanzas of eight lines. *SH* 1780 includes eight stanzas of four lines. The first seven stanzas are from *CPH* 1743 as follows: stanzas 1, 2, 6:5–8, and 7. Stanza 8 is a four-line doxology from *HGL* 1742, 56, with the title "[Gloria Patri] VI."

"O Love divine, how sweet thou art" (Hymn XCV: 231–33; CHAPEL) by Charles Wesley was first published in *HGF* 1746, 47–49, and subsequently in *HSP* 1749, 1:58–59, with the title [Desiring to Love.] "Hymn 5," and seven stanzas of six lines. *SH* 1780 includes all seven stanzas as they appear in *HSP* 1749. There are a few variants:

HGF 1746	*HSP* 1749
1:2, When shall I find my longing heart	When shall I find my willing heart
1:4, I thirst, I faint, and die, to prove	I thirst, and faint, and die to prove
7:2, Nothing on earth beneath desire	Nothing in earth beneath desire
7:5, Give me thine only love to know	Give me thy only love to know

SH 1780 follows the *HSP* 1749 text for 1:4, 7:2,5 and the *HGF* 1746 text for 1:2.

"O Love divine, what has thou done" (Hymn CV: 264–65; WELCH) by Charles Wesley was published in *HSP* 1742, 26–27, with the title "Another" [Desiring to Love], and four stanzas of six lines. *SH* 1780 includes all four stanzas as in *HSP* 1742 with some differences in punctuation. Stanza 4:2 was originally printed as "Of nothing think, or speak beside" and was changed to "Of nothing speak or think beside" in the second edition of 1745. *SH* 1780 follows this revision, but with a misprint in the line, "Of nothing speak or thing beside."

"O Sun of righteousness arise" (Hymn XXXIV: 72–73; BURFORD) probably by Charles Wesley was first published in *CPH* 1741, 32–33 with the title "A Prayer for the Light of Life," and five stanzas of four lines. *SH* 1780 includes all stanzas as in *CPH* 1741 with some differences in punctuation and one variant (probably a misprint): orig. 1:2, "With healing in thy wing" = "With healing in thy wings."

"O that my load of sin were gone" (Hymn LXIX: 158–59; EVESHAM) by Charles Wesley was published in *HSP* 1742, 91–92, with the title "Come unto me all you that labour, and are heavy laden, and I will give you rest. Mat[thew] xi:28," and fourteen stanzas of four lines. *SH* 1780 includes seven stanzas of the original fourteen (1–2, 4, 6–9) with some differences in punctuation and the following variant: orig. 4:2: "Saviour of all, if mine thou art" = 3:2 (*SH* 1780), "Saviour, if mine indeed thou art."

"O Thou holy Lamb divine" (Hymn XVI: 27; BRAY'S) by Charles Wesley was published in *HLS* 1745, 116, with the title "Hymn CXXXVI" and four stanzas of four lines. *SH* 1780 includes the four stanzas as in *HLS* 1745, with the exception of differences in punctuation. Interestingly John Wesley eliminates the question marks at the end of 1:2 and 2:2. Line four of stanza 4 involves an internal shifting of text: orig. 4:4, "Lift our souls with thee to heaven" = "Lift with thee our souls to heaven" in *SH* 1780.

"O Thou, our husband, brother, friend" (Hymn LXXV: 171–75; EVESHAM) by Charles Wesley was published in *HSP* 1749, 2:88–89, with the title [Hymns of Intercession.] "Hymn II," and nine stanzas of four lines. *SH* 1780 includes all nine stanzas with some differences in punctuation and spelling (orig. 5:3, "sanctified" = "sanctify'd").

"O thou, who when I did complain" (Hymn XXXVI: 76–77; LIVERPOOL) by Samuel Wesley, Sr., first appeared in *The Pious Communicant,* 1700 257–59 (stanzas 1–7). It was also published in *CPH* 1737, 8, with the title "VII. Psalm CXVI," and seven stanzas of four lines. *SH* 1780 includes all seven stanzas as in *CPH* 1737 with some differences in punctuation.

"O What shall I do, My Saviour to praise" (Hymn CX: 280–81; TALLY'S) by Charles Wesley was published in *HSP* 1742, 118–19, with the title "A Thanksgiving," and six stanzas of four lines. *SH* 1780 includes all six stanzas as they appear in *HSP* 1742 with some differences in punctuation.

"Our Lord is risen from the dead" (Hymn LXXX: 185–87; FULHAM) by Charles Wesley was published in *CPH* 1743, 69–70, a thirteen-stanza poem of four lines each titled "Psalm XXIV." "Our Lord is risen from the dead" is the first line of original stanza eight. *SH* 1780 includes stanzas 8–13 with some differences in punctuation and formatted as three stanzas of eight lines.

"Praise be to the Father given" (Hymn VIII: 14; HAVANT) by Charles Wesley was originally published in *HSP* 1740, 101–102, with the title "Another" [Hymn to the Trinity], and four stanzas of four lines. *SH* 1780 includes all four stanzas as in *HSP* 1740 with some differences in punctuation.

"Praise ye the Lord: 'Tis good to raise" (Hymn LXXII: 164–65; KETTLEBY'S) by Isaac Watts was published in *The Psalms of David* (1719), 385–86, with the title "Psalm CXLVII. First Part. The Divine Nature, Providence and Grace" and eight stanzas of four lines. John Wesley published the hymn in *CPH* 1737, 10–11, with the title "X. Psalm CXLVII," and seven of Watts' stanzas, omitting stanza 2 and adding an eighth stanza, namely, the four-line Doxology of Bishop Thomas Ken. *SH* 1780 includes six stanzas as they appear in *CPH* 1737 plus the aforementioned Doxology, for a total of seven stanzas. There are some differences in punctuation and spelling ("clothes" for original "cloathes") and one variant: Watts orig. 7:3, "The nimble wit, the active limb" = "The piercing wit, the active limb" (*CPH* 1737 & *SH* 1780).

"Praise ye the Lord y'immortal choir" (Hymn LIV: 118–21; HALLELUJAH) by Isaac Watts was published in *Horae Lyricae*, 32–34, with the title "The Universal Hallelujah: Psalm cxlviii," and fourteen stanzas. When John Wesley first published this Watts hymn in *CPH* 1738, 70–71, with the title "The Same" [Psalm CXLVIII], he included eleven of Watts' original fourteen stanzas (2–4, 6–13), and revised greatly Watts stanza 2 as stanza 1, and added repetitions of "Hallelujah."

Horae Lyricae	*CPH* 1738
2. Gabriel, and all th'immortal Choir That fill the Realms above Sing; for he form'd you of his Fire, And feeds you with his Love.	1. Praise ye the Lord, ye immortal quire, That fills the realms above: Praise him who form'd you of his fire, And feeds you with his love.

SH 1780 includes the same stanzas as in *CPH* 1738, however, the opening line of stanza 1 is slightly changed: "Praise ye the Lord, y'immortal choir." *SH* 1780 also follows the variant of line 2:3 as it appears in *CPH* 1738: Watts orig., 3:3, "Or veil your little twinkling eyes" = 2:3 "Or veil in shades your thousand eyes" in *SH* 1780.

"Regent of all the worlds above" (Hymn LIX: 134–35; STANTON) by Isaac Watts was published in *Horae Lyricae* (1709), 45–47, with the title "Sun, Moon, and Stars, praise ye the Lord." John Wesley included the hymn in *CPH* 1737, 70–71, Hymn IX, with the title "Sun, Moon and Stars, Praise Ye the Lord" and nine stanzas of four lines. *SH* 1780 includes the nine stanzas of *CPH* 1737 with some differences in punctuation. Once again John Wesley alters Watts's text in the opening stanza and elsewhere.

Horae Lyricae	*CPH* 1737

Fairest of all the Lights above,
  Thou Sun, whose Beams adorn the Spheres
And with unweary'd Swiftness move,
  To form the Circles of our Years.
	Regent of all the worlds above,
	  Thou, sun, whose rays adorn our sphere
	And with unwearied swiftness move
	  To form the circle of the year.

2:2, That dress'd thine Orb in golden Rays 2:4, If he forgets his Maker's praise 3:3, Whose gentle Beams, and borrow'd Light	Who decks thy orb with borrow'd rays When he forgets his Maker's praise Whose paler fires and female light

Stz. 5 Ye twinkling Stars, who gild the Skies When Darkness has its Curtains drawn Who keep your Watch, with wakeful Eyes, When Business, Cares, and Day are gone:	Ye glittering stars that gild the skies When darkness has her curtain drawn That keep the watch with wakeful eyes, When business, cares and day are gone.

SH 1780 follows the version published in *CPH* 1737.

"Rejoice, the Lord is King!" (Hymn XC: 216–18; RESURRECTION) by Charles Wesley was published in *HLR* 1746, 12–13, Hymn 8, with six stanzas of six lines. *SH* 1780 includes the six stanzas as in *HLR* 1746 with differences in punctuation.

"Sinners, obey the gospel word" (Hymn LX: 136–38; INVITATION) by Charles Wesley was first published in *HSP* 1749, 1:259–60, with the title "[Hymns for Believers.] Hymn XLIII. 'Come, for all things are now ready'" [Luke xiv. 7.], and ten stanzas of four lines. The text was published previously in *HGF* 1746, 44–46. *SH* 1780 includes all ten stanzas as in *HSP* 1749 with some differences in punctuation and one variant: orig. 5:2, "Is ready with their shining host" = "Are ready with their shining host" in *SH* 1780.

"Sinners, rejoice, your peace is made" (Hymn CVIII: 272–74; SHEFFIELD) by Charles Wesley was published in *HAD* 1746, 10–11, Hymn VI, with seven stanzas of six lines. *SH* 1780 includes four stanzas (1, 2, 4, and 7) with some differences in punctuation and spelling: *SH* 1780 uses "Jesu" in place of "Jesus"; *HAD* 1746 uses "thro'" in place of "through" while *SH* 1780 uses both. There are a number of variants.

HAD 1746	*SH* 1780
1:5, Hath Grace thro' Him and Blessing given	1:5, Hath grace thro' Christ and blessings giv'n
2:4, Confer'd on You some Gift unknown,	2:4, Confer'd on you some gifts unknown;
2:5, Your Joys thro' Jesus' Pains abound,	2:5, Your joy through Jesu's pain abounds,
2:6, Ye triumph by his Glorious Wound.	2:6, Ye triumph by his glorious wounds.
7:4, The Bliss wherein thro' Christ ye live,	4:4, The bliss wherein through Christ they live;

"Soldiers of Christ, arise" (Hymn CXXIV: 323–29; HANDEL'S MARCH) by Charles Wesley was published in *HSP* 1749, 1:236–39, with the title "[Hymns for Believers.] Hymn 28. 'The whole armour of God. Ephesians 6'" and sixteen stanzas of eight lines. This hymn was first published by Charles as a broadsheet in 1742, and not long thereafter it was appended to John Wesley's *The Character of a Methodist,* 1742. *SH* 1780 includes all sixteen stanzas with some differences in punctuation, spelling (*SH* 1780, 9:5 "apply'd" for *HSP* 1739, 10:5, "applied"), one misspelling (*SH* 1780, 4:5, "gaurd" for *HSP* 1739 5:5, "guard"). There is one variant: *HSP* 1739, 15:8, "Ingrasping all mankind" = *SH* 1780, 14:8, "In grasping all mankind." The stanzas of *SH* 1780 in block text are numbered 2 through 15, but should be numbered 3 through 16, since the first two stanzas are musically scored.

"Some seraph, lend your heav'nly tongue" (Hymn LI: 110–111; MITCHAM) by Isaac Watts, *Horae Lyricae* 1706, Book 1, 40–41, with the title "The Infinite" and seven stanzas of four lines. *SH* 1780 includes stanzas 1–4, 6–7 as in *Horae Lyricae,* however, formatted as three stanzas of eight lines.

"Son of God, thy blessing grant" (Hymn XV: 26–27; BRAY'S) by Charles Wesley was first published in *HLS* 1745, 36, Hymn XLIX, with four stanzas of four lines. Stanzas 1–4 appear in *SH* 1780 as in *HLS* 1745, with the exception of some differences in punctuation.

"**Stand and adore! how glorious He**" (Hymn LII: 112–14; SMITH'S) by Isaac Watts was published in *Horae Lyricae* 1706, Book 1, 57–58, with the title "God only known to himself" and six stanzas of four lines. *SH* 1780 includes all stanzas as in *Horae Lyricae* but formatted as three stanzas of eight lines. "Hallelujah" is repeated six times, i.e. at the conclusion of each stanza.

"Sweet is the mem'ry of thy Grace" (Hymn XLII: 88–89; ALDRICH) by Isaac Watts was published in *The Psalms of David* 1719, 380–81, with the title "Psalm CXLV. Second Part. The Goodness of God." John Wesley included it in *CPH* 1738, 16, with the title "Psalm CXLV. Verse 7, &c. Part I," and five stanzas of four lines. *SH* 1780 includes all five stanzas as in *CPH* 1738 with some differences in punctuation.

"**The God of Abraham Praise**" (Hymn LVIII: 130–33; THE GOD OF ABRAHAM PRAISE), paraphrase by Thomas Olivers (ca. 1770) from the Yigdal of Daniel ben Judah (ca. 1400). It was originally published as a leaflet titled "A Hymn to the God of Abraham." In Three Parts: Adapted to a celebrated Air, sung by the Priest, Signior Leoni, etc., at the Jews' Synagogue in London with twelve stanzas. See Augustus Toplady, *Psalms and Hymns* 1776 and John Wesley's *A Pocket Hymn Book* 1785. *SH* 1780 includes the twelve stanzas, though the last two stanzas are numbered "11." The last stanza should be numbered "12."

"The Lord Jehovah reigns" (Hymn LXXXIX: 214–15; FONMON) by Isaac Watts was published in *Hymns and Spiritual Songs,* 1709, 279–80 (Book 2, no. 169). John Wesley included it in *CPH* 1738, 23, with the title: "XIX. The Divine Perfections," and four stanzas of six lines. *SH* 1780 includes the four stanzas as in *CPH* 1738 which has some differences in punctuation from Watts's original text, as well as a few variants:

Watts	*SH* 1780 & *CPH* 1738
3:1, "Thro' all his ancient works"	3:1, "Through all his mighty works"
3:6, "His great Decrees, His sov'reign will"	3:6, "His great decrees and sov'reign will"
4:1, "And can this mighty King"	4:1, "And can this sov'reign King"

"The Lord my pasture shall prepare" (Hymn CII: 256–57; OLD 23rd PSALM TUNE) by Joseph Addison was published in *The Spectator,* No. 441 (July 26, 1712). The hymn was published in George Whitefield's *Journal of a Voyage* 1738, 58 (the first part of Whitefield's Journal) and subsequently the same year in *CPH* 1738, 4–5, with the title "Psalm XXIII," and four stanzas of six lines. *SH* 1780 includes the four stanzas as they appear in *The Spectator* and in *CPH* 1738, with some differences in punctuation and spelling (*SH* 1780 uses "Though" for "tho'" in *The Spectator* and *CPH* 1738; *SH* 1780 and *CPH* 1738 use "thro'" for "through" in *The Spectator*).

The Hymn Texts

"The spacious firmament on high" (Hymn LXXXIV: 197–99; LONDON) by Joseph Addison was published in *The Spectator,* 1711–14, 465, (Aug. 23, 1712). John Wesley published the hymn in *CPH* 1737, 59–60, with the title "[Hymn] II of 'The Same [Psalm XIX],'" and three stanzas of eight lines. *SH* 1780 prints the three stanzas as they originally appeared in *The Spectator* with one variant: orig. 3:3, "What tho' nor real Voice nor Sound" = "What though no real voice nor sound." The *CPH* 1737 version printed 3:3 as in the original, but it has two lines that are different from *The Spectator* version: orig. 1:2, "With all the blue Etherial Sky" = And all the wide ethereal sky"; orig. 2:5, "Whilst all the Stars that round her burn" = "While all the stars that round her burn." Wesley did not, however, continue these variants in *SH* 1780.

"The voice of my beloved sounds" (Hymn CXXVI: 334–40; CHESHUNT) by Charles Wesley is a three-stanza hymn published in *SH* 1762, 1:295, based on the Song of Solomon 2:8, "The voice of my beloved!" and 2:11, "Lo, the winter is past, the rain is going, &c." Stanzas 1 and 2 are poems 934 and 936 (1:296) in *SH* 1762 respectively. Stanza 3 is a repetition of stanza 1, with some differences in punctuation. *SH* 1780 includes the texts as they appear in *SH* 1762.

"Thee, Jesu, thee, the sinner's friend" (Hymn XCVII: 238–41; SNOWFIELDS) by Charles Wesley was published in *HSP* 1742, 242–44, with the title "Desiring Love" [Part I.], and eleven stanzas of six lines. *SH* 1780 includes all eleven stanzas as in *HSP* 1742 with some differences in punctuation and spelling (orig. 7:5, "mystick" = 7:5 "mystic"), and there is one variant: orig. 8:3, "The Lord, the gracious Lord" = 8:3, "O Lord, the gracious Lord."

"Thee we adore, Eternal Name" (Hymn XXXII: 68–69; BURSTAL) by Isaac Watts was published in *Hymns and Spiritual Songs,* 2nd edition (1709), 178–79 (Book 2, no. 55) with the title "Frail Life and succeeding Eternity." See also *CPH* 1738, 53–54 with the title "Life and Eternity," and seven stanzas of four lines. *SH* 1780 includes all stanzas as in *CPH* 1738 with the exception of some punctuation differences and two variants: orig. 6:1, "Or endless joy, or endless woe" = "Infinite joy or endless woe"; orig. 7:4, "May we be found with God" = "May they be found with God," a change which was made in the version of *CPH* 1741, 15.

"Thee will I love, my strength, my tow'r" (Hymn CIII: 258–60; CARY'S) is a translation by John Wesley of a hymn by Johann Scheffler that was published in the *Herrnhut Gesangbuch* (1737), 540–41, No. 610. Wesley's translation was published in *HSP* 1739, 198–200, with the title "Gratitude for Our Conversion. From the German," and seven stanzas of six lines. *SH* 1780 includes the seven stanzas as in *HSP* 1739 with some differences in punctuation and spelling (*SH* 1780 uses "though" for "tho'" in 7:5).

"Thou God of glorious majesty" (Hymn XCVIII: 242–44; WOOD'S) by Charles Wesley was published in *HSP* 1749, 1:34–35; Hymn VII, with the title "An Hymn for Seriousness," and six stanzas of six lines. *SH* 1780 includes the six stanzas as in *HSP* 1749 with some differences in punctuation and spelling (orig. 5:2, "insure" = 5:2, "ensure"; orig. 5:6, "indure" = 5:6, "endure."

"**Thou God of harmony and love**" (Hymn XCVI: 234–37; MUSICIAN'S) by Charles Wesley was published in *RH* 1747, 34–36, with the title "Hymn XXV. The Musician's" in ten stanzas of six lines. There are some alternative readings: orig. 2:4, "steward" = "servant" (the errata in *RH* 1747 says to change "steward" to "servant" which appears in *SH* 1780); orig. 7:3, "Who chant the praise above" = "Who chant thy praise above" (in *RH* 1747 & *SH* 1780, except the latter has "chaunt" in place of "chant"). *RH* 1747, 1:6, "The heavenly choristers" = *SH* 1780, 1:6, "Thy heavenly choristers." There are some differences in punctuation and in spelling: (orig. 6:3 & 8:6, "Jesus'" = 6:3 & 8:6, "Jesu's"; orig. 8:1, "extasy" = 8:1, "extacy").

"Thou God of truth and love" (Hymn LXXXVIII: 211–13; CARDIFF) by Charles Wesley was published in *HSP* 1749, 2:279–80, with the title "[Hymns for Christian Friends.] Hymn XIII," and seven stanzas of six lines. *SH* 1780 includes all seven stanzas as in *HSP* 1749 with some differences in punctuation and one variant: orig. 6:1, "O might thy Spirit seal" = 6:1, "O might the Spirit seal."

"Thou hidden love of God whose height" (OLD 112TH PSALM TUNE: 261–63) is a translation of a hymn, "Verborgne Gottes Liebe du," by Gerhard Tersteegen published in the *Herrnhut Gesangbuch* (1737), 483–84, No. 542. John Wesley first published his translation in *CPH* 1738, 51–53, [Hymn] 6, with the title "From the German: *Verborgne Gottes Liebe du,*" and eight stanzas of six lines. He subsequently published it in *HSP* 1739, 78–80, with the title "Divine Love. From the German," and eight stanzas of six lines. *SH* 1780 includes the eight stanzas as they appear in *HSP* 1739 with some differences in punctuation and spelling (*SH* 1739 uses "through" in place of "thro'"). There are two variants:

CPH 1738 / *HSP* 1739	*SH* 1780
2:4, "Be fix't"	2:4, "Seems fix'd"
8:6, "To taste thy love is all my choice"	8:6, "To taste thy love be all my choice."

In *HSP* 1739 John Wesley changed the last four lines of stanza four which he used in *SH* 1780 as well.

CPH 1738	*HSP* 1739 / *SH* 1780
Ah tear it thence, that thou alone	Ah! tear it thence, and reign alone,
May'st reign unrival'd monarch there.	The Lord of ev'ry motion there:
From earthly loves I must be free,	Then shall my heart from earth be free,
E'er I can find repose in thee.	When it has found repose in thee.

"Thou hidden source of calm repose" (Hymn CVII: 269–71; BIRMINGHAM) by Charles Wesley was published in *HSP* 1749, 1:245–46, [Hymns for Believers.] "Hymn XXXI." with four stanzas of six lines. *SH* 1780 includes the four stanzas as in *HSP* 1749 with some differences in punctuation.

"Thou, Jesu, art our King" (Hymn LXXXV: 200–01; IRENE) by Johann Scheffler was published in the *Herrnhut Gesangbuch* (1737), 68–69 (No. 68). John Wesley translated the hymn and first published it in *CPH* 1738, 36–38, with the title "From the German: Dich, Jesu, loben wir." The translation consisted of thirteen stanzas of six lines. This version subsequently appeared in *HSP* 1739, 175–78, with the title "The Saviour glorified by All. From the German" and thirteen stanzas of six lines. Of the thirteen translated stanzas Wesley includes eight (1–3, 5–6, 11–13) as they appeared in *CPH* 1738 with some differences in punctuation and one difference in spelling: orig. 6:3, "quires" = *SH* 1780, 5:3, "choirs."

"Thou shepherd of Israel, and mine" (Hymn LXXXI: 188–90; THOU SHEPHERD OF ISRAEL) by Charles Wesley was published in *SH* 1762, 1:294–95 (#931), with three stanzas of eight lines, based on the Song of Solomon 1:7, "Tell me, O thou whom my soul loveth, where thou feedest, where thou makest thy flock to rest at noon." *SH* 1780 includes the three stanzas as in *SH* 1762 with some differences in punctuation.

"Thou very paschal Lamb" (Hymn X: 16–17; BRENTFORD) by Charles Wesley was originally published in *HLS* 1745, 37, Hymn LI, with four stanzas of four lines. *SH* 1780 includes the four stanzas as in *HLS* 1745 with minor differences in punctuation.

"Tis finished! 'tis done" (Hymn CXII: 284–85; THE TRIUMPH) by Charles Wesley was published in *FH* 1746, 8–9, with the title "Hymn VI," and five stanzas of eight lines. *SH* 1780 includes all five stanzas with some differences in punctuation and spelling (*FH* 1746 in 2:4 uses "thro'" while *SH* 1780 uses "through"). There is one variant: orig. 1:6, "In Jesus's love" = 1:6, "Thro' Jesus his love." In this variant John Wesley is following a change that was made in the fourth edition of *FH* 1765.

"When all the mercies of my God" (Hymn XLIV: 92–94; MORNING SONG) by Joseph Addison and Richard Steele first appeared in *The Spectator* (August 9, 1712), 453. John Wesley published the hymn in *CPH* 1737, 26–27, with nine stanzas of the original (1, 3–7, 10–11, 13) and the title "XXVII. Thanksgiving for God's Particular Providence." *SH* 1780 includes eight stanzas as in *CPH* 1737, omitting stanza 7, with some differences in punctuation.

"When, gracious Lord, when shall it be" (Hymn LXVIII: 156–57; COMPLAINT), by Charles Wesley was published in *HSP* 1742, 204–06, with the title "Come, Lord Jesus!" and thirteen stanzas of four lines. However, the first line reads originally "When, dearest Lord, when shall it be." *SH* 1780 includes eight of the original thirteen stanzas (1–3, 9–13) with some differences in punctuation and one variant: orig. 10:1, "When man forsakes, Thou wilt not leave" = "Whom man forsakes, Thou wilt not leave."

"When shall thy lovely face be seen" (Hymn LXXX: 182–84; GUERNSEY) by Isaac Watts was published with twelve stanzas in *Horae Lyricae* (1709), with the title "Come, Lord Jesus." John Wesley first published the hymn in *CPH* 1738, with the title "XLI. Come, Lord Jesus" in eight stanzas of four lines, omitting original stanzas two, five, seven, and twelve. *SH* 1780 includes the eight stanzas of *CPH* 1738, but with some differences in punctuation and spelling (orig. "crystal" = "chrystal") and the text is formatted as four stanzas of eight lines. There are variants with Watts's original text that are identical in *CPH* 1738 and *SH* 1780. Watts, orig. 9:1–2, "O for a Shout of violent Joys, / To join the Trumpet's thund'ring Sound!" = *SH* 1780, 3:5 (*CPH* 1738, 6:1), "Hark! what a shout of vi'lent joys, / Joins with the mighty trumpet's sound!" Watts 11:4, "Active and young, and fair as they" = *SH* 1780, 4:8 (*CPH* 1736, 8:4), "To reign with him in endless day."

"Who in the Lord confide" (Hymn XIII: 20–21; OULNEY) by Charles Wesley was first published in *CPH* 1743, 90–91, with the title "Psalm CXXV," and six stanzas of eight lines. *SH* 1780 includes stanzas 1 and 2 as in *CPH* 1743 with some differences in punctuation.

"With glory clad, with strength array'd" (Hymn LXX: 160–61; ZOAR) by Nahum Tate and Nicholas Brady appeared in *A New Version of the Psalms of David,* 1698, 192. John Wesley published the text in *CPH* 1741, 10, with the title "Psalm XCIII," and four stanzas of four lines. *SH* 1780 includes the four stanzas as in *CPH* 1741 with some differences in punctuation and one variant: orig. 3:2, "And toss the troubled waves on high" = "And toss their troubled waves on high."

"Wretched, helpless and distrest" (Hymn CXV: 292–95; KINGSWOOD) by Charles Wesley was published in *HSP* 1742, 43–45, with the title "Another" [Wretched, and miserable, and poor, and blind, and naked. Revelation iii. 17], and eight stanzas of eight lines. *SH* 1780 includes all eight stanzas as in *HSP* 1742 with some differences in punctuation and one variant: orig. 8:5, "Let thy image be restor'd" = "Let thine image be restor'd" which follows the change made in the second edition of 1745.

"Ye servants of God" (Hymn CXIII: 287–89; WALSALL) by Charles Wesley was published in *HTT* 1744, 43, with the title "Hymns to be Sung in a Tumult. [Hymn] I," and six stanzas of four lines. *SH* 1780 includes all six stanzas as in *HTT* 1744 where they appear in eight lines of 5.5.5.5.5.5.5.5 meter. In *SH* 1780 the stanzas are reformatted into four lines of 10.10.10.10 meter and it does not follow the change from "triumphs" to "triumph" which was made in the second edition of 1745.

"Ye simple souls, that stray" (Hymn XIV: 22–25; CHESTER) by Charles Wesley was first published in *RH* 1747, 21–22, with the title "Hymn XVI. To: 'Spirit of truth, descend'" (i.e., the setting by John Lampe to that hymn in *HGF* 1746), and seven stanzas of eight lines. *SH* 1780 includes the original seven stanzas as in *RH* 1747, with the exception of differences in punctuation and one variant: original 5:7, "alway" = "always" in *SH* 1780.

"Ye who dwell above the skies" (Hymn XXIV: 44–45; MINORIES) by George Sandys first appeared in his *A Paraphrase upon the Psalms of David* (1676), 238–39. The hymn consists of forty lines, which are not numbered in Sandys' publication. With extensive editing Wesley shaped them into nine stanzas of four lines, which means that four lines have been omitted, merged, or partially used. Wesley first published the hymn in *CPH* 1741, 93–94 with the title "The Same" [Psalm CXLVIII], and nine stanzas of four lines. *SH* 1780 includes all nine stanzas as in *CPH* 1741 with some differences in punctuation and with one variant: orig. 6:2, "You, inured to obey" = "You accustom'd to obey" in *SH* 1780.

The Music of *Sacred Harmony* 1780

SH 1780 is essentially a harmonized edition of *SH* 1761 that contained Methodist societies' common core of unison tunes, broad in sources, styles, and poetic meters.[1] The musically-scored section of *SH* 1761 was titled *Sacred Melody,* [*SM* 1761; 1765].

The 354-paged *SH* 1780 includes 97 tunes from *SH* 1761, 10 from *SM* 1765,[2] and 15 from other sources.[3] Commentary on the 122 tunes in *SH* 1780 is included on pp. 51–70.[4]

While Wesley's motivations for publishing *SH* 1780 are unknown, we can assume they include:

1. To provide an alternative for precentors, choirs, organists[5] and other keyboardists, using Thomas Butts' 211-page *HS* 1754, the source of the majority of tunes in *SH* 1761, to lead hymn singing in Methodist class meetings, preaching-houses,[6] and in social worship. Notably, *HS* 1754 continued to be sold at the Foundery as late as 1777.
2. Expanding the "common core" to include settings that became popular in class-meetings and preaching services since the publication of *SH* 1761 and

---

[1] Wesley constantly references it as "our tune-book" and "our tunes." For example, see answers 12 and 8 to question 39 in the "Large" *Minutes,* "(12) Recommend our tune-book everywhere; and if you cannot sing yourself choose a person or two in each place to pitch the tune for you. (8) In every large society let them learn to sing; and let them always learn our own tunes first." *Minutes of several Conversations . . . 1741–1780,* 27.

[2] CANTERBURY, CHESHUNT, CHIMES, COMPLAINT, HOTHAM, MANCHESTER, OLIVERS, THOU SHEPHERD OF ISRAEL, TRAVELLER, YORKSHIRE.

[3] ARNE, ATHLONE, CHESTER, DEDICATION, DERBY, HAMILTON'S, MACCABEES, MITCHAM, MUSICIANS, PARIS, SMITH'S, THE GOD OF ABRAHAM, THE 100 PSALM, TRUE ELIJAH, TRUMPET.

[4] See also Clarke, "John Wesley and Methodist Music in the Eighteenth Century." 325–92; and Nicholas Temperley, *Hymn Tune Index,* "Sacred Harmony," code, #SHCCPH a, http://hymntune.library.uiuc.edu/

[5] Lightwood comments, "In Wesley's life time organs were installed in three Methodist chapels and other worship spaces," *Methodist Music Of The Eighteenth Century* 40. Amateur music making in homes, where Methodist preaching services were held, was often accompanied at the harpsichord or the smaller but similar virginal.

[6] Frank Baker has commented on the derivation and history of the term preaching-house. "At first Wesley preferred this term to 'chapel' in order to insist . . . Methodists would attend their parish church for full sacramental worship, and on the other hand to avoid the dissenting term 'meetinghouse.' The 1748 Conference firmly set its face against preaching without forming Societies, and thus make a meeting-place essential. . . . Preaching-houses were few compared with the huge number of cottages, farm-kitchens and barns used for Methodist fellowship and worship. Only a dozen had been erected by 1750, increased to forty by 1760 and to 120 by 1770. At Wesley's death in 1791 there were some 470 preaching-houses in England, 14 in Wales, 16 in Scotland, and 88 in Ireland." Davies and Rupp, *A History of the Methodist Church in Great Britain,* 1:228.

Clive Norris states that a Methodist society in 1780 with 40 members would worship in a chapel with 200 seats, accommodating members and "hearers"; of which half were "free" the other hundred rented. Excerpt from a paper "Economics of Methodism." 2017.

SM 1765; notably, theater tunes, ARNE and MACCABEES, an extended anthem, THE 100 PSALM, and a traditional melody, ATHLONE.
3. To supply a musical resource that met the emerging needs of indigenous song leaders and singers to lead effectively congregants who were gathered in new and adapted spaces during the expansion of British Methodism in the two decades encompassing *SH* 1761 and *SH* 1780.[7] This expansion in turn called for training new indigenous music leaders with technical, theoretical, and practical skills needed to teach the common core cited above.[8] Notably, Methodist preaching services initially held on Sunday afternoons to avoid competing with Anglican parish worship, began to meet on Sunday mornings.[9] George W. Dolbey traces this development.

> [while] most of the early chapels were in the country areas and inevitably small, . . . with the erection of City Road Chapel, London, (1778) it is evident that the movement was securing greater support in the larger towns, for after 1778 there are more large chapels. Simple increase in numbers was no doubt responsible for this but it may well have been that in the more densely populated areas the Established Church was unable—through lack of churches or willingness to co-operate where there were churches—to meet the worshipping needs of the Methodists, many of whom were still desiring to attend the parish for Communion and Sunday service. Internal pressures within Methodism for separation from the church of England were becoming stronger and these larger chapels expressed and reinforced a greater consciousness of separate identity.[10]

An example of the aforementioned movement towards separate identity is seen Wesley's provision for Word and Sacrament. The three-level pulpit provided for the Word read, sung, and preached. The precentor led the singing of psalms and hymns from first level. The lessons and appropriate liturgy were read from the second level, with one exception. Since the lessons could be heard at the parish

---

[7] Membership increased from 20,000 to 44,440, see, Richard P. Heitzenrater "Membership of Methodist Societies" in *Wesley and the People Called Methodists*, 264. Maldwyn Edwards comments on the reason for the growth. "[Wesley] was able to profit from the parochialism and conservatism of the Church of England. Its strength lay in the south, and in the eighteenth century the centre of population shifted from the south to the north, and the discovery that iron might be smelted with coal led to the phenomenal growth of population in Lancashire and Yorkshire," Davies and Rupp, *A History of the Methodist Church in Great Britain*, 62.

[8] This was presumably taught from *The Gamut, or Scale of Music* in *SH* 1761, or similar instructions included at the frontmatter of collections. While Wesley has received high praise from commentators for including, possibly originating this simplified pedagogical tool in *SH* 1761, the editors of this facsimile edition have established that Wesley, perhaps assisted by Thomas Butts, copied it word for word, note for note from *DM* 1754, 1–11.

[9] See Baker "From Society to Church," in *John Wesley and The Church of England*, 283–303; and Richard P. Heitzenrater, "The Maturing of Methodism (1758–1775)," in *Wesley and The People Called Methodists*, 199–260.

[10] [Many of these larger chapels were patterned after] the plain auditory type recommended by [Christopher[Wren], Dolbey, *The Architectural Expressions of Methodism*, 83–4.

church, they were usually omitted from the preaching-service. The sermon was preached from the third level. The communion table (Wesley referenced it as an altar) and kneeling rail were placed in the apse behind the pulpit. These provisions imply "that the full Anglican service was now [1778] regarded as customary by the Methodists."[11]

4. As the musical companion to the 1780 *Collection,* See Introduction p. 51.

5. While the title *Sacred Harmony* suggests hymns sung in harmony, the format of the collection expresses John Wesley's strong and abiding conviction for the primacy of unison singing.[12] For example the collection's mostly two-voice settings consist of a bass line without figures constructed from root position notes and thirds and sixths supporting the melody sung by male and female voices,[13] and the absence of instructions such as portions sung by the female voice alone. This flexible format suggests Wesley intended the tunes be sung in harmony with or without accompaniment.

Wesley produced a revised edition of *Sacred Harmony* in 1789,[14] (See cover in Appendix E) for reasons he did not relate. Perhaps he surmised there was a need for a more portable volume than the 354 pages in *SH* 1780. Consequently, Wesley significantly reduced the size of the parent collection to 157 pages by only including one interlined stanza of each hymn, contrasted to *SH* 1780 that included one interlined stanza, with the balance of the hymn in text blocks. Wesley deleted BRISTOL and EPWORTH, and in a gesture to the expanding presence of choirs included an additional three anthems, SPRING, THE DYING CHRISTIAN, and YARMOUTH,[15] and added dynamic markings and performance notes.[16]

---

[11] Dolbey, *The Architectural Expressions of Methodism,* 50.

[12] Wesley's views on the primacy of unison singing are set forth in his essay, "Thoughts on the Power of Music" (1789]). Wesley's text and the author's commentary are included in Young, *Music of the Heart,* 84–93.

[13] Nicholas Temperley comments on the derivation of the format *SH* 1780, which was carried into the nineteenth century: "The tune, in the G clef, was on the middle staff, the upper staff carried a subordinate part in the G clef; and the lower staff carried the vocal bass . . . This arrangement of the score seems to have been invented by Independents, later known as Congregationalists. It had the advantage for keyboard players of placing the tune right over the bass. . . . The congregation, male and female, sing the tune in two octaves. The upper [third] part is available for altos, singing an octave below the written notes." Temperley and Banfield, *Music and the Wesleys* (2010), 8–9.

[14] *Sacred Harmony* (1789). The cover of *SH* 1789 is included in Appendix F.

[15] Martin V. Clarke comments these tunes "stretched the definition of [early Methodist] congregational music to its limit and can be seen as a determined effort to reach a compromise between those who wanted to perform more elaborate settings as a part of worship and Wesley's theological and doctrinal principles concerning the necessity of full congregational participation (Clarke, "John Wesley and Methodist Music in the Eighteenth Century," 384).

Nicholas Temperley comments that the original purpose of training singers was to scatter them within the congregation "to encourage a more disciplined and inspiring congregational praise. . . But the singers, once they got their own way, wanted to sing together from their own pew or gallery, and then aspired more difficult music [often supported by a keyboard and bass viol, that resulted in] congregations [tending] to fall silent and listen to the music." (Nicholas Temperley, *The Music of the English Parish Church,* 1:151–52.

Particularly significant is the extended anthem "The Dying Christian," pages 139–47, a setting of Alexander Pope's "Dying Christian to his Soul" ("Vital spark of heavenly flame"), widely sung in Great Britain and in USA singing schools. Percy Scholes comments that this was apparently one of Wesley's favorite anthems: On one occasion (Bolton, 1787) he says, "I desired forty or fifty children to come in and sing *Vital spark of heavenly flame.* Although some of them were silent, not being able to sing for tears, yet the harmony was such as I believe could not be equalled in the King's Chapel."[17]

A third edition of *Sacred Harmony* (*SH* 1822) prepared by John Wesley's nephew, Charles, Jr. contained 120 "revised," "edited" figured-bass-with-melody tunes for 145 texts from *SH* 1789.[18] Only one stanza of each hymn is interlined. This two-part format expresses John Wesley's intended prominence of the melody as previously stated in point 5.

The first three pages of the twelve-page "Preface to The Present Edition,"[19] cite the neglect of *SH,* reject the popular tunes of the day, and advocate a return to its 'simple melodies,' as seen in the excerpt in Appendix F. This conservative third edition did little to assuage the encroachment of a new repertory[20] as described by Nicholas Temperley,

> The typical tune that emerged was melodious, even pretty, and in the major mode. It often had a second, equally tuneful subordinate part, moving mostly in parallel 3rds or 6ths, either of similar compass or in a treble-tenor relationship; the bass was inclined to be static. In other words, the texture was that of the 'galant' or early classic style, and for the most part the compositional rules of that style were well observed; but it long outlived the departure of *galanterie* in secular music.[21]

John Wesley's *Journal* includes a number of his jaded opinions of choirs, including [Neath, Thursday, August 9, 1768] "I began reading prayers at six, but was greatly disgusted at the manner of singing: (1) twelve or fourteen persons kept it to themselves, and quite shut out the congregation; (2) these repeated the same words, contrary to all sense and reason, six or eight or ten times over; (3) according to the shocking custom of modern music, different persons sung different words at one and the same moment; an intolerable insult on common sense, and utterly incompatible with any devotion" (*JWW* 3:339).

[16] For parallel developments of choirs in Anglican parishes, urban and country, see iii, v. https://archive.org/details/imslp-music-reformed-arnold-john.

[17] Ward, *Oxford Companion,* 632.

[18] *Sacred Harmony, a set of Tunes Collected by the late Rev. John Wesley* (1822). The cover of *SH* 1822 and an excerpt from the Preface are included in Appendix F.

[19] Richard Watson (1781–1833) is cited as the author of the Preface in Stephen B. Wickens, *The Life of Rev. Richard Watson,* 200. Much of the text is taken from "Mr. Watson on Congregational Singing," 31–34. Watson was the author of *Theological Institutes,* (1829), the first attempt to include John Wesley's thought in a systematic theology; and co-compiler with Thomas Jackson, (1783–1873), Methodist biographer and historian, of the first authorized supplement to John Wesley's concluding and abiding volume (1831). https://catalog.hathitrust.org/Record/100907635.

[20] This simpler style is exemplified in two collections by Methodist musician, James Leach (1761–1798), *A new sett of hymns and psalm tunes* (1789), and, *A Second Sett . . .* (1794); and Edward Miller's (1735–1807) *David's Harp.*

In consequence, few melodies from the three editions of *Sacred Harmony* were included in British Methodist hymnals beyond mid-nineteenth century when Victorian-style tunes become the normative style.

---

[21] "Methodist Church Music," *Grove Music Online,* accessed August 18, 2018.

The Hymn Tunes[1]

Oliver A. Beckerlegge and Frank Baker in *JWW*, 7:772–87, provide sources and annotations for 104 of the 119 tunes in *Sacred Harmony* 1780, the companion to the 1780 *Collection*. Since all but a few of the designated tunes are included in the discussion of tunes in the facsimile reprint of *SH* 1761, Beckerlegge and Baker's work serves as a companion to this facsimile edition. Following a brief history of each tune a list is provided of the hymns in the 1780 *Collection* to which it was set by John Wesley. The commentaries are included with the kind permission of Abingdon Press.[2]

The following abbreviations are used in the notes on the tunes.
Adams—'The Musical Sources for John Wesley's Tune-Books', 1974
Booth—*Wesleyan Psalmist*, 1857
Companion—*Companion to the Wesleyan Hymn Book*, 1847
Div. Mus. Misc.—*Divine Musical Miscellany*, 1754
Festival H.—*Hymns on the Great Festivals*, 1746 (J. Lampe)
Foundery C.—*A Collection of Tunes Set to Music, As they are commonly Sung at the Foundery*, 1742
Harm. Sac.—*Harmonia Sacra* (Butts, c. 1754; 2nd ed., c.k 1765; 3rd ed., 1770; references are to the first edition unless otherwise noted)
Madan—Martin Madan, *A Collection of Psalm and Hymn Tunes Never Published Before . . . to be had at the Lock Hospital* (London, ca. 1763, 1769)
Playford—*Divine Companion*, 1701
SH—*Sacred Harmony*, 1780
SM—*Sacred Melody*, 1761 (Note: While the contents of *Sacred Melody* are included in the hymn tune section of *SH* 1761 [*Select Hytmns with Tunes Annext*], the engraved title page of *Sacred Melody* appears only from the second edition onwards.)
The arabic numerals within the notes refer to the pages in the various volumes unless specified otherwise.

---

[1] Copyright restrictions prevented the editors from updating, deleting or adding to this commentary. Seventeen of the hymn tunes in *SH* 1780 are not addressed in the commentaries of Beckerlegge and Baker. Commentaries for these tunes are provided in this edition of *SH* 1780 and immediately follow the last of the tune commentaries, ZOAR, for which Abingdon Press has granted copyright permission.

[2] Published by Abingdon Press © 1989. All rights reserved. Used by permission, granted by Pamala Reed.

Alphabetical List of Tunes

ALDRICH
SM, 27–8; SH, 88. Possibly Welsh? Appeared in *Harm. Sac.*, 31, where spelt 'Aldridge'; and originally in *Div. Mus. Misc.*, as 'Elenborough'. (Adams, 137.) 85, 86, 119, 288, 338, 394, 490

AMSTERDAM
SM, 90; SH, 219. *Foundery C.*, 29–30, a slightly more elaborate version. Founded on a German chorale, found in a collection by J. G. Hille (Cantor in Glaucha, near Halle), 1739, a version of which appears in C. J. Latrobe's collection of tunes, published for the use of English Moravians, *c.* 1800; also in *Harm. Sac.*, 153–4. (Adams, 112.) 18, 53, 175, 185, 206, 212, 234, 263, 266, 269, 348, 349, 361, 371, 372, 390, 395, 475, 492

ANGEL HYMN (also ANGEL SONG, ANGEL'S SONG)
SM, 44–5; SH, 145. Wesley, who had already included it in the *Foundery C.*, possibly knew it through Patrick's version of the Psalms (1744), (though it is earlier than Patrick) where, entitled 'Angel's Song Tune', it is set to Psalm 104. In Wesley's publications the tune is somewhat simplified; it appears in the *Companion* in its modern form. It was composed by Orlando Gibbons and, entitled 'Song 34', was set in 1624 to Wither's versification of Luke 2:13, 'Thus angels sung and thus sing we'—hence its name. (Adams, 100.) 4, 17, 276, 315, 410, 458

ANGLESEY
SM, 46; SH, 148. Originally appeared in *Harm. Sac.*, 70, named 'Anglesea', and *Div. Mus. Misc.*, where it is named 'Clifton'. Possibly of Welsh origin. (Adams, 147.) 92

ARNE'S
SH, 64–6. By Thomas Augustine Arne (1710–78), an adaptation of the aria 'Waters parted from the sea', from his opera *Artaxerxes*. The same aria was adapted as 'Clayton' in the *Primitive Methodist Hymn-book* of 1889, but with no indication as to its source. Its first appearance as a hymn tune was in Thomas Knibb's *Psalm Singer's Help* (*c.* 1775). (Adams, 189.) 13, 74

ASCENSION
SM, 18–19; SH, 56–7, *Festival H.*, No. 11. It was composed by John Frederick Lampe (1703–1751), who settled in England about 1725. He played in Handel's operatic orchestras and collaborated with Henry Carey. In November 1745 he came under the influence of the Wesleys, was converted, and in 1746 published at his own expense *Hymns on the Great Festivals*, a collection of twenty-four original tunes set to Charles Wesley's words, of which this tune is No. 11. He seems to have edited also the tunes in *A Collection of Hymns and Sacred Poems*, published in Dublin in 1749, when

The Hymn Tunes

both Wesley and he were there. The tune was republished in *Harm. Sac.*, 20, as 'Ascension Hymn'. (Adams, 402.) 50, 228, 504

ATHLONE

SH, 152–3. This is an adaptation of an air 'Roisin Dubh' by Turlogh O'Carolan (1670–1738), which Wesley may have heard in Athlone, whence its name. (Adams, 192.) 16, 80, 149, 282, 358, 396, 442

BEXLEY

SM, 24; *SH*, 74. Already used in the *Foundery C.*, 15, it was composed by William Tans'ur (*c.* 1700–83), and appeared in 1735 under the name of 'Colchester', set to Psalm 150 in one of his collections of Psalm tunes. This version is very different from the original, and it has been hazarded that Wesley heard the tune, and noted it down by ear; he possibly called it 'Bexley' in reminiscence of a pleasant week he spent there in 1740. It appeared also in one of Aaron Williams's Collections in 1760, and in *Harm. Sac.*, 23. (Adams, 92.) 39, 313, 350, 393

BIRMINGHAM

SM, 82–3; *SH*, 269–71; and previously in *Harm. Sac.*, 135, named 'Stafford'. It has the florid style of Lampe—or is it perhaps of Welsh origin? *Div. Mus. Misc.* names it 'Somerton'. (Adams, 166.) 193, 201

BIRSTALL (orig., 'Birstal')

SM, 22; *SH*, 68. Nothing seems to be known of the origin of this tune. (Adams, 136.) It appears in Toplady's *Gospel Magazine* for 1777. 1, 34, 35

BRADFORD

SM, 79; *SH*, 251–2. Composed by Jeremiah Clark (1670–1707), the organist of St. Paul's, it originally appeared in Playford in a four-line form, as it also appeared in the *Foundery C.*, 28, called 'Clark's', and later in *Harm. Sac.*, 80, where it is named 'Uffington'. It is now known as 'Uffingham'. (Adams, 109.) 109, 170, 365, 419, 433

BRAY'S

SM, 12–13; *SH*, 26. Wesley had published it in the *Foundery C.*, 9, under the title 'London New Tune', but its first appearance was in Playford, set to 'How uneasie are we here'. A contemporary manuscript note in a copy of *Harm. Sac.* (where a slightly different setting occurs, 11), ascribes it to Jeremiah Clark, as does Adams. 81. 152, 386

BRENTFORD

SM, 9; *SH*, 16. It appears in Green's *Book of Psalmody* (5th edn., 1721), an earlier form appearing in Chetham's Psalmody (1718). Wesley had included it in the *Foundery C.*, 3, calling it 'Fetter Lane Tune', recalling the pioneer London society. It was printed also by Butts in *Harm. Sac.*, 7, under the name of 'Wirksworth', which it still bears. The composer is unknown, though a contemporary manuscript note ascribes it to J. Chetham; another early note gives it the alternative name 'Aylesbury'. (Adams, 74.) 90, 93, 102, 147, 256, 398, 409, 438, 447, 473

BROCKMER'S

SM, 30–1; *SH*, 95–6. Its first appearance was in the *Foundery C.*, 23–4, as 'Leipsick Tune', and it was reprinted in *Harm. Sac.*, 43, in *Div. Mus. Misc.*, and in Hutton's Moravian Collection, *c.* 1745, which possibly indicates a German origin. (Adams, 104.) 62, 63, 121, 134, 135, 359, 404, 453, 518

BROOK'S

SM, 33–4; *SH*, 100–1. It appeared first in Francis Timbrell's *Divine Musick Scholar's Guide* (*c.* 1725), and in a book of the same title by John Sreeve (1740). *Harm. Sac.*, 62, first gave it the name 'Brook's'. (Adams, 140.) 81, 239, 250, 347, 489

BUILTH

SM, 72–3; *SH*, 225–6. It appeared first in either the *Div. Mus. Misc.* (where it is called 'Beuelth', and is in a more sedate form than in *SM*), or in *Harm. Sac.*, 117. Builth, near Garth, Brecon, the home of Charles Wesley's wife, gave its name to the tune. (Adams, 160.) 221, 476, 478, 486

CALVARY

SM, 93–4; *SH*, 299–300. It is No. 5 of Lampe's *Festival H.*, and was reprinted in *Harm. Sac.*, 158, where Butts named it 'For the Sacrament'. In the *Companion* it is called 'Crucifixion.' (Adams, 396.) 103, 111, 158

CANON

SM, 41; *SH*, 127–8, and in the *Foundery C.*, 22. Composed by Thomas Tallis (1510?–85), it first appeared in a much longer form in Parker's version of the Psalms (*c.* 1558, composed while Archbishop Parker was in a country retreat on account of his being married, and therefore deprived of his benefice and orders by Queen Mary); it was reduced to its present form in Ravenscroft's *Psalter* (1621). The form in *SM* and *SH* (and in *Harm. Sac.*, 68) is somewhat different from that in the *Foundery C.* and in modern books, where it is now known as 'Tallis's Canon'. Wesley may have met it in Playford's *Whole Book of Psalms* (1677—or a later edn.) unless indeed he had been familiar with it from childhood. (Adams, 101.) 11, 56, 183, 270

CANTERBURY

SM (1765), 106; *SH*, 311–12, and previously in *Harm. Sac.* (2nd and 3rd edn.), 219, named 'London'. It first appeared in Israel Holdroyd's *Spiritual Man's Companion* (1753) in a four-part anthem style. (Adams, 179.) 115, 289, 319, 367, 429, 430, 497

CARDIFF

SM, 69–70; *SH*, 211–12. It appeared first in *Harm. Sac.*, 109, and in the *Div. Mus. Misc.* as 'Thornbury', and is quite different from 'Cardiff Tune' in the *Foundery C.*, 28–9, and of course from the six-lines-eights tune of the same name of later date, found in Booth. (Adams, 159.) 484

The Hymn Tunes

CAREY'S
> *SM*, 80; *SH*, 258–9. It appeared first in John Church's *Introduction to Psalmody* (1723), in Gawthorn's *Harmonia Perfecta* (1730), and then in *Harm. Sac.*, 133. Henry Carey (*c*. 1692–1743), after whom the tune was apparently named, though it is spelt 'Cary' in the original, collaborated with Lampe in a series of operas. As with 'Old Twenty-third', this tune was set to Addison's 'The Lord my pasture shall prepare.' (Adams, 163.) 31, 116, 117, 171, 275, 335, 362

CHAPEL (orig. 'Chappel')
> *SM*, 74–5; *SH*, 231–2. It is No. 19 of Lampe's *Festival H.*, and was reprinted in *Harm. Sac.*, 120. (Adams, 410.) 61, 66, 139, 141, 273, 311, 514

CHIMES
> *SM* (1765), 102; *SH*, 80–1. It appeared in *Harm. Sac.* (2nd edn., 1765), 85, and the author, if it be not Butts, is unknown. In some collections, however, it was known as 'Whitton's', and this may in fact indicate the composer. In *Harm. Sac.* it is headed 'Psalm 150, by King James'; the tune apparently first appeared in Moore's *The Psalm-Singer's Pocket Companion* (1756), and *The Psalm-Singer's Delightful Pocket Companion* (*c*. 1762), where it is called 'King David's Delight', and set to Watts' version of Psalm 150. (Adams, 174.) 40, 405

COMPLAINT
> *SM* (1765), 103–4; *SH*, 156. In *Harm. Sac.* (2nd edn., 1765), 221; in the 3rd edn. it is called 'Wantage'. It is thus a question as to which of the two 1765 volumes appeared first, and which thus first printed the tune. (Adams, 176.) 25, 128, 151, 277, 443

COOKHAM
> *SM*, 16; *SH*, 41. Originally, in a slightly different version, in *Harm. Sac.*, 14, and in *Div. Mus. Misc.*, as 'Huntington.' Like 'Arne's', it is said to be derived from Arne's song, 'Waters parted from the sea'; but that presupposes that the song was known before the opera *Artaxerxes* was first produced in 1762. Adams, 135, doubts the identification. 388, 507

CORNISH
> *SM*, 29–30; *SH*, 98–9. Its first appearance seems to be in Knapp's *Collection* (1738), in an anthem-like style, as 'Dorchester' (Knapp was a Dorset man); about 1750 it was set to 'Come, let us join our cheerful songs'; as 'Weston Favel', it appears in a more elaborate form in Evison's *Compleat Book of Psalmody* (1754), and it is found in *Harm. Sac.*, 34. By an unknown composer, it is possibly, as its name implies, of Cornish origin. (Adams, 139.) 200, 229, 434

DEDICATION
> *SM*, 71–2, entitled 'Self Dedication'; *SH*, 222–3. It appeared first in *Harm. Sac.*, 114. (Adams, 159.) 20, 98, 150, 166, 379, 399, 418, 451, 498

DERBY
Appearing first in *SH*, 10, its composer and original source are alike unknown. Now known as 'Derbe', the *Companion* attributes it to Lampe. (Adams, 187.) 210, 485

DRESDEN
SM, 57; *SH*, 179–80. Almost certainly adapted from a German (Moravian) chorale, found in a manuscript collection of 1743, and printed in Hutton's *Tunes for the Hymns* (*c*. 1745). It was printed by Butts, *Harm. Sac.*, 95–6, in a different form. (Adams, 153.) 24, 151, 385

EVESHAM
SM, 48–9; *SH*, 158. It continued in use as late as the *Companion* (1847), which rightly indicates its source as *Harm. Sac.*, 73, where it appears in 2/2 time, as it is, in a more altered form, in the *Foundery C.*, 36. Its first appearance, however, was in the 3rd edn. of Playford (1709), where it is set to 'Hymn XIV, To the Holy Ghost'. The name may be a reminiscence of a visit Wesley paid to Evesham in 1742. Its use seems to have been confined to Methodists. (Adams, 118.) 127, 218, 353, 384, 450, 479

FETTER LANE
SM, 22–3; *SH*, 70. A quite different tune from that named 'Fetter Lane Tune' in the *Foundery C.*, 3 (see 'Brentford', above). It is a German chorale by Kriegers (1667), and was used by Hutton, Butts, (*Harm. Sac.*, 22) and the *Div. Mus. Misc.*, where it is named 'Marienborn Tune'. (Adams, 93.) 22, 88, 113, 488

FONMON
SM, 68–9); *SH*, 214–15. It appeared in the *Foundery C.*, 7, which was possibly its first appearance. Butts prints it, *Harm. Sac.*, 108, and it appears also in *Div. Mus. Misc.* Fonmon Castle was several times visited by Wesley; situated near Cardiff, it was the home of Robert Jones, who had the dining-room fitted out as a chapel. (Adams, 79.) 194, 496

FOUNDERY
SM, 21; *SH*, 46–7. In *Harm. Sac.* (2nd edn), 222, entitled 'For the Epiphany', and *Div. Mus. Misc.* By Lampe? (Adams, 136.) 28, 107, 112, 137, 176, 415, 467, 468, 494, 508

FRANKFORT (i.e. Frankfurt?)
SM, 77–8; *SH*, 248–9). It is included in Booth where the source is given simply as *SH*. It is, however, a German chorale: 'Wer weiss, wie nahe mir mein Ende', published by G. R. Wittwe (Hamburg, 1690). Wesley no doubt met it in use among the Moravians on his visit to Germany, and in his copy of Freylinghausen's *Gesangbuch* (1704), and he included it in the *Foundery C.*, 34, as 'Swift German Tune'; there it is in 2/4 time, whereas, as 'Frankfort', it is in 3/2 time. Now used as a long-metre tune, it is called 'Winchester New' (the name first appears in 1754). Butts included it in his *Harm. Sac.*, 128. The

tune named 'Frankfort' in the *Foundery C.*, 12, is entirely different. (Adams, 116.) 29, 30, 87, 130, 202, 369, 462, 463

FULHAM

SM, 59–60; *SH,* 185–7. Originally, in a slightly different version in *Harm. Sac.,* 208. Possibly an adaptation of a song. (Adams, 155.) 224, 444, 445

FUNERAL

SM, 62–3; *SH,* 191–2. By Lampe, No. 22 of his *Festival H.,* 1746. Written for 'Ah, lovely appearance of death' (Hymn 47), the title is taken from the subject. It appeared in *Harm. Sac.,* 92–3, entitled 'Funeral Hymn'. (Adams, 413). 47, 75, 76, 167

GUERNSEY

SM, 58–9); *SH,* 182–3. It appeared in *Harm. Sac.,* 100–1, and was an adaptation of a tune by Henry Holcombe, called 'When here Lucinda', from 'Arno's Vale', in his *Musical Medley*. This appeared also in the *Gentleman's Magazine* for 1745. (Adams, 154.) 125

HALLELUJAH

SM, 39–40; *SH,* 118–20. Appearing in *Harm. Sac.,* 60–1, and *Div. Mus. Misc.,* it was taken from Robinson's *Divine Companion* (1738), and was composed by William Markham (*c.* 1725) for Psalm 119. It takes its name from the elaborate doxology with which the tune concludes. (Adams, 143.) 217, 243, 254

HAMILTON'S

SM (1765), 87–8; *SH,* 296–7. It appears in *Harm. Sac.,* 155, as 'Clarke's'. Perhaps by Lampe, as Charles Wesley, Jun., suggested. (Adams, 168.) 57, 156, 233, 402, 465

HANDEL'S MARCH

SM, 101–2; *SH,* 323–6. Already in the *Foundery C.,* 5–6, named 'Jericho Tune', it was adapted from a march in Handel's *Ricardo Primo* (1727)—the earliest example of a popular tune being seized on by Wesley. *Harm. Sac.,* 176–8, names it 'March'. (Adams, 76.) 258, 259, 260, 268, 305, 306

HOTHAM

SM (1765), 107; *SH,* 50–1. Also in *Harm. Sac.* (2nd edn.), 75; the tune is by Martin Madan (1726–90), who seems to have assisted Wesley in the preparation of *SM.* It was later reprinted, set to 'Jesu, Lover of my soul', in Toplady's *Gospel Magazine,* in 1776, and was the accepted tune to that hymn for a century afterwards. Butts (in his 3rd edn.) calls it 'Oatham'. (Adams, 180.) 6 ['Hotham's'], 7, 8, 199, 223, 339, 495, 515, 524

INVITATION

SM, 42–3; *SH,* 136. No. 18 of *Festival H.,* it takes its name from the opening theme of the words, 'Come, sinners, to the Gospel feast', Hymn 2. The tune was reprinted in *Harm. Sac.,* 65. (Adams, 409.) 2, 9, 280, 383, 493

IRENE

SM, 65–6; *SH*, 200–1. It had already appeared, in an altered version, in the *Foundery C.*, 8–9, as 'Savannah Tune'. It first appeared in Freylinghausen's *Gesangbuch* (1704), 1066, and was no doubt learned by Wesley from the Moravians on board the *Simmonds*. In 1742 a party of Moravians passed through London *en route* for America; some ascended the gallery of St. Paul's Cathedral and sang to this tune a hymn of intercession for the teeming population below. They then proceeded to their vessel, the *Irene*, and Wesley, in commemoration of this incident, changed the name of the tune from 'Savannah' to 'Irene'. It appears under the latter name in *Harm. Sac.*, 104. The *Companion* wrongly attributed it to Lampe; it is in any case quite unlike his florid style. (Adams, 80.) 51, 84, 184, 342

ISLINGTON

SM, 47–8; *SH*, 154. It first appeared in Andrew Roner's *Melopeia Sacra*, *c.* 1720. Roner was a music master and a friend of Handel. Wesley used it in the *Foundery C.*, 26–7. Butts included it in *Harm. Sac.*, 72, and it was printed as late as Booth (1857); Gauntlett wrongly attributed it to Martin Madan. The name echoes Wesley's frequent visits to Islington, then, as still, an Evangelical stronghold. (Adams, 108.) 129, 195, 255, 455

ITALIAN

SM, 52–3; *SH*, 168–9. Originally in *Harm. Sac.*, 75, in a slightly different version, and in the *Div. Mus. Misc.*, as 'Maryland'). A very florid tune, perhaps adapted from an operatic aria. (Adams, 151.) 231, 232, 284, 425

JUDGMENT

SM, 54–5; *SH*, 174–5. It is an adaptation of an air by Henry Carey written to a popular patriotic song to celebrate Admiral Vernon's capture of Portobello in 1739: 'He comes! he comes! the hero comes!' As with 'Love divine, all loves excelling' (see Hymn 374), the words are a parody by Charles Wesley, specially written to make use of the tune; it was thus probably written some time before its first known printed appearance. Carey's tune appears, set to the same words, in *Harm. Sac.*, (2nd edn. *c.* 1765), 110, entitled 'Trumpet Tune'. (Adams, 152.) 55

KETTLEBY'S

SM, 51; *SH*, 164–5. Found originally in *Harm. Sac.*, 79, it is almost certainly named after its composer. (Adams, 149.) 44, 216

KINGSWOOD

SM, 95; *SH*, 292–3. It has similarities with the tune 'Barnabas' which is derived from a setting of Ps. 75 in the French *Psalter* of 1561, from which perhaps it was adapted by Campion in one of his books of songs issued in 1613; it was used by Nathaniel Gawthorn, in his *Harmonia Perfecta* (1730), and is interesting as being the first '7's and 6's' hymn and tune ever printed together. The name of course commemorates Wesley's school near Bristol. *Harm. Sac.*

also reprinted it, 160–1. (Adams, 169.) 60, 95, 105, 106, 108, 160, 161, 168, 172, 180, 181, 235, 236, 283, 286, 290, 316, 326, 327, 344, 357, 401, 406, 411, 412, 436, 437, 452, 517

LAMPE'S

SM, 9–10; *SH,* 18–19. Composed by J. F. Lampe, it forms No. 1 of his *Festival H.; Harm. Sac.* (2nd edn.), 155, includes it under the name 'Nativity Hymn'. (Adams, 392.) 12, 41, 83, 94, 100, 133, 146, 257, 291, 292, 294, 314, 331, 414, 441B, 466, 470, 521

LEEDS

SM, 25–6; *SH,* 82. In a much simpler form it appears as 'Jera' in the *Foundery C.,* 24, being originally a chorale going back to 1554. It appeared in the first edn. of *Harm. Sac.,* 183, named 'Bloxham', and in the *Div. Mus. Misc.,* which retains the original triple metre: from Butts onward it is, in its elaborated form, in quadruple metre. (Adams, 105.) 82, 322, 397

LIVERPOOL

SM, 24–5; *SH,* 76. It was composed by William Weale of Bedford, and first appeared in the *Divine Music Scholar's Guide* (*c.*1715). *Harm. Sac.,* 37, calls it 'Edmonton', but 'Bedford Tune' is the name given to it in the *Foundery C.,* 15, as in Broome's *Collection:* and from the *Companion,* Booth, etc., onwards it has been known as 'Bedford'. (Adams, 90.) 36, 205, 207, 267, 373, 403, 420, 523

LONDON

SM, 64–5; *SH,* 197–9. By John Sheeles, it first appeared in *The Skylark* (*c.* 1730), set, as in *SM,* to 'The spacious firmament on high'. It was also used in the *Div. Mus. Misc.* and *Harm. Sac.,* (94–5), in the latter being given the name 'Kettering' by which it is still known. (Adams, 157.) 'London New Tune', in *Foundery C.,* 9, is a different tune, for which see 'Bray's'. 225, 226

LOVE-FEAST

SM, 17–18; *SH,* 53–4. It had already appeared in the *Foundery C.,* 12–13, and varies slightly from volume to volume. It appears to be founded on a melody by J. G. Hille, 1739, called 'O ihr auserwählten Kinder' (but may even go back to an untitled collection of 1733), and Wesley presumably heard it on his visit to Herrnhut. Its name comes from the words to which it was first set by Wesley (Hymn 505):

> Come, and let us sweetly join . . .
> Celebrate the feast of love.

Harm. Sac. reprints it, 21, named 'Lambeth', and the *Div. Mus. Misc.* calls it 'Philadelphia'. (Adams, 87.) 49, 73, 189, 501, 505, 506

MAGDALEN

SM, 19–20; *SH,* 60–1. By J. F. Lampe. It takes its title from the words to which it was first set, as No. 10 of *Festival H.:* 'Happy Magdalen, to whom/Christ the

Lord vouchsafed to appear'; in *Harm. Sac.*, 18–19. (Adams, 401.) 37, 178, 209, 278

MARIENBORN (also spelt 'Marienburn')

SM, 77; *SH*, 245–6. It appeared in a somewhat different form in the *Foundery C.*, 30–1, entitled 'Slow German Tune'—'Marienborn Tune' therein, 16, is entirely different. It seems to be an elaborated form of the tune 'Bremen'; composed by Georg Christian Neumark (1621–81) for his own hymn 'Wer nur den lieben Gott lässt walten' (1657), and first appeared in England in J. C. Jacobi's *Psalmodia Germanica* (1722), which contained a large number of German chorales, together with English translations of German hymns. Wesley came across it, however, in Freylinghausen's *Gesangbuch*. *Harm. Sac.*, 129, called the tune both 'Marienbourn' and 'Publick Worship'. (Adams, 113.) 67, 274, 323, 382, 431, 461, 499

MINORIES

SM, 16–17; *SH*, 44. This seems first to have appeared in the *Foundery C.*, 10–11, entitled 'Penmark', then came into *Div. Mus. Misc.*, as 'Alcester', where the range and rhythm were improved, and thence to *SM* and *SH*. It appears also in *Harm. Sac.*, 15, with the same title and set to the same hymn as in *SM* and *SH*. In his 2nd edn., 153, Butts altered the name to 'Doxology'. (Adams, 84.) 293

MISS EDWIN'S

SM, 67–8; *SH*, 203–4. Apparently taken from *Harm. Sac.*, 107, where it has the same name and is set to the same hymn. It seems originally to have appeared in *Div. Mus. Misc.*, 1754, where it is named 'Bethesda'. (Adams, 158.) 219

MITCHAM

SH, 110–11. Possibly influenced by Handel—cf. his Water Music. It appears earlier in *Harm. Sac.* (2nd edn.), 123. (Adams, 190.) 101, 131, 132, 312, 333, 351, 423, 456

MORNING SONG

SM, 29; *SH*, 92–3. It first appeared in *Harm. Sac.*, 33, and in the *Div. Mus. Misc.*, and is derived from one of Corelli's concertos. (Adams, 138.) 208

MOURNER'S

SM, 86–7; *SH*, 275–6. (The tune of the same name in the 1822 edition of the *SH*, and later works, by Charles Wesley, Jun., is entirely different.) The earlier tune is found in *Harm. Sac.*, 142, and in the *Div. Mus. Misc.*, entitled 'Leeds'. (Adams, 166.) 32, 96, 126, 142, 148, 169, 285, 363, 439, 449

MUSICIAN'S

SH, 234–5; the 1822 edition ascribed it to Lampe, and Dr. Miller, in *David's Harp*, to Arne. It owes its name to the theme of Hymn 196, to which, among others, it is set. Its earliest appearance is in *SH*, that of the same title in *Harm. Sac.*, 122–3, being quite different. (Adams, 194.) 138, 196, 300, 392, 512

NEWCASTLE

SM, 88; SH, 282. The tune has strong similarities to the folksong, 'The lass with the delicate air'. It appeared first either in *Harm. Sac.*, 149, or the *Div. Mus. Misc.*, as 'Halifax'. Though Adams claims to have found it in Hutton's *Collection* (1745) and in two Moravian chorale collections of the end of the century, the present writer cannot believe it was originally a chorale. (Adams, 167.) 5, 10, 203, 469

NEW YEAR'S DAY

SM, 7–8; SH, 12–13. No. 3 of Lampe's *Festival H.*, it was reprinted in *Harm. Sac.*, 152–3. (Adams, 394.) 45, 482.

NORWICH

SM, 81–2; SH, 266–7. By Robert King, a royal musician under Charles II and William and Mary. He was one of the contributors to the *Divine Companion* (1701), from which this tune is taken. In a simplified form it is now known as 'David's Harp', and in a similar form as 'King's' in *Harm. Sac.*, 130. (Adams, 164.) 182, 247, 261, 317, 389, 471, 480

OLD GERMAN

SM, 5; SH, 2. It would appear to be another adaptation—or reminiscence—of Georg Neumark's 'Wer nur den lieben Gott lässt walten' (cf. note on 'Marienborn'). *Harm. Sac.* prints it, 2. If this assumption is correct, 'Old German' is a form of the first half of the original chorale; its first appearance is in a manuscript chorale book of 1720. (Adams, 133.) 197

OLNEY

SM, 10–11; SH, 20–1. (Often spelt 'Oulney' in these and other early edns.) In the *Foundery C.*, 4, it appears in a simpler form as 'The Resignation Tune'. It is a German chorale, found in Jacobi, and in Freylinghausen's *Gesangbuch*. *Harm. Sac.* prints it, 10. In its origin it may perhaps go back to a chorale by W. Figulus of 1575. (Adams, 75.) 21, 54, 72, 99, 165, 244, 262, 287, 296, 302, 309, 356, 376, 424, 435, 440, 448

PALMI'S

SM, 50; SH, 162–3. Originally in *Harm. Sac.*, 78, it appears in Arnold's *Complete Psalmodist* (7th edn., 1779), and it is possible that the unknown first edition may (if it contains the tune) precede *Harm. Sac.* (Adams, 148.) 43, 174, 227, 238, 307, 318, 332, 407, 408, 413, 464

PARIS

SH, 32. The *Companion* attributes it to a certain Weldon. Its first appearance seems to have been in *SH*. (Adams, 187.) 370

PASSION

SM, 5–6; SH, 4–5. No. 4 of Lampe's *Festival H.*, it was reprinted in *Harm. Sac.*, 4–5, under the title 'All ye that pass by'. (Adams, 395.) 154

PLYMOUTH

SM, 14; *SH*, 30. It appeared in the *Foundery C.*, 12, as 'Frankfort Tune', and is first found in a publication in 1693 by J. Ch. Bach, and then in Jacobi's *Psalmodia Germanica* (1722); it is thus an old German melody, and Wesley found it in his own German hymn-book. *Harm. Sac.* prints it, 13, as does *Div. Mus. Misc.*, both naming the tune 'Plymouth'. (Adams, 86.) 345, 500

23rd PSALM

SM, 78–9; *SH*, 256–7. Now known as 'Old Twenty-third', it originally appeared in Andrew Roner's *Melopeia Sacra* (*c.* 1720 — see 'Islington' above) in a very elaborate form, and was republished in *Div. Mus. Misc.* where it was christened 'Kingswood Tune', and set to Addison's version of Psalm 23: 'The Lord my pasture shall prepare'—hence the later name. *Harm. Sac.* also prints it, 132. On the other hand Moore's *Psalm Singer's Compleat Tutor* (1750) states that it is 'by T. M'. (Adams, 162.) 163, 264, 321, [354[4]]

112th PSALM

SM, 84, as 'Old 112th Psalm Tune'; *SH*, 261–2, in which the tune is altered to 3/2 time. Wesley first used it in the *Foundery C.*, 33–4, called 'Playford's Tune.' Now known as 'Vater Unser', it first appeared in *Geistliche Lieder* (1539), thence came into the Anglo-Genevan Psalter of 1561, thence to the English Psalter of 1562, set to Kethe's version of Psalm 112: 'The man is blest that God doth fear'. Playford published a version of it in his *Psalms and Hymns in solemn Musick* (1671) — hence the title in the *Foundery C.*, though it had appeared in many other earlier collections. In *Harm. Sac.*, 131. It is sometimes attributed to Luther. (Adams, 114.) 27, 69, 70, 110, 143, 164, 297, 364, 368, 511

113th PSALM

SM, 98–9; *SH*, 314–17, entitled '(Old) 113th Psalm Tune'. It had already appeared in the *Foundery C.*, 35–6, and can be traced back to the *Strassburg Psalter* of 1536; it was possibly composed by Matthias Greiter. Set in *SM*, etc., to 'I'll praise my Maker', it may thus very easily have been the last tune Wesley sang, for he sang (or attempted to sing) this hymn on his deathbed. Though it appeared in England in 1558 in a book of *26 Psalms and other Songs,* the Anglo-Genevan Psalter of 1561, Day's Psalter of 1563, and very many later collections, it may well be that Wesley learned it directly from the Moravians. *Harm. Sac.* reprints it, 172–3. (Adams, 117.) 179, 215, 343, 366, 428, 510

PUDSEY

SM, 44; *SH*, 142–3. It appears in an altered version in the *Foundery C.*, 22–3, named 'First German Tune'—a chorale that can be traced back to 1544, composed by Georg Rhaw, though considerably altered. (Adams, 103.) 23, 173, 281, 330

The Hymn Tunes

PURCELL'S
SM, 53–4; SH, 171–2. It appears in *Harm. Sac.*, 66, and is derived from 'When charming Chloe', by Thomas Gladwin. (Adams, 152.) 46, 303, 304, 329, 377, 509

RESURRECTION
SM, 70–1; SH, 216–17. No. 8 of Lampe's *Festival H.* In *Harm. Sac.*, 110 (Adams, 399.) 336

ST. LUKE'S
SM, 55–6; SH; 176–7; *Foundery C.*, 32–3. Its origin and history are quite unknown, as is the reason for the name, though it might commemorate the Wren parish church where the Methodists from the Foundery worshipped. It is first found in Tate and Brady's *Supplement* (1703), the *Supplement to the New Version* (1708), and later appears in *Harm. Sac.*, 97–8. (Adams, 114.) 123, 188, 375

ST. PAUL'S
SM, 34–5; SH, 102–3. It appeared first in *Harm. Sac.*, 51. (Adams, 141.) 91, 124, 301, 334, 352, 457

SALISBURY
SM, 15; SH, 38–9; *Foundery C.*, 11, set to 'Christ the Lord is risen today'. It first appeared in *Lyra Davidica* (1708), but no name of composer or compiler is known, and the source of the tune is not further known. In 1708 it was called 'The Resurrection', and nowadays 'Easter Morn'. *Harm. Sac.* prints it, 17, headed 'For Christmas Day'. Two contemporary manuscript notes ascribe its composition (*a*) to Dr. Worgan (impossible, as he was born later than the tune's first appearance) and (*b*) Henry Carey. (Adams, 85.) 252, 502, 503

SAVANNAH
SM, 13–14; SH, 28. In the *Foundery C.*, 10, it is named 'Herrnhuth Tune'. It was composed about 1690 by G. C. Strattner, who died in 1705. The *Foundery C.* probably marked its first appearance in England, the tune having been brought back by Wesley after his visit to Herrnhut—hence the earlier name. In *Harm. Sac.*, 12, as 'Savannah'. (For the tune named 'Savannah' in the *Foundery C.*, 8–9, see 'Irene'.) (Adams, 83.) 162, 340, 422

SHEFFIELD
SM, 85–6; SH, 272–3. Composed by J. F. Lampe for *Festival H.*, No. 13, entitled 'On the Ascension', and taken over into *Harm. Sac.*, 136–7. Later Butts set it to 'Infinite God, to thee we raise' (CW's version of the *Te Deum*), and entitled it 'Te Deum Laudamus'. (Adams, 404.) 198, 214, 253, 481

SION
SM, 63–4; SH, 194–5. Later sometimes called 'New Jerusalem', the tune is (perhaps incorrectly) reputed to have been composed by Benjamin Milgrove (c. 1731–1810). Its first appearance was in *SM*. (Adams, 156.) 48, 52, 71, 77

SMITH'S
> *SH*, 112–14. Found originally in *Harm. Sac.*, 90–1. (Adams, 190.) 97, 246, 400, 446

SNOWSFIELDS
> *SM*, 73–4; *SH*, 238. This may be based on the tune 'Innsbruck' ('Nun ruhen alle Wälder') by Heinrich Isaac (1450–1527), which first appeared in 1539. It had previously appeared in *Hymns and Sacred Poems,* in which Butts and Lampe had collaborated in 1749, in *Harm. Sac.*, 121, and *Div. Mus. Misc.* Named after the third of Wesley's London chapels, obtained in 1743. (Adams, 161.) 42, 58, 114, 140, 213, 272, 324, 325, 454, 459, 513

SPITALFIELDS
> *SM*, 35–6; *SH*, 108–9. Found first in *Harm. Sac.*, 45, and in the 2nd edn. 107, set to a different hymn and entitled 'A Request to the Divine Being'. Probably named after one of Wesley's early London chapels. (Adams, 142.) 15, 242, 416

STANTON
> *SM*, 42; *SH*, 134. (Adams, 145.) Presumably named after the Cotswold village beloved by JW in his Oxford days. 14, 237

SWANLING BAR
> Nothing whatever seems to be known of this tune; it is quite unidentifiable, and appears in neither *SM* nor *SH*, nor does Adams know it. It takes its name from a town in Ireland, often visited by Wesley; the town contained an ironworks, founded by Messrs. Swann, Ling, and Barr—hence the name. 474

TALLIS'S
> *SM*, 87; *SH*, 280–1, entitled 'Tally's 104th Psalm' in *SM*, and 'Tally's' in *SH*. It first appeared in the 6th edn. of Tate and Brady's *New Version* of the Psalms (1708), and is almost certainly by William Croft (1678–1727). But earlier it was frequently attributed to Handel; the *Companion* (which first after Gawthorn (1730) called it by its modern name of 'Hanover'), and Booth ('104th Psalm') and a contemporary manuscript note in *Harm. Sac.* (68, entitled 'Cannon'), all so attribute it. Charles Wesley, Jun.'s edition of *SH* (1822), queries whether it be by Purcell. Broome's *Collection* (by 1748) names it 'St. George's Tune', but does not ascribe it to Croft, though many tunes in that collection are so ascribed. Wesley had printed it in the *Foundery C.,* 6, under the name 'Bromswick Tune', in deference to the ruling house of Brunswick. In *Harm. Sac.*, 101, named '104th Psalm Tune', as also in almost all psalm and tune books of the eighteenth century. (Adams, 77.) 3, 19, 192, 472

THOU SHEPHERD OF ISRAEL
> *SM* (1765), 108; *SH*, 188–9; in the 1822 edn. of the latter collection it is named 'Salters', and in the *Companion*, 136, 'Invocation'. It takes its name from the hymn, 'Thou Shepherd of Israel, and mine', for which it was originally intended by Wesley. It appeared in *Harm. Sac.* (2nd edn.), 108, named

'At Lying Down', and is derived from Arne's *Eliza* (1754). (Adams, 181.) 68, 159, 211, 360

TRAVELLER'S

SM (1765), 105; *SH*, 228–9. Adapted from 'A Thought in a Grotto' by Henry Holcombe (born *c*. 1690), as the 1822 edn. of *SH* indicates. (An anthem based on another tune of Holcombe also appears in *SH*.) Presumably the title was given because it was set to 'Come on, my partners in distress', Hymn 324. In *Harm. Sac.*, 126–7, it is named 'St. Michael's'. Hymn 136, 'Come, O thou Traveller unknown', is also set to be sung to 'Traveller's', but this is clearly an error, as the only tune in Wesley's publications of that name is this tune in the 88.6.D metre (cf. Hymns 118, 295, 460); but the error was continued in edition after edition. In Coke's 1816 (Dublin) edition of the hymn-book, Hymn 136 is set to a tune 'Wrestling Jacob'—perhaps the tune so named in Booth, composed by William Jackson of Masham. In the *Foundery C.*, 28–9, Hymn 136 is set to 'Cardiff Tune' (the same as 'Welsh', for which see below). (Adams, 178.) 118, 295, 460

TRINITY

SM, 38; *SH*, 115–17. No. 17 of Lampe's *Festival H*. The name is derived from the title there given, 'On the Trinity', the tune being set to 'Hail, holy, holy, holy Lord', Hymn 251. *Harm. Sac.*, 50, calls it 'Hymn to the Trinity' in the 3rd edn., 104. (Adams, 408.) 240, 241, 248, 249, 251, 378

TRIUMPH

SM, 88–9; *SH*, 284–5. No. 23 of Lampe's *Festival H*. The title is derived from the theme of the hymn to which it is there set—'On the Death of a Believer'. *Harm. Sac.* prints it, 150, with the title 'Marlbrough', changed in the 2nd edn. to 'On the Death of a Believer', as in Lampe. (Adams, 414.) 38, 191, 204, 265, 483

TRUMPET

SH, 219–20. In Isaac Smith's *Collection* (*c*. 1770), A. Williams' *New Universal Psalmodist* (1770), the *Companion*, and Booth, it is named 'Portsmouth', the *Companion* attributing it to Lampe. *Harm. Sac.* (2nd edn.), 77, marks its first appearance, under the title 'On the Death of a Believer'. (Adams, 193.) 33, 64, 222, 519, 522

WALSALL

SM, 89–90; *SH*, 287–8. It has no connection with the tune 'Walsall' which appeared in Anchor's *Collection* (*c*. 1721). Often ascribed to Purcell, it is in fact No. 21 of Lampe's *Festival H*. *Harm. Sac.* prints it, 151, and Toplady printed Hymn 190 set to this tune in his *Gospel Magazine* for 1777. (Adams, 123, 412). 190

WEDNESBURY

SM, 37; *SH*, 105–6, the 1822 edn. of which ascribes it with real probability to Lampe. It appeared originally in *Harm. Sac.*, 52. Named after the

Staffordshire town, the scene of some of Methodism's earliest triumphs. (Adams, 142.) 89, 104, 144, 320, 337, 391, 487, 525

WELLING
SM, 52; SH, 166–7. Of Welsh origin? Harm. Sac., 74, names it 'Harwich', and Div. Mus. Misc., 'Kingsbridge'. (Adams, 150.) 122, 155, 308, 328

WELSH
SM, 80–1; SH, 264–5. In both these it is called 'Welch', as it is in Harm. Sac., 134. It appeared originally in a very corrupt form in the Foundery C., 28–9 named 'Cardiff Tune', set to 'Come, O thou Traveller unknown' (Hymn 136), possibly appearing there for the first time (cf. note on 'Traveller's'). Probably of German origin. (Adams, 110.) 79, 245, 310 (orig., 'Welch'), 421, 432

WENVOE (originally 'Wenvo')
SM, 26–7; SH, 86–7. It first appeared in a slightly different form in the Foundery C., 17–18. It is of unknown origin, but may be a Welsh melody — cf. the name of a village near Cardiff, and the parish of one of Wesley's early clerical coworkers, the Revd. John Hodges. The tune is of interest as being the first Methodist tune with 'repeats' at the end of each verse. Harm. Sac. reprints it, 30, as does Div. Mus. Misc. (Adams, 96.) 78, 177, 298, 299, 346

WESTMINSTER
SM, 96; SH, 302–3. It is an adaptation of Purcell's tune, 'Fairest isle, all isles excelling', for which the words, 'Love divine, all loves excelling', were first published in 1747 — Hymn 374, which see. Purcell's music is taken from his opera, 'King Arthur' (1691), set to words by Dryden. It is the best known of those of Charles Wesley's hymns which imitated earlier poems, and were written to make use of popular tunes. Harm. Sac. prints it, 162–3, set to the original Wesley words, also naming it 'Westminster', while the Div. Mus. Misc. sets it to 'Loving Saviour, Prince of peace', under the name 'Dublin'. (Adams, 170.) 59, 374, 387, 516

WEST STREET
SM, 66–7; SH, 206–7. Possibly adapted from Handel, it takes its name from West Street Chapel, one of Wesley's early London chapels (still standing, though now put to secular use). It appeared first in Harm. Sac., 106. (Adams, 158.) 26, 65, 145, 186, 187

WHIT SUNDAY
Though composed by Lampe, No. 14 of his Festival H., it does not appear in either SM or SH. Harm. Sac. prints it, 138–9, 'For Whitsunday', and another hymn in this metre, named 'Whitsuntide', attributed to Kimber, appears in the Companion, 88. (Adams, 405.) 153, 220, 417

WOOD'S
SM, 75–6, SH, 242–3. It appeared originally in Harm. Sac., 124. (Adams, 162.) 120, 279

YORK
> *SM,* 99–101; *SH,* 318–21. It appeared first in *Harm. Sac.,* 174–5, as 'Castor'. (Adams, 171.) 341, 355, 426, 427, 477

ZION
> see 'Sion'

ZOAR
> *SM,* 49–50; *SH,* 160–1. Of unknown origin, it may come from Handel. *Harm. Sac.,* where it first appeared, 81, entitled it 'Hoxton'. Zoar was the name of one of Wesley's London chapels, obtained in 1755. (Adams, 148.) 230, 271, 380, 381, 491

O.A.B.
F.B.

Seventeen Additional Tune Commentaries

BRISTOL first appeared as BRISTOL TUNE at p. 16 in *Foundery C*. It was adapted from William Croft's (1678–1727) setting of Ps. 116, in Playford. The appended triple-time traveling chorus "Hallelujah. Amen" suggests an early-Methodist practice of adding refrains. Thomas Butts (fl. mid-18th century)[1] includes a slightly modified version of the tune and reconstructed chorus at p. 32 in *Harm. Sac.* John Wesley includes that version of the tune and chorus at p. 28, in *SH* 1761, and the two-voice version in *SH* 1780 includes a new bass line minus figures.

CAMBRIDGE, one of two tunes based on the song *Charming Chloe* ("When charming Chloe"), published ca. 1730. The first tune, named VIRGINIA, 2225a, appeared at p. 49, in *Div. Mus. Misc.*, with figured bass and melody, and at p. 76, in *Harm. Sac.*, with a slightly different figured bass, melody, and a second voice. The second tune, named PERCALL'S, 2225b, appeared at p. 66 in *Harm. Sac.* in a three-voice setting that at p. 43 in *SH* 1761was reduced to melody and renamed CAMBRIDGE. Wesley included the melody of VIRGINIA, with a new bass, in *SH* 1780, and misnamed the tune CAMBRIDGE.

CHESHUNT is an anthem slightly abridged from "A thought on a Spring morning," in Henry Holcombe's (ca. 1693–ca. 1750) *The Musical Medley*[2] [1755], pp. 2–4. It appeared at pp. 195–98 in *Harm. Sac.*, named CHESUNT, in three parts with figured bass. John Wesley includes the melody and spelling of the tune name at pp. 110–112 in *SH* 1765. A marginal note to the tune on p. 334 in *SH* 1780, presumably John Wesley's, indicates the insertion of an "h" to correct the misspelling of the tune name.

CHESTER appears for the first time in *SH* 1780. There is no information about the composer or source of this tune.

DYING STEPHEN first appeared at p. 50, hymn 20, "The Triumph of Faith," in John F. Lampe's (1702/3–1751) *Festival H*.[3] 1746. Thomas Butts included the tune at p. 170 in Harm. Sac, under the name ST. STEPHENS with a new figured bass and a third voice. The melody was included at p. 97 in *SH* 1761, renamed DYING STEPHEN, and appears at p. 308 in *SH* 1780 with a slight variant of Lampe's figured bass.

EPWORTH, according to the Hymn Tune Index, is based on the "Gavotte" from John Humphries's (1707–1733) *Concerto* Op. 2, No. 7, published ca. 1755. The tune first appeared at p. 169 in *Harm. Sac.*, named OUNDELL, under the

---

[1] Bookkeeper and a steward at The Foundery, and a traveling companion of the Wesleys, that in addition probably "collaborated with Wesley in the production of *The Gamut, or Scale of Music*, the precedes the interlined hymns in *SH* 1765.

[2] *The Musical Medley*, 1755. https://books.google.com/books?id=2s_jc0BO0M8C&printsec=frontcover&source=gbs_ge_summary_r&cad=0#v=onepage&q&f=false.

[3] Lampe, *Hymns on the Great Festivals*, 1746; facsimile reprint, Madison, New Jersey: the Charles Wesley Society, 1996.

heading "For a Dying Believer." Wesley included the melody with "Hallelujah's," renamed EPWORTH, at p. 40 in *SH* 1761, with a new bass at p. 122 in *SH* 1780.

THE GOD OF ABRAHAM is a traditional melody for the Hebrew *Yigdal* that was transcribed by cantor Meyer Lyon (1751–1796), for Thomas Olivers (1725–1799), ca. 1770. *The Hymn Tune Index* cites the first appearance of the tune with the text, "The God of Abraham praise," in a music insert for *The Gospel Magazine, or Treasury of Divine Knowledge*, vol. 2 (London, 1775). The tune first appeared in 1775 named HYMN and APRIL, and in 1778 appeared as YELDING and LEONI. JW first named it THE GOD OF ABRAHAM in *Sac. H.* 1780.

HAVANT. The melody named HAVANT TUNE appeared with figured bass at p. 26 in *Div. Mus. Misc.*, and at p. 4 in *Harm. Sac.*, with a different figured bass and a third voice. The melody is included at p. 8 in *SH* 1761, and appears with a new bass at p. 14 in *SH* 1780. The composer or source of this tune is unknown. The publication of an identical tune in the same year suggests that the music leaders at the Wesleys' Foundery and George Whitefield's (1741–1768) nearby Tabernacle, may have developed a core of tunes.

LEOMINSTER first appeared at p. 179 in *Harm. Sac.*, and Wesley included it at p. 102 in *SH* 1761. There is no information about the composer or source of this tune.

MACCABEES was adapted from the chorus, "See, the conqu'ring hero comes" in G. F. Handel's (1685–1759) famous oratorio *Judas Maccabaeus,* composed in 1746, premiered London, 1747. The chorus also appeared in the composer's less performed oratorio, *Joshua,* which premiered the same year. "Christ the Lord is risen today," which is notably absent from *SH* 1761 and his final *Collection* (1780), first appeared with this tune at p. 194 in Thomas Butts's *Harm. Sac.* under the heading "For Easter Day." One problem of this setting is that Handel's tune is 24 bars in length, and only 16 bars are needed to sing a stanza of Wesley's 77.77 text. Thus, to prevent each stanza ending on the dominant chord "V", Butts directs the singer to "end with the first part," meaning to repeat the first eight bars of music along with the last two lines of each stanza. The music editor of *SH* 1780 includes the complete tune and interlines the final two lines of each stanza. Wesley, perhaps having second thoughts, in his personal copy scratched out MACABBEAS and added "Easter," suggesting that the hymn as set at p. 11 in *Foundery C.* to EASTER HYMN [SALISBURY TUNE] with its rousing "Hallelujahs," is a better setting.

MANCHESTER is cited by the Hymn Tune Index as adapted from a setting in William East's *The Second Book of the Voice of Melody*. Wesley included it at page 102 in *SH* 1765.

OLIVERS, named by John Wesley after Thomas Olivers (1725–1799), first appeared in a three-part setting with figured bass under the name HELMS-

LEY, page 16 in Madan 1763. It was probably based on other tunes, including the opening line of "Country Dance," at p. 29 in Thomas A. Arne's (1710–1778) opera, *Thomas and Sally,* 1761. It is thought that the name HELMSLEY was given by Richard Conyers (1725–1786), a friend of Wesley and rector at Helmsley, a small town in Yorkshire, England.

Ps. 100 is a seven-page, three-voice, homophonic anthem setting of John Wesley's version of Isaac Watts' (1674–1748) metrical paraphrase of Psalm 100, "Before Jehovah's awful throne."[4] The setting first appeared at p. 94 in Madan 1769 where it is called DENMARK.[5] It is one of two set-pieces[6] in *SH* 1780; the other is CHESHUNT, which John Wesley had included in *SH* 1765. Wesley's inclusion of anthems appears to contradict his life-long advocacy of the primacy of congregational song. Sally Drage speculates that Wesley's "inclusion of set pieces in his tune books may indicate that he expected them to be sung congregationally . . . for domestic worship or for use at class meetings."[7]

SACRAMENT first appeared at p. 3 in *HS* 1754. Wesley included the melody at pp. 6–7 in *SH* 1761, and the melody with the bass from *HS* 1754. See Appendix C for the three versions of this tune. There is no information about the composer or source of this tune.

STOCKTON first appeared at p. 46 in *SH* 1761. The composer and source are unknown.

YORKSHIRE first appeared at p. 101 in *SH* 1765. The composer and source are unknown.

TRUE ELIJAH first appeared at pp. 305–306 in *SH* 1780. The composer and source are unknown.

---

[4] The hymn is no. 77 in *SH* 1761, to be sung to ISLINGTON, see p. 47 *SH* 1765.

[5] Nicholas Temperley comments, "Martin Madan, an early associate of John Wesley, was hospital chaplain and music director of its chapel. He formed the congregation as the choir because at Lock, unlike the Foundling and Magdalen Hospitals with choirs composed of inmates, the patients—men, women, and children—were frail victims of venereal disease, many of whom were too ill to attend chapel at all." Temperley, "The Lock Hospital Chapel," 44-72. http://www.jstor.org/stable/766542

[6] Woods, Drage, and Roads, "West Gallery Music." *Canterbury Dictionary of Hymnology,* https://hymnology.hymnsam.co.uk/w/west-gallery-music?q=West+Gallery+music.

[7] Drage "The Set Piece," 2010.

INDEX.

A

	Page
Afcenfion	56
Arne	64
Aldrich	88
Angels Song	145
Anglefea	148
Athlone	152
Amfterdam	290

B

Brentford	16
Brays	26
Burftal	68
Burford	72
Bexly	74
Briftol	90
Brochmer	95
Broock's	100
Builth	225
Bradford	251
Birmingham	269

C

Chefter	22

	Page
Cookham	41
Chimes	80
Cornish	98
Cannon	127
Cambridge	139
Complaint	156
Cardiff	211
Chapel	231
Cary	258
Calvary	299
Canterbury	311
Chesunt	334

D

Derby	10
Dresden	179
Dedication	222
Dying Stephen	308

E

Epworth	122
Evesham	158
~~Evesham~~ *Durrell*(?)	171

F

Foundry	46
Fetter Lane	40
Fulham	185
Funeral	191
Fonmon	214
Frankfort	28

G

| Guernsey | 182 |

	Page
H	
Havant	14
Hotham	50
Hallelujah	118
Hamilton's	296
Handel's March	323
I	
Invitation	136
Iflington	154
Italian	168
Judgment	174
Jerene	200
K	
Kettleby's	164
Kingfwood	292
L	
Lamp's	18
Love-Feaſt	53
Liverpool	76
Leeds	82
London	197
Leominſter	334
M	
~~Maccabees~~ *Eaſter*	34
Minories	44
Magdalen	60
Manchefter	84
Morning Song	92
Mitcham	100
Miſs Edwin's	203

	Page
Muſician's	234
Marienbourn	245
Mourner's	275

N

New year's Day	12
Norwich	266
Newcaſtle	282

O

Old German	2
Gulney	20
Olivers	124
Old 112th Pſalmn tune	261
Old 113th Pſalm tune	314

P

Paſsion	4
Plymouth	30
Paris	32
Pudſey	142
Palmi's	162

R

Reſurrection	216

S

Sacrament	8
Savannah	28
Saliſbury	38
St Paul's	102
Spittlefields	108
Smith's	112
Stanton	134
Stockton	150

	Page
S.t Luke's — — — —	176
Sion — — — —	194
Snowfields — — — —	238
Sheffield	272

T

	Page
Trinity — — — —	115
The God of Abraham — —	130
Thou Shepherd of Ifrael — —	188
Trumpet — — — —	219
Traveller — — — —	225
Twenty-third Pfalm — —	254
Tally's — … — —	280
The Triumph — — — —	284
True Elijah — — — —	305
The 100 Pfalm — — —	342

W

	Page
Wenvo — — — —	80
Wednefbury — — — —	105
Welling — — — —	166
Weft-Street — — —	206
Wood's — — — —	242
Welch — — — —	264
Walfall — — — —	287
Weftminfter — — —	302

Y

	Page
Yorkfhire — — — —	78
York — — — —	318

Z

	Page
Zoar — — — —	160

HYMN I.

Old German

ALL glo--ry and praise, To the Ancient of Days, Who was born and was slain to re-deem a lost race.

    2   Salvation to God,
         Who carried our load,
And purchas'd our lives with the price of his blood.

    3   And shall he not have,
         The lives which he gave
Such an Infinite ransome for ever to save.

4   Yes, Lord, we are thine,
And gladly rifign
Our fouls to be fill'd with the fulnefs divine.

5   How, when it fhall be
We cannot forefee:
But, O let us live, let us die unto thee.

HYMN II.

1   MY God I am thine,
What a comfort divine,
What a blefsing to know that my Jefus is mine.

2   In the heavenly Lamb
Thrice happy I am,
And my heart doth rejoice at the found of his Name

3   True pleafures abound
In the raptures found,
And whoever hath found it, hath paradife found.

4   My Jefus to know,
And feel his blood flow,
'Tis life everlafting, 'tis heaven below.

5   Yet onward I hafte
To the heav'nly feaft:
That, that is the fulnefs; but this is the tafte.

6   And this I fhall prove,
Till with Joy I remove
To the Heaven of Heaven's in Jefus's love.

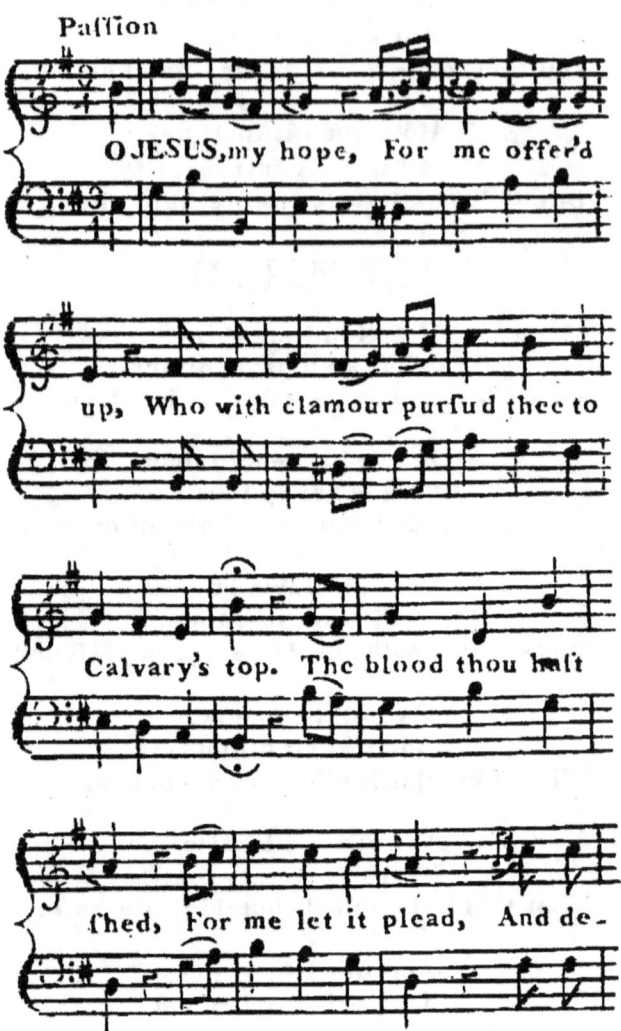

HYMN III.

Passion

O JESUS, my hope, For me offer'd up, Who with clamour pursu'd thee to Calvary's top. The blood thou hast shed, For me let it plead, And de-

2   Thy blood, which alone
For fin could atone
For the infinite evil I madly have done:
That only can feal
My pardon, and fill
My heart with a power of obeying thy will.

3 Now, now let me know
  Its virtue below;
Let it wash me, and I shall be whiter than snow.
  Let it hallow my heart,
  And throughly convert,
And make me, O Lord, in the world as thou art.

4 Each moment apply'd,
  My weakness to hide,
Thy blood be upon me, and always abide:
  My advocate prove
  With the Father above,
And speak me at last to the throne of thy love.

HYMN IV.

1 ALL ye that pass by,
  To Jesus draw nigh:
To you is it nothing that Jesus should die.
  Your ransom and peace,
  Your surety he is:
Come, see if there ever was sorrow like his.

2 For what you have done
  His blood must atone:
The Father hath punish'd, for you, his dear Son:
  The Lord, in the day
  Of his anger, did lay
Your sins on the Lamb, and he bore them away.

3   He anſwer'd for all,
      O come at his call;
And lo, at his feet with aſtoniſhment fall.
      Ye all may receive
      The peace he did leave
Who made interceſſion, "My Father forgive!"

4   For you and for me,
      He pray'd on the tree:
The prayer is accepted: the ſinner is free.
      The ſinner am I,
      Who on Jeſus rely,
And come for the pardon: God cannot deny.

5   My pardon I claim;
      For a ſinner I am,
A ſinner believing on Jeſus's name:
      He purchas'd the grace
      Which now I embrace:
O Father, thou know'ſt, he hath died in my place.

6   His death is my plea,
      My advocate fee,
And hear the blood ſpeak that hath anſwer'd for me
      Acquitted I was,
      When he hung on the croſs,
And by loſing his life he hath carried my cauſe.

HYMN V.

Sacrament

AH tell us no more, The Spirit and pow'r Of Jesus our God, Is not to be found in this life-giving food!

2   Did Jesus ordain
    His supper in vain?
    And furnish a feast,
For none but his earliest servants to taste?

3   Nay, but this is his will,
    We know it and feel
    That we should partake
The banquet for all he so freely did make.

4   'Tis God we belive,
    Who cannot deceive:
    The witness of God
Is present, and speaks in the mystical blood.

5   Receiving the bread,
    On Jesus we feed:
    It doth not appear
His manner of working; but Jesus is here.

6   O that all men would haste
    To this spiritual feast;
    At Jesus's word,
Do this, and be fed with the love of their Lord.

7   True light of mankind,
    Shine into their mind,
    And clearly reveal
Thy perfect, and good and acceptable will.

8   Bring near the glad day,
    When all shall obey
    Thy dying request,
And eat of thy supper and lean on thy breast.

9   To all men impart
    One way and one heart;
    Thy people be shown
All righteous, and spotless, and perfect in one.

10 Then, then let us see
    Thy glory, and be
    Caught up in the air,
This heavenly supper in heaven to share.

2   The pledge of our Lord
       To his heaven reſtor'd,
       Is ſent from the ſky,
And tells us, our Head is exalted on high.

3   Our advocate there
       By his blood and his pray'r
       The gift hath obtain'd,
For us he hath pray'd and the Comforter gain'd.

4   Our glorify'd head
       His Spirit hath ſhed,
       With his people to ſtay;
And never again will he take him away.

5   Our heavenly guide
       With us ſhall abide:
       His comfort impart,
And ſet up his kingdom of love in our heart.

6   The heart that believes,
       His kingdom receives,
       His pow'r and his peace,
His life and his joy's everlaſting increaſe.

7   Then let us rejoice
       In heart and in voice,
       Our leader purſue
And ſhout as we travel the wildernefs through:

8   With the Spirit remove
       To the Sion above;
       Triumphant ariſe,
And walk with our God till we fly to the ſkies.

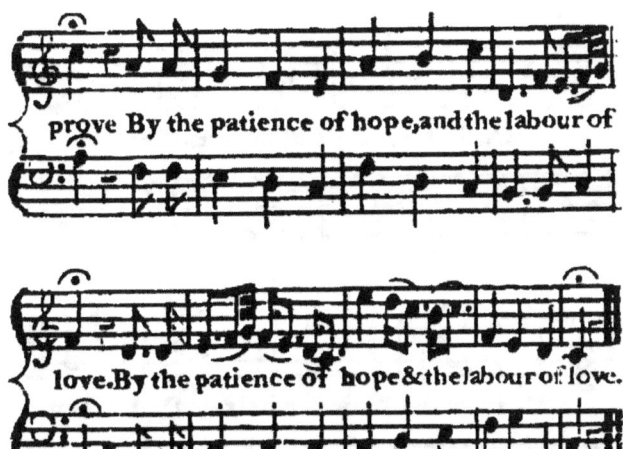

prove By the patience of hope, and the labour of love. By the patience of hope & the labour of love.

  2 Our life is a dream,
   Our time as a ftream
   Glides fwiftly away,
And the fugitive moment refufes to ftay.
   The arrow is flown,
   The moment is gone;
   The millenial year
Rufhes on to our yiew, and eternity's here.

  3 O that each in the day
   Of his coming may fay,
   "I have fought my way through,
"I have finifh'd the work thou didft give me to do."
   O that each from his Lord,
   May receive the glad word,
   "Well and faithfully done,
"Enter into my joy, and fit down on my throne."

HYMN VIII.

Havant

PRAISE be to the Father given; Christ he gave, Us to save, Now the heirs of heaven.

2 Pay we equal adoration
   To the Son: He alone,
Wrought out our salvation.

3 Glory to the eternal Spirit;
   Us he seals, Christ reveals,
And applies his merit.

4 Worship, honour, thanks and blessing,
   One and Three, Give we Thee
Never, never ceasing.

HYMN IX.

1 JESUS, come, thou hope of glory;
   Purify Me, that I
 May with faints adore thee.

2 Big with earneft expectation,
   Still I fit, At thy feet,
 Longing for falvation.

3 My poor heart vouchfafe to dwell in:
   Make me thine, Love divine,
 By thy Spirit's fealing.

4 Thou haft laid the fure foundation
   Of my hope, Build me up;
 Finifh thy creation.

5 From this inbred fin deliver;
   Let the yoke, Now be broke,
 Make me thine for ever.

6 Partner of thy perfect nature
   Let me be, Now in thee,
 A new, fpotlefs creature.

7 Perfect when I walk before thee,
   Soon or late, Then tranflate
 To the realms of glory.

HYMN X.

Brentford

THOU very paschal Lamb, Whose blood for us was shed, Through whom we out of Egypt came, Thy ransom'd people lead.

2   Angel of gospel-grace,
      Fulfil thy character;
    To guard and feed the chosen race
      In Israel's camp appear.

3   Throughout the desart way
      Conduct us by thy light:
    Be thou a cooling cloud by day,
      A chearing fire by night.

4 Our fainting fouls fuftain
  With bleffings from above,
And ever on thy people rain
  The Manna of thy love.

HYMN XI.

1 COME ye that love the Lord,
    And let your joys be known:
  Join in a fong with fweet accord,
    While ye furround his throne.

2 Let thofe refufe to fing,
    Who never knew our God:
  But fervants of the heavenl King
    May fpeak their joys abroad.

3 The God that rules on high,
    And all the earth furveys,
  That rides upon the ftormy fky,
    And calmes the roaring feas:

4 This awful God is ours,
    Our Father and our love;
  He fhall fend down his heav'nly pow'rs
    To carry us above.

5 There we fhall fee his face,
    And never never fin:
  There from the rivers of his grace
    Drink endlefs pleafures in.

6 Then let our fongs abound,
    And ev'ry tear be dry:
  We're marching thro' Immanuel's ground
    To fairer worlds on high.

HYMN XII

2 Thy blood and righteousness
   I make my only plea:
 My present and eternal peace
   Are both deriv'd from Thee.
 Rivers of life divine
   From Thee their fountain flow,
 And all who know that love of thine,
   The joy of angels know.

3 Come then, impute, impart
   To me thy righteousness,
 And let me taste how good thou art,
   How full of truth and grace:
 That thou canst here forgive,
   Grant me to testify,
 And justify'd by faith to live,
   And in that faith to die.

HYMN XIII.

WHO in the Lord confide, And feel his sprinkled blood, In storms and hurricanes abide Firm as the mount of God: Stedfast and fixt, and sure His Sion, cannot move:

2   As round Jerusalem
     The hilly bulwarks rise,
  So God protects and covers them
     From all their enemies.
  On ev'ry side he stands,
     And for his Israel cares;
  And safe in his almighty hands
     Their souls for ever bears.

HYMN XIV.

Chester

YE simple souls, that stray, Far from the path of peace, That unfrequented way, To life and happiness How long will ye your folly

2   Madness and misery
      Ye count out life beneath,
    And nothing great can see,
      Or glorious in our death:
As born to suffer and to grieve,
    Beneath your feet we lie,
And utterly condemn'd we live,
    And unlamented die.

3   Poor pensive sojourners
      O'erwhelm'd with grief and woes,
    Perplex'd with needless fears,
      And pleasure's mortal foes;
More irksome then a gaping tomb,
    Our sight we cannot bear,
Wrapt in the melancholy gloom
    Of fanciful despair.

4   So wretched and obscure,
    The men whom ye despise,
    So foolish weak and poor,
    Above your scorn we rise:
Our conscience in the Holy Ghost
    Can witness better things;
For he, whose blood is all our boast,
    Hath made us priests and kings.

5   Riches unsearchable
    In Jesu's love we know,
    And pleasures, from the well
    Of life, our soul's o'erflow;
  From him the Spirit we receive
    Of wisdom grace and pow'r,
  And always sorrowful we live,
    Rejoicing evermore.

6   Angels our servants are,
    And keep in all our ways,
    And in their hands they bear
    The sacred sons of grace;
  Our guardians to that heavenly bliss.
    They all our steps attend;
  And God himself our father is,
    And Jesus is our frind.

7   With him we walk in white,
    We in his image shine,
    Our robes are robes of light,
    Our rightousness divine;
  On all the grov'ling kings of earth
    With pity we look down,
  And claim in virtue of our birth,
    A never fading crown.

HYMN XV.

Bray's

SON of God, thy blessing grant, Still supply my every want; Tree of life thine influence shed, With thy sap my spirit feed.

2 Tenderest branch, alas! am I,
Wither without thee and die,
Weak as helpless infancy;
O confirm my soul in thee.

3 Unsustain'd by thee I fall;
 Send the help for which I call:
 Weaker than a bruised reed,
 Help I ev'ry moment need,

4 All my hopes on thee depend;
 Love me, save me to the end:
 Give me the continuing grace;
 Take the everlasting praise.

HYMN XVI.

1 O Thou holy Lamb divine,
 How canst thou and sinners join.
 God of spotless purity
 How shall man concur with thee.

2 Offer up one sacrifice,
 Acceptable to the skies.
 What shall wretched mortals bring
 Pleasing to the glorious King.

3 Only sin we call our own:
 But thou art the darling Son:
 Thine it is our God t'appease;
 Him thou dost for ever please.

4 We on Thee alone depend,
 With thy sacrifice ascend,
 Render what thy grace hath given;
 Lift with thee our souls to heaven.

HYMN XVII.

Savannah.

HOLY Lamb who thee recive, Who in thee begin to live, Day and night we cry to thee As thou art so let us be.

2 Jesu, see my pantin breast,
  See I pant in the to rest;
  Gladly would I now be clean:
  Clense me now from ev'ry sin.

3 Fix O fix my way'rin mind;
  To thy cross my Spirit bind,
  Earthly passions far remove:
  Swallow up my soul in love.

4 Dust and ashes tho' we be,
  Full of Sin and Misery,
  Thine we are thou Son of God,
  Take the purchase of thy Blood.

5 Boundless wisdom pow'r divine,
  Love unspeakable are thine:
  Praise by all to thee be giv'n,
  Sons of earth and hosts of Heav'n.

2 Thee to laud in songs divine,
  Angels and archangels join:
  We with them our voices raise,
  Echoing thy eternal praise.

3 Holy holy holy Lord,
  Live by heaven and earth ador'd;
  Full of thee they ever cry,
  Glory be to God most high.

HYMN XIX.

1 LORD if thou the grace impart,
  Poor in spirit meek in heart;
  I shall as my Master be,
  Rooted in humility.

2 From the time that Thee I know,
  Nothing shall I seek below;
  Aim at nothing great or high,
  Lowly both my heart and eye:

3 Simple, teachable, and mild,
  Aw'd into a little child:
  Quiet now without my food,
  Wean'd from ev'ry creature good.

4 Hangs my new born soul on Thee,
  Kept from all idolatry;
  Nothing wants beneath above,
  Happy, happy in thy love.

5 O that all may seek and find
  Every good in Jesus join'd.
  Him let Israel still adore;
  Trust him, praise him evermore.

HYMN XX.

2 Thou, who haft our place prepar'd,
　Make us meet for our reward;
　Then with all thy faints defcend,
　Then our earthly trials end.

3 Mindful of thy chofen race,
　Shorten thefe vindictive days,
　Who for full redemption groan,
　Hear us now and fave thine own.

4 Now deftroy the man of fin,
　Now thine antient flock bring in,
　Fill'd with righteoufnefs divine,
　Claim a ranfom'd world for thine.

5 Plant the heavenly kingdom here,
　Glorious in thy faints appear,
　Speak the facred number feal'd,
　Speak the myftery fulfil'd.

6 Take to thee thy royal pow'r,
　Reign when fin fhall be no more,
　Reign when death no more fhall be,
　Reign to all eternity.

HYMN XXI.

2 Love's redeeming work is done,
   Fought the fight the battle's won,
   Lo! our Sun's eclips is o'er,
   Lo! he sets in blood no more.

3 Vain the stone, the watch, the seal;
   Christ hath burst the gates of hell;
   Death in vain forbids his rise;
   Christ hath open'd Paradise.

4 Lives again our glorious King;
   Where O death is now thy sting?
   Once he died our souls to save,
   Where thy victory O Grave!

5 Soar we now where Christ hath led,
   Following our exalted head;
   Made like him, like him we rise;
   Ours the Cross, the Grave, the Skies!

6 Hail the Lord of earth and heav'n!
   Praise to thee by both be giv'n;
   Thee we greet triumphant now;
   Hail the Resurrection thou!

HYMN XXII.

2 Sov'reign Father, heav'nly king,
  Thee we now presume to sing,
  Glad thine attributes confess,
  Glorious all and numberless.

3 Hail by all thy works ador'd!
  Hail the everlasting Lord!
  Thee with thankful hearts we prove!
  Lord of power, and God of love.

4 Christ our Lord and God we own;
  Christ the Father's only Son;
  Lamb of God for sinners slain,
  Saviour of offending man.

5 Bow thine ear, in mercy bow,
  Hear, the world's atonement thou:
  Jesu in thy name we pray,
  Take, O take our sins away.

6 Pow'rful advocate with God,
  Justify us by thy blood,
  Bow thine ear, in mercy bow,
  Hear, the world's atonement thou.

7 Hear, for thou O Christ alone,
  With thy glorious Sire art one;
  One the Holy Ghost with thee,
  One supreme, eternal Three.

HYMN XXIII.
Cookham

CLAP your hands ye peo-ple all,

Praise the God on whom ye call,

Lift your voice and shout his praise,

Triumph in his sov'reign grace.

2 Glorious is the Lord Most High,
  Terrible in majesty,
  He his sov'reign sway maintains,
  King o'er all the earth he reigns.

3 He the people shall subde,
  Make us kings and conq'rors too;
  Force the nations to submit,
  Bruise our sins beneath our feet.

4 He shall bless his ransom'd ones,
  Number us with Israel's sons;
  God our heritage shall prove,
  Give us all a lot of love.

5 Jesus is gone up on high,
  Takes his seat above the sky:
  Shout the angels quires aloud,
  Echoing to the trump of God.

6 Sons of earth the triumph join,
  Praise him with the host divine,
  Emulate the heavn'ly pow'rs,
  Their victorious Lord is ours.

7 Shout the God enthron'd above,
  Trumpet forth his conq'ring love,
  Praises to our Jesus sing,
  Praises to our glorious King.

8 Pow'r is all to Jesus giv'n,
  Pow'r o'er hell and earth and heav'n:
  Pow'r he now to us imparts:
  Praise him with believing hearts.

9 Heathens he compels t' obey,
  Saints he rules with mildest sway;
  Pure and holy hearts alone
  Chuses for his quiet throne.

10 Peace to them and pow'r he brings,
   Makes his subjects priests and kings:
   Guards while in his worship join'd,
   Bids them cast the world behind.

11 On himself he takes their care,
   Saves them not by sword or spear:
   Safely to his house they go,
   Fearless of th' invading foe.

12 God keeps of the hostile bands,
   God protects their happy lands,
   Stands as keeper of their fields,
   Stands as twice ten thousand shields.

13 Wonderful in saving pow'r,
   Him let all our hearts adore:
   Earth and heav'n repeat the cry,
   Glory be to God Most High.

HYMN XXIV.

Minories

YE who dwell a-bove the skies,

Free from hu-man miser-ies,

Ye whom highest heaven em-bow'rs

Praise the Lord with all your pow'rs

2 Angels your clear voices raise:
Him ye heav'nly armies praise;
Sun and moon with borrow'd light;
All ye sparkling eyes of night.

3 Waters hanging in the air,
  Heav'n of heav'ns his praise declare:
  His deserved praise record;
  His who made you by his word.

4 Let the earth his praise resound:
  Monstrous whales and seas profound:
  Vapours, lightning, hail, and snow,
  Storms which where he bids you blow

5 Flow'ry hills and mountains high;
  Cedars, neighbours to the sky;
  Trees and cattle, creeping things,
  All that cut the air with wings.

6 You who awful scepters sway,
  You accustom'd to obey,
  Princes, judges of the earth,
  All of high and humble birth.

7 Youths and Virgins, flourishing
  In the beauty of your spring;
  Ye who were but born of late,
  Ye who bow with age's weight.

8 Praise his name with one consent:
  O how great! how excellent!
  Than the earth profounder far!
  Higher than the highest star.

9 He will his to glory raise,
  Ye his saints Resound his praise;
  Ye his sons his chosen race,
  Bless his love and sov'reign grace.

HYMN XXV.

GOD of all redeeming grace, By thy pard'ning love compell'd, Up to thee our souls we raise, Up to thee our bodies

2 Just it is, and good, and right,
   That we should be wholly thine;
In thy only will delight,
   In thy blessed service join.
O that every thought and word
   Might proclaim how good thou art!
Holiness unto the Lord
   Still be written on our heart.

HYMN XXVI.

1 COME thou high and lofty Lord,
Lowly, meek, Incarnate Word,
Humbly stoop to earth again,
Come, and visit abject man:
Jesu, dear expected guest,
Thou art bidden to the feast:
For thyself our hearts prepare,
Come and sit and banquet there.

2 Jesu, we thy promise claim,
We are met in thy great name;
In the midst do thou appear,
Manifest thy presence here:

Sanctify us, Lord, and bless:
Breathe thy Spirit, give thy peace:
Thou thyself within us move,
Make our feast a feast of love.

3 Let the fruits of grace abound,
Let us in thy bowels found:
Faith and love and joy increase,
Temperance and gentleness.
Plant in us thy humble mind;
Patient, pitiful, and kind:
Meek and lowly let us be,
Full of goodness, full of thee.

4. Make us all in thee complete,
Make us all for glory meet,
Meet t'appear before thy sight,
Partners with the saints in light:
Call, O call us all by name,
To the marrige of the Lamb,
Let us lean upon thy breast;
Love be there our endless feast.

HYMN XXVI.

2 Other refuge have I none,
    Hangs my helpless soul on thee:
Leave, ah! leave me not alone,
    Still support and comfort me:

All my truſt on thee is ſtay'd,
    All my help from thee I bring:
Cover my defenceleſs head,
    With the ſhadow of thy wing.

3 Thou, O Chriſt, art all I want,
    More than all in thee I find:
Raiſe the fallen, chear the faint,
    Heal the ſick, and lead the blind;
Juſt and holy is thy name,
    I am all unrighteouſneſs;
Falſe, and full of ſin I am,
    Thou art full of truth and grace.

4 Plenteous grace with the is found,
    Grace to cover all my ſin;
Let the healing ſtreams abound,
    Make and keep me pure within;
Thou of life the fountain art,
    Freely let me take of thee;
Spring thou up within my heart,
    Riſe to all eternity.

HYMN XXVII

53

Love feast

COME, and let us sweetly join, Christ to praise in, Christ to praise in hymns divine: Give we all with one ac-cord, Glo-ry to our, Glo-ry to our common Lord;

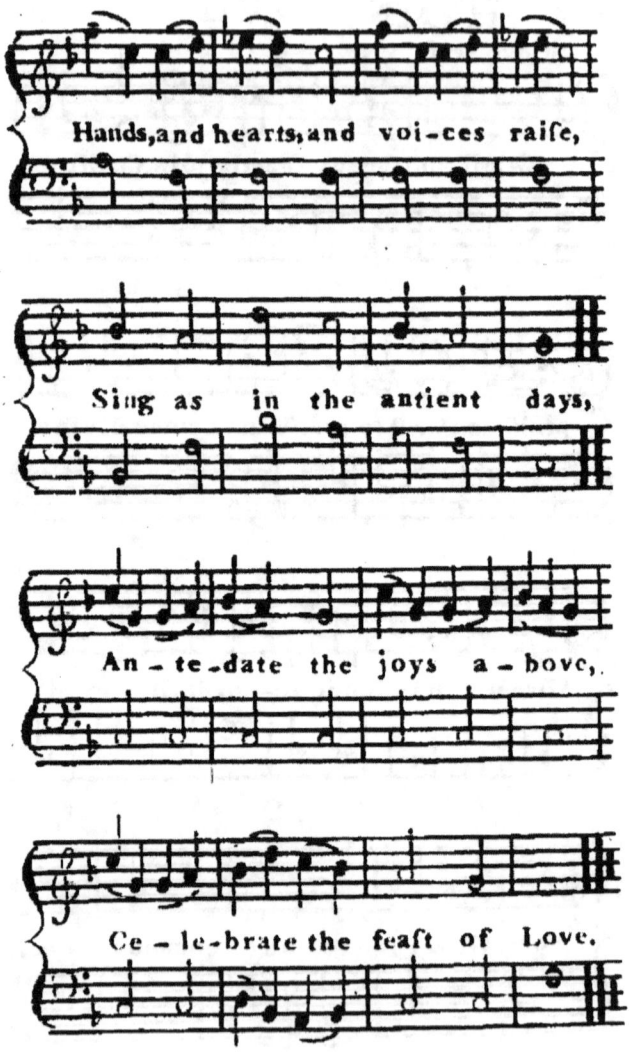

2 Strive we, in affection strive,
Let the purer flame revive,
Such as in the Martyrs glow'd,
Dying champions for their God.
We like them may live and love,
Call'd we are their joys to prove;
Sav'd with them from future wrath,
Partners of like precious faith.

3 Sing we then in Jesu's name,
Now as yesterday the same,
One in ev'ry age and place,
Full for all of truth and grace.
We for Christ, our master, stand,
Lights in a benighted land:
We our dying Lord confess;
We are Jesu's witnesses.

4 Witnesses that Christ hath dy'd,
We with him are crucify'd:
Christ hath burst the bands of death,
We his quick'ning Spirit breathe:
Christ is now gone up on high;
(Thither all our wishes fly:)
Sits at God's right hand above;
There with him we reign in love.

HYMN XXVIII

2 Circled round with angel-powers,
  Their triumphant Lord and our's;
  Conq'ror o'er death, hell and sin,
  Take the King of Glory in.
  Him though highest heav'n receives,
  Still he loves the earth he leaves,
  Though returning to his throne,
  Still he calls mankind his own.

3 See, he lifts his hands above;
  See, he shews the prints of love;
  Hark! his gracious lips bestow
  Blessings on his Church below.
  Still for us he intercedes,
  Prevalent his death he pleads;
  Next himself prepares our place,
  Harbinger of human race.

4 Master (will we ever say)
  Taken from our head to day,
  See, thy faithful servants see,
  Ever gazing up to thee.
  Grant, though parted from our sight,
  High above yon azure height,
  Grant, our hearts may thither rise;
  Following thee beyond the skies.

5 Ever upward let us move,
  Wafted on the wings of love;
  Looking when our Lord shall come,
  Longing gasping after home!
  There we shall with thee remain,
  Partners of thine endless reign;
  There thy face unclouded see,
  Find our heav'n of heav'ns in thee.

HYMN XXIX.

CHRIST, our head gone up on high
Be thou in thy Spirt nigh;
Advocate with God give ear,
To thine own effectual prayer;
Hear the founds thou once didſt breathe,
In thy days of fleſh beneath:
Now, O Jeſus, let them be
Strongly echoed back to thee!

We, O Chriſt, have thee receiv'd;
Have the goſpel-word believ'd,
Juſtly then we claim a ſhare
In thine everlaſting prayer.
One the Father is with thee,
Knit us in like unity;
Make us, O uniting Son,
One as Thou and He art one.

Thee he lov'd ere time begun,
Thee, the co-eternal Son:
He hath to thy merit given
Us th' adopted heirs of heaven.
Thou haſt will'd that we ſhould riſe,
See thy glory in the ſkies;
See thee by all heaven ador'd,
Be for ever with our Lord.

Still O Lord, for thine we are,
Still to us his name declare;
Thy revealing Spirit give,
Whom the world cannot receive;
Fill us with the Father's love,
Never from our ſouls remove,
Dwell in us, and we ſhall be
Thine to all eternity.

HYMN XXX.

Magdalen

HAPPY Mag-da-len, to whom Christ the
Lord vouchsaf'd t'appear! Newly ri-sen
from the tomb, Would he first be
seen of her. Her by seven

2 Yes, to her the Mafter came,
   Firft his welcome voice fhe hears:
Jefus calls her by her name;
   He the weeping finner chears;
Lets her the dear tafk repeat,
   While her eyes again run o'er,
Lets her hold his bleeding feet,
   Kifs them, and with joy adore.

3 Highly favor'd foul. To her
   Further ftill his grace extends,
Raifes the glad meffenger,
   Sends her to his drooping friends:
Tidings of their living Lord
   Firft in her report they find;
She muft fpread the gofpel word,
   Teach the teachers of mankind!

4 Who can now prefume to fear?
   Who difpair his Lord to fee?
Jefus, wilt thou not appear,
   Shew thyfelf alive to me?
Yes, my God I dare not doubt:
   Thou fhalt all my fins remove:
Thou haft caft a legion out;
   Thou wilt perfect me in love.

5 Surely thou haſt called now,
    Now I hear the voice divine.
At thy wounded feet I bow,
    Wounded for whoſe ſins but mine.
I have nail'd him to the tree;
    I have ſent him to the grave
But the Lord is riſ'n for me;
    Hold of him by faith I have.

6 Here for ever would I lie,
    Didſt thou not thy ſervant raiſe,
Send me forth to teſtify
    All the wonders of thy graice.
Lo! I at thy bidding go,
    Gladly to thy followers tell,
They their riſing God may know,
    They the life of Chriſt may feel.

7 Hear ye brethren of the Lord.
    (Such he you vouchſafes to call)
O belive the goſpel word,
    Chriſt hath died and roſe for all.
Turn ye from your ſins to God.
    Haſte to Galilee and ſee
Him who bought thee with his blood,
    Him who roſe to live in thee.

HYMN XXXI.

2 O that I might so believe,
  Stedfastly to Jesus cleave,
  On his only love rely,
  Smile at the destroyer nigh.
  Free from sin and servile fear,
  Have my Jesus ever near;
  All his care rejoice to prove,
  All his paradise of love.

3 Jesus seek thy wand'ring sheep,
  Bring me back, and lead, and keep,
  Take on thee my ev'ry care,
  Bear me on thy bosom, bear.
  Let me know my shepherd's voice,
  More and more in thee rejoice:
  More and more of thee receive,
  Ever in thy spirit live.

4 Live till all my life I know,
  Perfect as my Lord below,
  Gladly then from earth remove,
  Gather'd to the fold above:
  O that I at last may stand
  With the sheep at thy right hand,
  Take the crown so freely giv'n,
  Enter in by thee to heav'n.

HYMN XXXII.

THEE we adore, E-ternal Name,
And humbly own to thee,
How feeble is our mortal frame,
What dying worms we be.

2 Our wasting lives grow shorter still,
    As days and months increase;
And ev'ry beating pulse we tell
    Leaves but the number less.

3 The year rolls round and steals away
    The breath that first it gave:
Whate'er we do, where'er we be,
    We're trav'ling to the grave.

4 Dangers stand thick thro' all the ground
    To push us to the tomb;
And fierce diseases wait around,
    To hurry mortals home.

5 Great God, on what a slender thread
    Hang everlasting things;
Th' eternal states of all the dead,
    Upon life's feeble strings.

6 Infinite joy or endless woe
    Attend on ev'ry breath;
And yet how unconcern'd we go,
    Upon the brink of death.

7 Waken O Lord, our drowsy sense,
    To walk this dang'rous road:
And if our souls are hurry'd hence.
    May they be found with God.

HYMN XXXIII.

2 But there's a voice of sov'reign grace
　　　Sounds from the sacred word;
　Ho! ye despairing sinners, come,
　　　And trust upon the Lord.

3 My soul obeys th' almighty call,
　　　And runs to this relief:
　I would believe thy promise, Lord,
　　　O help my unbelief.

4 To the blest fountain of thy blood,
　　　Incarnate God, I fly:
　Here let me wash my spotted soul
　　　From sins of deepest dye.

5 Stretch out thine arm, victorious King,
　　　My reigning sins subdue;
　Drive the old dragon from his seat,
　　　With his infernal crew.

6 A guilty, weak, and helpless worm,
　　　Into thy arms I fall;
　Be thou my strength and righteousness,
　　　My Jesus and my all.

HYMN XXXIV.

2 These clouds of pride and sin dispel
    By thy all piercing beam;
 Lighten mine eyes with faith, my heart
    With holy hope inflame.

3 My mind by thy all quickning pow'r
    From low desires set free;
 Unite my scatter'd thoughts, and fix
    My love entire on thee.

4 Father thy long lost son receives
    Saviour, thy purchase own;
 Blest Comforter, with peace and joy
    Thy new-made creature crown.

5 Eternal, undivided Lord,
    Co-equal One and Three,
 On thee all faith, all hope be plac'd,
    All love be paid to thee.

2 Thy all surrounding sight surveys
    My rising and my rest,
My public walks, my private ways,
    The secrets of my breast.

3 My thoughts lie open to thee, Lord,
    Before they're form'd within:
And ere my lips pronounce the word,
    Thou know'st the sense I mean.

4 O wondrous knowledge deep and high!
    Where can a creature hide?
Within thy circling arms I lie,
    Beset on ev'ry side.

5 So let thy grace surround me still,
    And like a bulwark prove,
To guard my soul from ev'ry ill,
    Secur'd by sov'reign love.

2 Since thou a pitying ear didst give,
   And heard me when I pray'd,
  I'll call upon thee while I live,
   And never doubt thy aid.

3 Pale death, with all its ghastly train,
   My soul encompass'd round;
  Anguish and sin, and dread, and pain,
   On ev'ry side I found.

4 To thee, O Lord of life, I pray'd,
   And did for succour flee;
  O save, in my distress I said,
   The soul that trusts in thee.

5 How good thou art! how large thy grace!
   How easy to forgive!
  The helpless thou delight'st to raise:
   And by thy love I live.

6 Then O my soul be never more
   With anxious thoughts distrest;
  God's bounteous love doth thee restore
   To ease, and joy, and rest.

7 My eyes no longer drown'd in tears,
   My feet from falling free;
  Redeem'd from death and guilty fears,
   O Lord I'll live to thee.

HYMN XXXVII.

O for an heart to praise my God! An heart from sin set free, An heart that always feels thy blood So free——ly spilt for me.

2 An heart resign'd, submissive, meek,
　　My dear Redeemer's throne,
　Where only Christ is heard to speak,
　　Where Jesus reigns alone.

3 An humble, lowly, contrite heart,
　　Believing, true, and clean,
　Which neither life, nor death can part
　　From him that dwells within.

4 An heart in ev'ry thought renew'd,
　　And fill'd with love divine,
　Perfect, and right, and pure, and good,
　　A copy, Lord, of thine.

5 Thy tender heart is still the same,
　　And melts at human woe:
　Jesu, for thee distrest I am,
　　I want thy love to know.

6 My heart, thou know'st, can never rest,
　　Till thou create my peace;
　Till of my Eden re-possess'd,
　　From self and sin I cease.

7 Fruit of thy gracious lips, on me
　　Bestow the peace unknown,
　The hidden Manna, and the tree
　　Of life, and the white stone.

8 Thy nature, gracious Lord, impart,
　　Come quickly from above;
　Write thy new name upon my heart,
　　Thy new best name of Love.

thefe cold hearts of ours.

2 Look how we grovel here below,
　　Fond of thefe earthly Toys:
　Our Souls how heavily they go
　　To reach eternal Joys.

3 In vain we tune our formal Songs,
　　In vain we ftrive to rife;
　Hofannas languifh on our tongues,
　　And our devotion dies.

4 Father, fhall we then ever live
　　At this poor dying rate;
　Our love fo faint, fo cold to thee,
　　And thine to us fo great?

5 Come, Holy Spirit, heav'nly dove,
　　With all thy quick'ning pow'rs:
　Come fhed abroad a Saviour's love,
　　And that fhall kindle ours.

2 With steady course the shining sun
   Keeps his appointed way;
   And all the hours obedient run
   The circle of the day.

3 But ah! how wide my spirit flies,
   And wanders from her God;
   My soul forgets the heav'nly prize
   And treads the downward road.

4 The raging fire and stormy sea
   Perform thy awful will,
   And ev'ry beast and ev'ry tree
   Thy great design fulfil.

5 While my wild passions rage within,
   Nor thy commands obey;
   But flesh and sense, enslav'd to sin,
   Draw my best thoughts away.

6 Shall creatures of a meaner frame
   Pay all their dues to thee!
   Creatures that never knew thy name,
   That ne'er were lov'd like me.

7 Great God, create my soul anew,
   Conform my heart to thine;
   Melt down my will, and let it flow,
   And take the mould divine.

8 Seize my whole frame into thine hand,
   Here all my pow'rs I bring;
   Manage the wheels by thy command,
   And govern ev'ry spring.

9 Then shall my feet no more depart,
   Nor my affections rove;
   Devotion shall be all my heart,
   And all my passions love.

2 Still will I call with lifted eyes,
　　Come, O my God, and King,
　Till thou regard my ceaseless cries,
　　And full deliv'rance bring.

3 On thee, O God of purity,
　　I wait for hallowing grace:
　None without holiness shall see
　　The glories of thy face.

4 In souls unholy and unclean
　　Thou never canst delight;
　Nor shall they, while unsav'd from sin,
　　Appear before thy sight.

5 But all who put their trust in thee,
　　Thy mercy shall proclaim,
　And sing, with chearful melody,
　　Their dear Redeemer's name.

6 Protected by thy guardian grace,
　　They shall extol thy pow'r,
　Rejoice, give thanks, and shout thy praise,
　　And triumph evermore.

7 They never shall to evil yield,
　　Defended from above,
　And kept and cover'd with the shield
　　Of thine almighty love.

8 To Father, Son, and Holy Ghost,
　　Who sweetly all agree
　To save a world of sinners lost,
　　Eternal glory be.

HYMN XLI.

Wenvo

FROM whence thefe dire portents a-round That earth and heav'n a-maze! Wherefore do earthquakes cleave the ground? Why hides the Sun his rays? Why

hides the Sun Why hides the Sun his rays?

2 Not thus did Sinai's trembling head
  With facred horror nod,
Beneath the dark pavilion fpread
  Of legiflative God.

3 Thou earth, thy loweft center fhake,
  With Jefus fympathize.
Thou fun as hell's deep gloom be black:
  'Tis thy Creator dies.

4 See ftreaming from th' accurfed tree,
  His all-atoning blood.
Is this the Infinite! 'Tis he,
  My Saviour and my God.

5 For me thefe pangs his foul affail,
  For me the death is borne;
My fin gave fharpnefs to the nail,
  And pointed ev'ry thorn.

6 Let fin no more my foul enflave;
  Break, Lord, the tyrant's chain;
O fave me, whom thou cam'ft to fave;
  Nor bleed nor die in vain.

HYMN XLII.

Aldrich

SWEET is the mem'ry of thy grace, My God, my heav'nly King: Let age to age thy righteous-ness, Let age to age thy righteousness

In sounds of glory sing, In sounds of glory sing.

2 God reigns on high, but not confines
His goodness to the skies;
Through the whole earth his goodness shines,
And every want supplies.

3 With longing eyes thy creatures wait
On thee for daily food:
Thy lib'ral hand provides them meat,
And fills their mouths with good.

4 How kind are thy compassions Lord!
How slow thine anger moves!
But soon he sends his pard'ning word,
To cheer the soul he loves.

5 Creatures with all their endless race,
Thy pow'r and praise proclaim:
But we who taste thy richer grace,
Delight to bless thy name.

HYMN XLIII.

BEING of Beings, God of love, To thee our hearts we raise: Thy all-sustaining power we prove, And gladly sing thy praise. Hal-lelu-jah

Hal-lelujah Halle-lu-jah, A-men.

2 Thine, wholly thine, we pant to be,
    Our facrifice receive:
Made, and preferv'd, and fav'd by thee,
    To thee ourfelves we give.

3 Heav'n-ward our ev'ry wifh afpires,
    For all thy mercy's ftore;
The fole return thy love requires
    Is that we afk for more.

4 For more we afk; we open then
    Our hearts t' embrace thy will:
Turn and beget us, Lord, again:
    With all thy fulnefs fill.

5 Come, Holy Ghoft, the Saviour's love
    Shed in our hearts abroad!
So fhall we ever live and move,
    And be with Chrift in God.

HYMN XLIV.

Morning Song

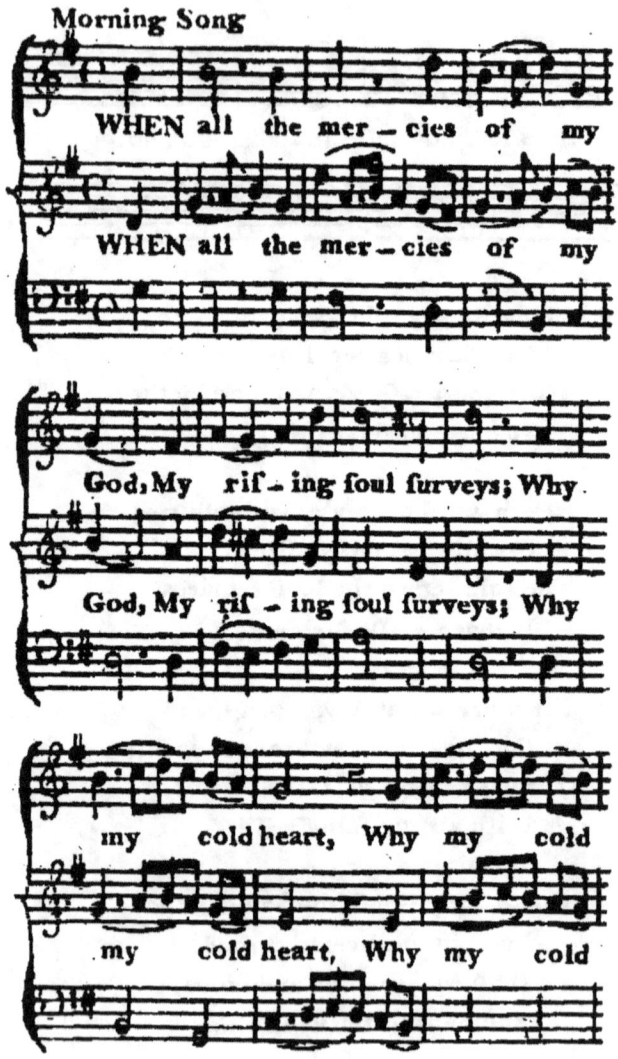

2 Thy providence my life suftain'd,
    And all my wants redreft,
Whilft in the filent womb I lay,
    And hung upon the breft.

3 To all my weak complaints and cries
    Thy mercy lent an ear,
Ere yet my feeble thoughts had learnt
    To form themfelves in prayer.

4 Unnumber'd comforts on my foul
    Thy tender care beftow'd,
Before my infant heart conceiv'd
    From whom thofe comforts flow'd.

5 When in the flippery paths of youth
    With heedlefs fteps I ran,
Thine arm, unfeen, convey'd me fafe,
    And led me up to Man.

6 Through hidden dangers, toils, and deaths,
    It gently clear'd my way;
And through the pleafing fnares of vice,
    More to be fear'd than they.

7 Through ev'ry period of my life,
    Thy goodnefs I'll purfue;
And after death in diftant worlds,
    The pleafing theme renew.

8 Through all eternity to thee
    A grateful fong I'll raife:
But O eternity's too fhort
    To utter all thy praife.

HYMN XLV.

2 If mercy is indeed with thee,
   May I obedient prove;
Nor e'er abuse my liberty,
   Or sin against thy love:
This choicest fruit of faith bestow
   On a poor sojourner,
And let me pass my days below
   In humbleness and fear.

3 Rather I would in darkness mourn
   The absence of thy peace,
Than e'er by light irrev'rence turn
   Thy grace to wantonness;
Rather I would in painful awe
   Beneath thine anger move,
Than e'er reject the gospel-law
   Of liberty and love.

4 But O thou wouldst not have me live
   In bondage, grief and pain:
Thou dost not take delight to grieve
   The helpless sons of men:
Thy will is my salvation Lord;
   And let it now take place,
And let me tremble at thy word
   Of reconciling grace.

5 Still may I walk as in thy sight,
   My strict observer see;
And thou by rev'rent love unite
   My child-like heart to thee.
Still let me till my days are past,
   At Jesu's feet abide;
So shall he lift me up at last,
   And seat me by his side.

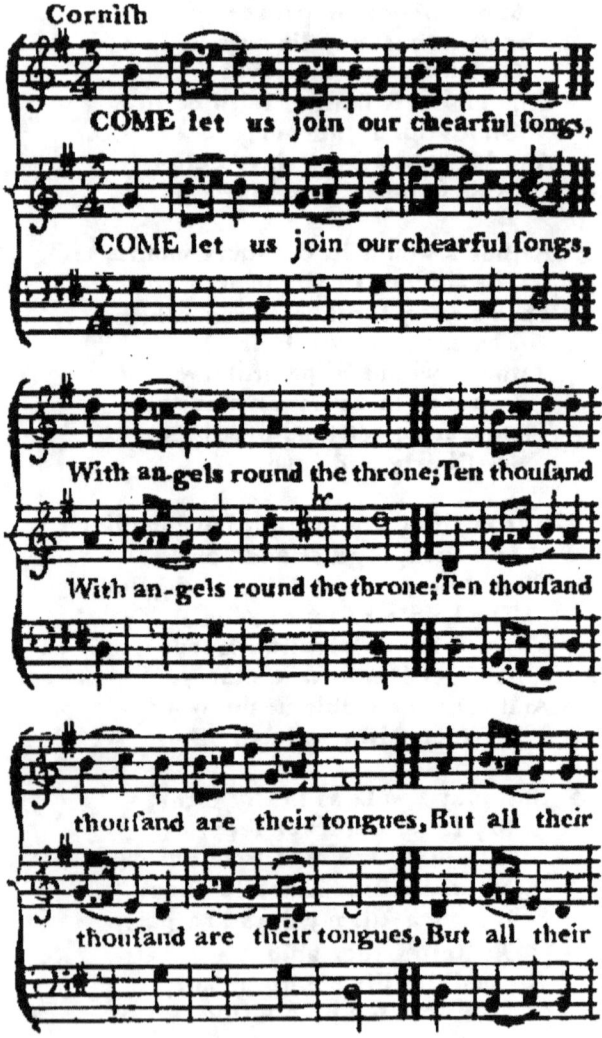

2 Worthy the Lamb that dy'd, they cry,
  To be exalted thus:
  Worthy the Lamb our hearts reply,
  For he was flain for us.

3 Jefus is worthy to receive
  Honour and pow'r divine:
  And bleffings more than we can give,
  Be, Lord, for ever thine.

4 The whole creation join in one,
  To blefs the facred name
  Of him that fits upon the throne,
  And to adore the Lamb.

HYMN XLVII.

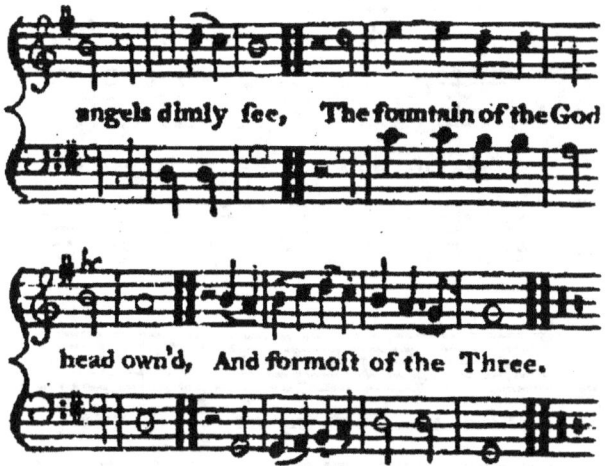

angels dimly see, The fountain of the God-head own'd, And foremost of the Three.

2 From thee, through an eternal now,
   The Son thine offspring flow'd:
And everlasting Father thou,
   As everlasting God.
Nor quite display'd to worlds above,
   Nor quite on earth conceal'd:
By wondrous unexhausted love,
   To mortal man reveal'd.

3 Supreme and all-sufficient God,
   When nature shall expire,
And worlds created by thy nod,
   Shall perish by thy fire:
Thy name, Jehovah, be ador'd
   By creatures without end,
Whom none but thy Essential Word
   And Spirit comprehend.

2 Part of thy name divinely stands
   On all thy creatures writ,
 They shew the labour of thy hands,
   Or impress of thy feet:
 But when we view thy strange design
   To save rebellious worms,
 Where vengeance and compassion join
   In their divinest forms:

3 Here the whole Deity is known,
   Nor dares a creature guess
 Which of the glories brightest shone,
   The justice or the grace.
 Now the full glories of the Lamb
   Adorn the heavenly plains,
 Bright seraphs learn Immanuel's name,
   And try their choicest strains.

4 O may I bear some humble part
   In that immortal song!
 Wonder and joy shall tune my heart,
   And love command my tongue.
 To Father, Son, and Holy Ghost,
   Who sweetly all agree
 To save a world of sinners lost,
   Eternal glory be.

HYMN XLIX.

2 Yet hear alas! in pain I live,
   Where Satan keeps his seat;
And day and night for those I grieve,
   Who will to sin submit:
With gushing eyes their deeds I see,
   Shut up in Sodom I,
And ask, with him who ransom'd me,
   Why will ye sin and die?

3 Jesus Redeemer of mankind,
   Display thy saving power,
Thy mercy let these outcasts find,
   And know their gracious hour.
Ah! give them, Lord, a longer space,
   Nor suddenly consume,
But let them take the proffer'd grace,
   And flee the wrath to come.

4 O wouldst thou cast a pitying look,
   (All goodness as thou art)
Like that which faithless Peter's broke,
   Or my obdurate heart.
Who thee beneath their feet have trod,
   And crucify'd afresh,
Touch with thine all-victorious blood,
   And turn the stone to flesh.

5 Open their eyes and ears to see
   Thy cross, to hear thy cries,
Sinner, thy Saviour weeps for thee,
   For thee he weeps and dies.
All the day long he meekly stands
   His rebels to receive;
And shews his wounds, & spreads his hands,
   And bids you turn and live.

God, Fountain for guilt and ſin,

Sprinkle me e-ver with thy blood, And

cleanſe and keep me clean.

2 Waſh me, and make me thus thine own,
　Waſh me, and mine thou art:
Waſh me, but not my feet alone,
　My hands, my head, my heart.
Th' atonement of thy blood apply,
　Till faith to ſight improve:
Till hope in full fruition die,
　And all my ſoul is love.

HYMN LI.

be. Great everlasting One. Boundless thy might and majesty, And unconfin'd thy throne.

2 Thy glories shine of wond'rous size,
    And wond'rous large thy grace:
Immortal day breaks from thine eyes,
    And Gabriel veils his face.
Thine essence is a vast abyss,
    Which angels cannot sound,
An ocean of infinities
    Where all our thoughts are drown'd.

3 Reason may grasp the massy hills,
    And stretch from pole to pole,
But half thy name our spirit fills,
    And over loads our soul.
In vain our haughty reason swells,
    For nothing's found in thee
But boundless unconceivables,
    And vast eternity.

113

2 Seraphs, the neareſt to the throne,
  Begin, and ſpeak the great unknown:
  Attempt the ſong, wind up your ſtrings,
  To notes untry'd and boundleſs things.
  You, whoſe capacious pow'rs ſurvey,
  Largely beyond our eyes of clay:
  Yet what a narrow portion too
  Is ſeen, or known, or thought by you.

3 How flat your higheſt praiſe fall
  Below th'immenſe original.
  Weak creatures we that ſtrive in vain
  To reach an uncreated ſtrain.
  Great God forgive our feeble lays,
  Sound out thine own eternal praiſe;
  A ſong ſo vaſt, a theme ſo high,
  Calls for the voice that tun'd the ſky.

HYMN LIII.

Trinity

HAIL, ho-ly, ho-ly, ho-ly Lord! Be endless praise to thee! Supreme, ef-sential one, a-dor'd In co-e-ternal three!

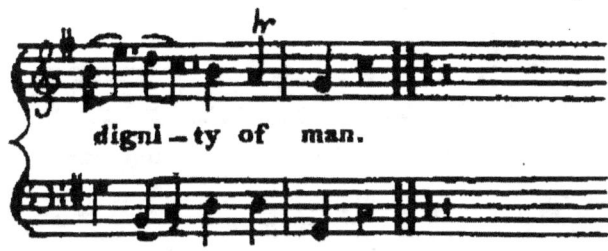

digni-ty of man.

2 To whom Isaiah's vision shew'd
    The seraphs veil their wings,
While thee, Jehovah, Lord and God,
    Th' angelic army sings.
To thee by mystic pow'rs on high,
    Were humble praises giv'n,
When John beheld, with favour'd eye,
    Th' inhabitants of heav'n.

3 All that the name of creature owns
    To thee in hymns aspire:
May we as angels on our thrones
    For ever join the choir.
Hail, holy, holy, holy Lord.
    Be endless praise to thee.
Supreme, essential One, ador'd
    In co-eternal Three.

3 Thou restless globe of golden light,
   Whose beams create our days,
   Join with the silver queen of night,
   To own your borrow'd rays.

4 Winds, ye shall bear his name aloud
   Through the ethereal blue;
   For when his chariot is a cloud,
   He makes his wheels of you.

5 Thunder and hail, and fires and ſtorms,
   The troops of his command,
Appear in all your dreadful forms,
   And ſpeak his awful hand.

6 Shout to the Lord, ye ſurging ſeas,
   In your eternal roar;
Let wave to wave reſound his praiſe,
   And ſhore reply to ſhore.

7 While monſters, ſporting on the flood,
   In ſcaly ſilver ſhine,
Speak terribly their Maker, God,
   And laſh the foaming brine.

8 But gentler things ſhall tune his name
   To ſofter notes than theſe,
Young zephyrs breathing o'er the ſtream,
   Or whiſp'ring through the trees.

9 Wave your tall heads ye lofty pines,
   To him that bids you grow;
Sweet cluſters bend the fruitful vines
   On ev'ry thankful bough.

10 Let the ſhrill birds his honours raiſe,
   And climb the morning ſky;
While grov'ling beaſts attempt his praiſe
   In hoarſer harmony.

11 Thus while the meaner creatures ſing,
   Ye mortals take the ſound;
Echo the glories of your King
   Through all the nations round.

HYMN LV

HAPPY soul, thy days are ended;
All thy mourning days be low; Go by
angels guards attended To the sight of
Jesus go. Halle--lu jah, Hal le-

123

-lu-jah, Halle - - lu-jah, Hal-le - -

-lu-jah, A - men.

2 Waiting to receive thy S*p*irit,
 Lo! the Saviour ftands above,
Shews the purchafe of his merit,
 Reaches out the crown of love.

3 Struggle through thy lateft paffion,
 To thy dear Redeemer's breaft,
To his uttermoft falvation,
 To his everlafting reft.

4 For the joy he fets before thee,
 Bear a momentary pain,
Die, to live a life of glory,
 Suffer with thy Lord to reign.

HYMN LVI.

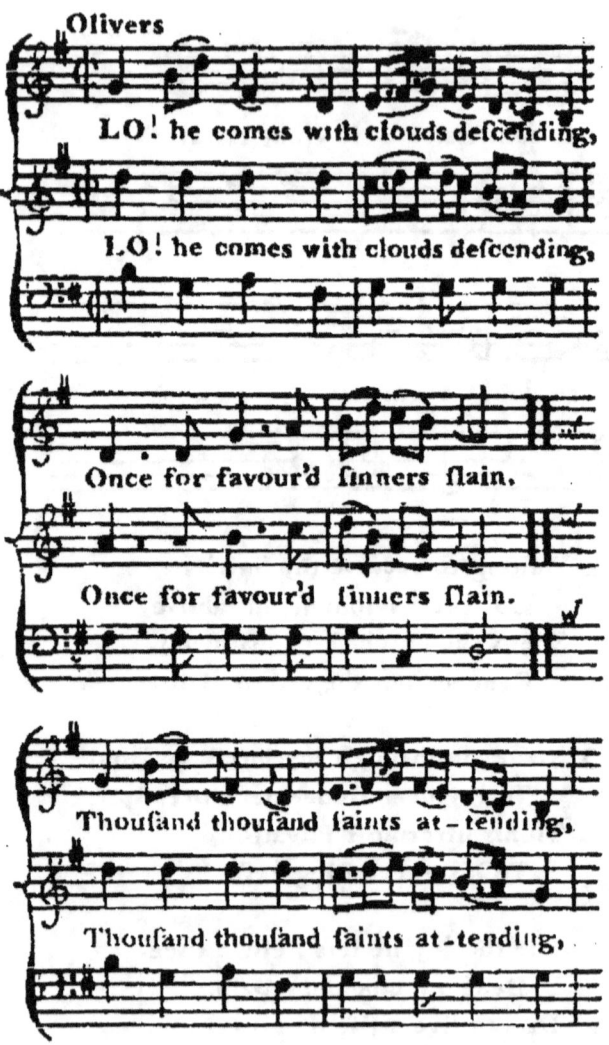

2 Ev'ry eye shall now behold him
   Rob'd in dreadful majesty;
Those who set at nought and sold him,
   Pierc'd and nail'd him to the tree,
      Deeply wailing
   Shall the true Messiah see.

3 The dear tokens of his passion
   Still his dazzling body bears,
Cause of endless exultation
   To his ransom'd worshippers:
      With what rapture
   Gaze we on those glorious scars.

4 Yea, amen; let all adore thee
   High on thine eternal throne;
Saviour, take the pow'r and glory,
   Claim the kingdom for thine own:
      JAH, JEHOVAH,
   Everlasting God, come down.

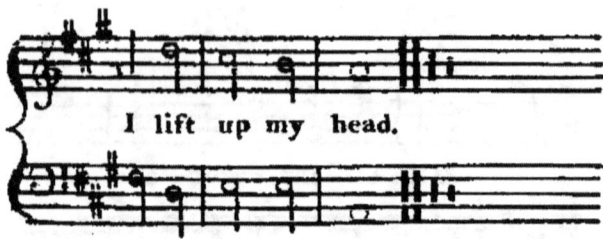

I lift up my head.

2 Bold shall I stand in thy great day,
  For who ought to my charge shall lay?
  Fully absolv'd through these I am;
  From sin and fear, from guilt and shame.

3 The deadly writing now I see
  Nail'd with thy body to the tree;
  Torn with the nails that pierc'd thy hands,
  Th' old Covenant no longer stands.

4 Though sign'd and written with my blood,
  As hell's foundation sure it stood;
  Thine hath wash'd out the crimson stains,
  And white as snow my soul remains.

5 Satan thy due reward survey,
  The Lord of life why didst thou slay?
  To tear the prey out of thy teeth,
  To spoil the realms of hell and death.

6 The holy, meek, unspotted Lamb,
  Who from the Father's bosom came,
  Who dy'd for me ev'n me, t' atone,
  Now for my Lord and God I own.

7 Lord, I believe thy precious blood,
  Which at the mercy seat of God
  For ever doth for sinners plead,
  For me, ev'n for my soul, was shed.

8 Yet nought whereof to boast I have,
  All, all thy mercy freely gave;
  No works, no righteousness are mine;
  All is thy work, and only thine.

9 Thou God of might, thou God of love,
  Let the whole world thy mercy prove;
  Now let thy word o'er all prevail,
  Now take the spoils of death and hell.

10 O let the dead now hear thy voice,
   Now bid thy banish'd ones rejoice,
   Their beauty this, their glorious dress,
   Jesu, thy blood and righteousness.

Rochford

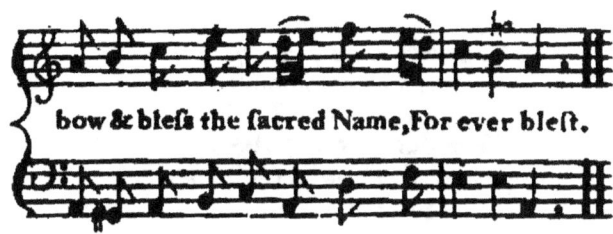

bow & bless the sacred Name, For ever blest.

2 The God of Abrah'm praise,
At whose supreme command,
From earth I rise — and seek the joys
At his right hand:
I all on earth forsake,
Its wisdom, fame and power;
And Him my only Portion make,
My shield and tower.

3 The God of Abrah'm praise,
Whose all-sufficient grace
Shall guide me all my happy days,
In all my ways.
He calls a worm his friend!
He calls himself my God!
And he shall save me to the end,
Thro' Jesu's blood.

4 He by Himself hath sworn,
I on his oath depend:
I shall, on eagle's wings up-born,
To heav'n ascend:
I shall behold his face,
I shall his power adore,
And sing the wonders of his grace
For evermore.

5   Tho' nature's strength decay,
      And earth and hell withstand,
   To Canaan's bounds I urge my way,
      At his command:
    The wat'ry deep I pass,
      With Jesus in my view;
   And thro' the howling wilderness
      My way pursue.

6   The goodly land I see,
      With peace and plenty bless'd;
   A land of sacred liberty,
      And endless rest:
    There milk and honey flow;
      And oil and wine abound;
   And trees of life for ever grow,
      With mercy crown'd.

7   There dwells the Lord our King,
      The Lord our righteousness,
   Triumphant o'er the world and sin,
      The Prince of peace:
    On Sion's sacred height,
      His kingdom still maintains;
   And glorious with his saints in light,
      For ever reigns.

8   He keeps his own secure,
      He guards them by his side,
   Arrays in garments white and pure
      His spotless bride.
    With streams of sacred bliss,
      With groves of living joys —
   With all the fruits of Paradise,
      He still supplies.

9   Before the great Three—One
      They all exulting ftand,
    And tell the wonders he hath done,
      Thro' all their land:
    The lift'ning fpheres attend,
      And fwell the growing fame;
    And fing, in fongs which never end,
      The wond'rous Name.

10 The God who reigns on high,
      The great arch-angels fing,
    And "Holy, Holy, Holy," cry,
      "Almighty King!
    "Who Was, and Is, the fame;
      "And evermore fhall be;
    "Jehovah—Father—Great I am!
      "We worfhip thee."

11 Before the Saviour's face
      The ranfom'd nations bow;
    O'erwhelm'd at his Almighty grace,
      For ever new:
    He fhews his prints of Love—
      They kindle—to a flame!
    And found thro' all the worlds above,
      The flaughter'd Lamb.

12 The whole triumphant hoft
      Give thanks to God on high;
    "Hail, Father, Son, and Holy-Ghoft,"
      They ever cry:
    Hail, Abraham's God—and mine.
      (I join the heav'nly lays,)
    All Might and Majefty are Thine,
      And endlefs Praife.

HYMN LIX.

Stanton

REGENT of all the worlds above:

Thou sun, whose rays adorn our sphere,

And with unwearied swiftness move, To

form the circle of the year.

2 Praise the Creator of the skies,
    Who decks thy orb with borrow'd rays:
Or may the sun forget to rise,
    When he forgets his Maker's praise.

3 Thou reigning beauty of the night,
    Fair queen of silence, silver moon,
Whose paler fires and female light
    Are softer rivals of the noon.

4 Arise, and to that sov'reign pow'r,
    Waxing and waning honours pay;
Who bade thee rule the dusky hours,
    And half supply the absent day.

5 Ye glitt'ring stars that gild the skies,
    When darkness has her curtain drawn,
That keeps the watch with wakeful eyes,
    When business, cares, and day are gone.

6 Proclaim the glories of your Lord,
    Dispers'd through all the heav'nly street,
Whose boundless treasures can afford
    So rich a pavement for his feet.

7 Thou heav'n of heavens, supremely bright,
    Fair palace of the court divine,
Where with inimitable light,
    The Godhead condescends to shine;

8 Praise thou the great inhabitant,
    Who scatters lovely beams of grace
On ev'ry angel ev'ry saint,
    Nor veils the lustre of his face.

9 O God of glory, God of love,
    Thou art the sun that mak'st our days;
'Midst all thy wond'rous works above
    Let earth and dust attempt thy praise.

HYMN LX.

2 Ready the Father is to own,
   And kifs his late returning fon:
   Ready your loving Saviour ftands,
   And fpreads for you his bleeding hands.

3 Ready the fpirit of his love
   Juft now the ftony to remove,
   T'apply and witnefs with the blood,
   And wafh and feal the fons of God.

4 Ready for you the angels wait,
   To triumph in your bleft eftate:
   Tuning their harps, they long to praife
   The wonders of redeeming grace.

5 The Father, Son, and Holy Ghoft:
   Are ready with their fhining hoft;
   All heav'n is ready to refound,
   "The dead's alive the loft is found."

6 Come then, ye finners, to your Lord,
   In Chrift to paradife reftor'd;
   His proffer'd benefits embrace,
   The plenitude of gofpel grace.

7 A pardon written with his blood,
　The favour and the peace of God,
　The feeing eye, the feeling fenfe,
　The myftic joys of penitence;

8 The godly grief, the pleafing fmart,
　The meltings of a broken heart,
　The tears that tell your fins forgiv'n,
　The fighs that waft you up to heaven;

9 The guiltlefs fhame, the fweet diftrefs,
　The unutterable tendernefs,
　The genuine, meek humility,
　The wonder, "why fuch love to me!"

10 Th' o'erwhelming pow'r of faving grace,
　The fight that veils the feraph's face,
　The fpeechlefs awe that dares not move,
　And all the filent heav'n of love!

2 Happy beyond description he,
    Who knows,"The Saviour died for me,"
    The gift unspeakable obtains,
    And heavenly understanding gains.

3 Wisdom divine! Who tells the price
    Of wisdom's costly merchandize!
    Wisdom to silver we prefer,
    And gold is drofs compar'd to her.

4 Better she is than richest mines,
    All earthly treasures she outshines,
    Her value above rubies is,
    And precious pearls are vile to this.

5 Whate'er thy heart can wish is poor,
   To wisdom's all-sufficient store:
   Pleasure, and fame, and health, and friends;
   She all created good transcends.

6 Her hands are fill'd with length of days,
   True riches and immortal praise,
   Riches of Christ on all bestow'd,
   And honour that descends from God.

7 To purest joys she all invites,
   Chaste, holy, spiritual delights:
   Her ways are ways of pleasantness,
   And all her flowry paths are peace.

8 He finds, who wisdom apprehends,
   A life begun that never ends;
   The tree of life divine she is,
   Set in the midst of paradise.

9 Happy the man who wisdom gains,
   Thrice happy—who his guest retains;
   He owns, and shall for ever own,
   Wisdom, and Christ, and heav'n are one.

thy prefence fet me free.

2 Loft and undone, for aid I cry;
In thy death, Saviour, let me die!
Griev'd with thy grief, pain'd with thy pain,
Ne'er may I feel felf-love again.

3 Jefu, vouchfafe my heart and will
With thy meek lowlinefs to fill;
No more her pow'r let nature boaft,
But in thy will may mine be loft.

4 In life's fhort day let me yet more
Of thy enliv'ning pow'r implore;
My mind muft deeper fink in thee,
My foot ftand firm, from wand'ring free.

5 Ye fons of men, here nought avails
Your ftrength; here all your wifdom fails;
Who bids a finful heart be clean?
Thou only, Lord, fupreme of men!

6 And well I know thy tender love,
 Thou never didst unfaithful prove;
 And well I know thou stand'st by me,
 Pleas'd from myself to set me free.

7 Still will I watch and labour still
 To banish ev'ry thought of ill;
 Till thou in thy good time appear,
 And sav'st me from the fowler's snare.

8 Already springing hope I feel;
 God will destroy the pow'r of hell;
 God, from the land of wars and pain,
 Leads me where peace and safety reign.

9 One only care my soul shall know,
 Father, all thy commands to do:
 Ah! deep engrave it on my breast,
 That I in thee ev'n now am blest.

10 When my warm thoughts I fix on thee,
 And plunge me in thy mercy's sea,
 Then ev'n on me thy face shall shine,
 And quicken this dead heart of mine.

11 So ev'n in storms my zeal shall grow,
 So shall I thy hid sweetness know:
 And feel (what endless age shall prove)
 That thou, my Lord, my God, are love.

HYMN LXIII.

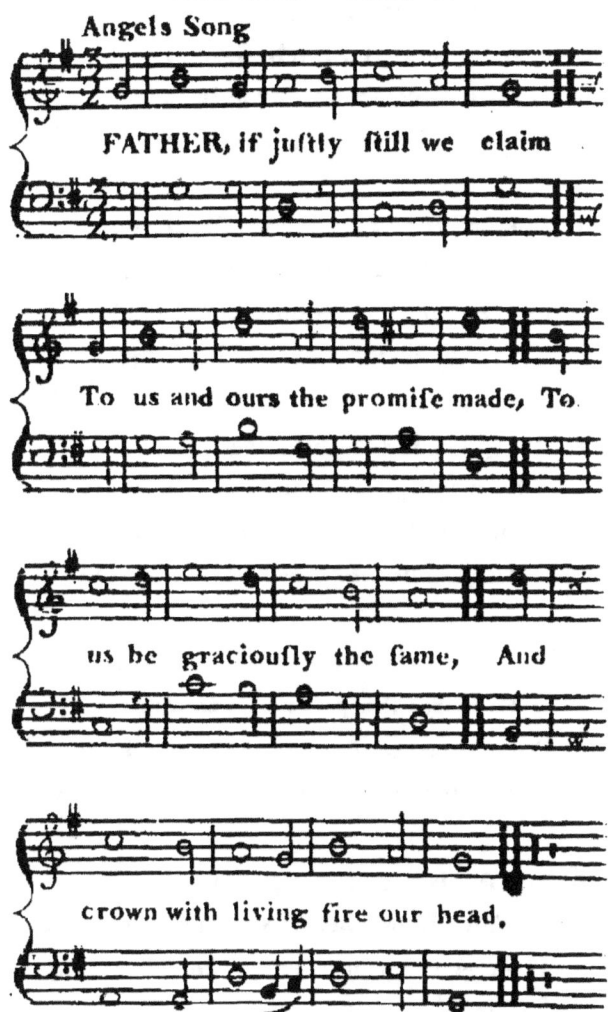

FATHER, if justly still we claim
To us and ours the promise made,
To us be graciously the same,
And crown with living fire our head.

2 Our claim admit, and from above
    Of holiness the spirit show'r,
  Of wise discernment, humble love,
    And zeal, and unity, and pow'r.

3 The Spirit of convincing speech,
    Of pow'r demonstrative impart,
  Such as may ev'ry conscience reach,
    And sound the unbelieving heart.

4 The spirit of refining fire,
    Searching the inmost of the mind,
  To purge all fierce and foul desire,
    And kindle life more pure and kind.

5 The spirit of faith in this thy day,
    To break the pow'r of cancel'd sin,
  Tread down its strength, o'erturn its sway,
    And still the conquest more than win.

6 The spirit breathe of inward life,
    Which in our hearts thy laws may write;
  Then grief expires, and pain, and strife,
    'Tis nature all, and all delight.

7 On all the earth thy spirit show'r,
    The earth in righteousness renew;
 Thy kingdom come, and hell's o'erpow'r,
    And to thy scepter all subdue.

8 Like mighty winds, or torrents fierce,
    Let it opposers all o'er-run,
 And ev'ry law of sin reverse,
    That faith and love may make all one.

9 Yea, let the Spirit in ev'ry place
    Its richer energy declare,
 While lovely tempers, fruits of grace,
    The kingdom of thy Christ prepare.

10 Grant this, O holy God, and true!
    The ancient seers thou didst inspire:
 To us perform the promise due,
    Descend and crown us now with fire.

HYMN LXIV.

ETERNAL depth of love divine, In Jesus God with us dis-play'd, How bright thy beaming glories shine! How wide thy hea - - - - - ling streams are spread!

2 With whom doſt thou delight to dwell?
    Sinners, a vile and thankleſs race:
O God! what tongue aright can tell
    How vaſt thy love, how great thy grace!

3 The dictates of thy ſov'reign will
    With joy our grateful hearts receive;
All thy delight in us fulfil,
    Lo! all we are to thee we give.

4 To thy ſure love, thy tender care,
    Our fleſh, ſoul, ſpirit we reſign;
O! fix thy ſacred preſence there,
    And ſeal th' abode for ever thine.

5 O King of Glory, thy rich grace
    Our ſhort deſires ſurpaſſes far!
Yea, ev'n our crimes, tho' numberleſs,
    Leſs num'rous than thy mercies are.

6 Still on thee, Father, may we reſt!
    Still may we pant thy Son to know!
Thy Spirit ſtill breathe into our breaſt,
    Fountain of peace and joy below.

7 Oft have we ſeen thy mighty pow'r,
    Since from the world thou mad'ſt us free
Still may we praiſe thee more and more,
    Our hearts more firmly knit to thee.

8 Still, Lord, thy ſaving health diſplay,
    And arm our ſouls with heavenly zeal:
So fearleſs ſhall we urge our way
    Through all the pow'rs of earth and hell.

2 Take this poor heart, and let it be
  For ever clos'd to all but thee!
  Seal thou my breast, and let me wear
  That pledge of love forever there.

3 How blest are they who still abide,
  Close shelter'd in thy bleeding side!
  Who life and strength from thence derive;
  And by thee move and in thee live.

4 What are our works but sin and death,
  Till thou thy quick'ning Spirit breathe?
  Thou giv'st the pow'r thy grace to move;
  O wond'rous grace! O boundless love!

5 How can it be, thou heav'nly King,
  That thou shouldst us to glory bring;
  Make slaves the partners of thy throne,
  Deck'd with a never-fading crown.

6 Hence our hearts melt, our eyes o'erflow,
  Our words are lost; nor will we know,
  Nor will we think of ought beside,
  My Lord my Love is crucify'd!

7 Ah! Lord enlarge our scanty thought,
  To know the wonders thou hast wrought!
  Unloose our stamm'ring tongue to tell
  Thy love immense, unsearchable.

8 First-born of many brethren thou!
  To thee, lo! all our souls we bow,
  To thee our hearts and hands we give,
  Thine may we die, thine may we live.

HYMN LXVI.

JESUS, in whom the Godhead's rays Beam forth with milder majesty, I see thee full of truth and grace, And come for all I

2 Wrathful, impure, and proud I am,
    Nor conftancy, nor ftrength I have:
But thou, O Lord, art ftill the fame,
    And haft not loft thy power to fave.

3 Save me from pride, the plague expel;
    Jefu, thine humble felf impart,
O let thy mind within me dwell;
    O give me lowlinefs of heart.

4 Enter thyfelf, and caft out fin;
    Thy fpotlefs purity beftow;
Touch me, and make the leper clean;
    Wafh me, and I am white as fnow.

5 Fury is not in thee my God,
    O why fhould it be found in thine!
Sprinkle me, Saviour, with thy blood,
    And all thy gentlenefs is mine.

6 Pour but thy blood upon the flame,
    Meek, and difpaffionate, and mild,
The leopard finks into a lamb,
    And I become a little child.

HYMN LXVII.

Islington

BROTHER in Christ, and well-belov'd,
To Jesus and his servants dear, Enter, and
shew thyself ap-prov'd; Enter, and
find, Enter, and find that God is here.

2 Scap'd from the world, redeem'd from sin,
 By fiends pursued, by men abhorr'd,
Come in, poor fugitive, come in,
 And share the portion of thy Lord.

3 Welcome from earth! — lo, the right hand
 Of fellowship to thee we give!
With open arms and hearts we stand,
 And thee in Jesu's name receive.

4 Say, is thy heart resolv'd as our's;
 Then let it burn with sacred love;
Then let it taste the heav'nly pow'rs,
 Partaker of the joys above.

5 Jesu, attend! thyself reveal!
 Are we not met in thy great name?
Thee in the midst we wait to feel,
 We wait to catch the spreading flame.

6 Thou God, that answerest by fire!
 The Spirit of burning now impart,
And let the flames of pure desire
 Rise from the altar of our heart.

7 Truly our fellowship below
 With thee and with the Father is:
In thee eternal life we know,
 And heav'n's unutterable bliss.

8 In part we only know thee here,
 But wait thy coming from above —
And I shall then behold thee near!
 And I shall all be lost in love.

HYMN LXVIII.

Complaint

WHEN, gracious Lord, when shall it be
That I shall find my all in thee?
The fulness of thy promise prove, The
seal of thine, The seal of thine eternal love?

2 A poor, blind child, I wander here,
   If haply I may feel thee near;
   O dark, dark, dark, (I still must say)
   Amidst the blaze of gospel day.

3 Thee, only thee I fain would find,
   And cast the world and flesh behind;
   Thou, only Thou to me be given,
   Of all thou hast in earth or heaven.

4 When from the arm of flesh set free,
   Jesu, my soul shall fly to thee:
   Jesu, when I have lost my all,
   My soul shall on thy bosom fall.

5 Whom man forsakes, Thou wilt not leave,
   Ready the outcasts to receive,
   Though all my simpleness I own,
   And all my faults to thee are known.

6 Ah! wherefore did I ever doubt?
   Thou wilt in no wise cast me out,
   An helpless soul that comes to thee
   With only sin and misery.

7 Lord, I am sick: my sickness cure:
   I want; do thou enrich the poor:
   Under thy mighty hand I stoop;
   O lift the abject sinner up.

8 Lord, I am blind; be thou my sight:
   Lord I am weak; be thou my might:
   An helper of the helpless be,
   And let me find my all in thee.

HYMN LXIX.

2 When shall mine eyes behold the Lamb,
   The God of my salvation see!
Weary, O Lord, thou know'st I am,
   Yet still I cannot come to thee.

3 Rest for my soul I long to find:
   Saviour, if mine indeed thou art,
Give me thy meek and lowly mind,
   And stamp thine image on my heart.

4 Fain would I learn of thee, my God,
   Thy light and easy burden prove,
The cross all stain'd with hallow'd blood,
   The labour of thy dying love.

5 This moment would I take it up,
   And after my dear Master bear,
With thee ascend to Calv'ry's top,
   And bow my head and suffer there.

6 I would, but thou must give the pow'r,
   My heart from ev'ry sin release;
Bring near, bring near the joyful hour,
   And fill me with thy perfect peace.

7 Come, Lord, the drooping sinner chear,
   Nor let thy chariot wheels delay,
Appear, in my poor heart appear,
   My God, my Saviour, come away!

HYMN LXX.

fa — — — — — — and the — — vast
fa — bric still sustains.

2 How sure establish'd is thy throne!
    Which shall no change or period see:
For thou O Lord and thou alone,
    Art King from all eternity.

3 The floods, O Lord, lift up their voice,
    And toss their troubled waves on high;
But God above can still their noise,
    And make the angry sea comply.

4 Thy promise, Lord, is ever sure,
    And they that in thy house would dwell,
That happy station to secure,
    Must still in holiness excel.

HYMN LXXI.

ETERNAL Pow'r, whose high abode, Becomes the grandeur of a God: Infinite lengths beyond the bounds Where stars — — — — revolve their

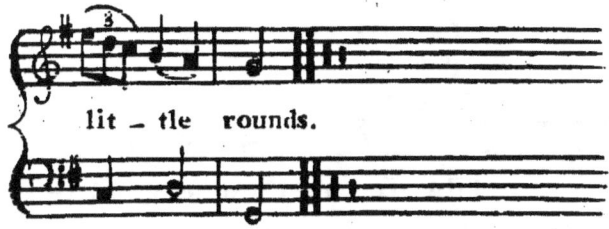

lit - tle rounds.

2 Thee while the firſt archangel ſings,
 He hides his face behind his wings,
 And ranks of ſhining thrones around
 Fall, worſhipping, and ſpread the ground.

3 Lord, what ſhall earth and aſhes do?
 We would adore our Maker too:
 From ſin and duſt to thee we cry,
 The Great, the Holy and the High!

4 Earth from afar has heard thy fame,
 And worms have learnt to liſp thy name:
 But O the glories of thy mind
 Leave all our ſoaring thoughts behind.

5 God is in heaven, and men below,
 Be ſhort our tunes; our words be few;
 A ſacred rev'rence checks our ſongs,
 And praiſe ſits ſilent on our tongues.

HYMN LXXII

Kettleby's

PRAISE ye the Lord: 'tis good to raise Our hearts and voices in his praise: His nature and his works in-vite, To make this duty our de-

165

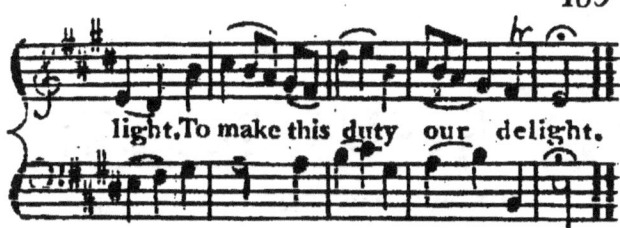

light. To make this duty our delight.

2 He form'd the stars, those heav'nly flames;
   He counts their numbers, calls their names,
   His wisdom's vast, and knows no bound,
   A deep where all our thoughts are drown'd.

3 Sing to the Lord, exalt him high,
   Who spreads his clouds around the sky;
   There he prepares the fruitful rain,
   Nor lets the drops descend in vain.

4 He makes the grass the hills adorn,
   And clothes the smiling fields with corn;
   The beasts with food his hands supply,
   And the young ravens when they cry.

5 What is the creature's skill or force,
   The sprightly man, or warlike horse?
   The piercing wit, the active limb,
   All are too mean delights for him.

6 But saints are lovely in his sight,
   He views his children with delight;
   He sees their hope, he knows their fear,
   And looks and loves his image there.

7 Praise God, from whom all blessings flow,
   Praise him all creatures here below,
   Praise him above, ye heavenly host,
   Praise Father, Son, and Holy Ghost.

HYMN LXXIII.

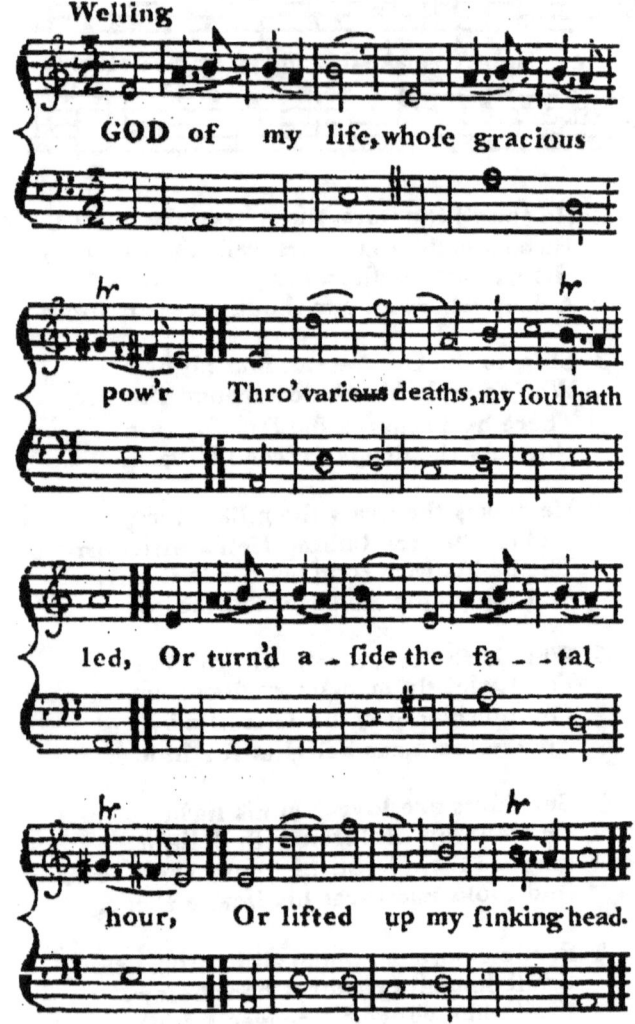

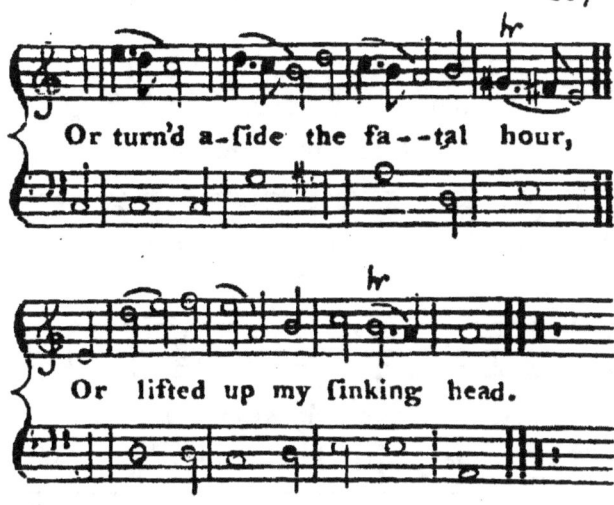

Or turn'd a-side the fa--tal hour,

Or lifted up my sinking head.

2 In all my ways thy hand I own,
   Thy ruling Providence I see:
O help me still my course to run,
   And still direct my paths to thee.

3 Foolish, and impotent, and blind,
   Lead me a way I have not known;
Bring me where I my heaven may find,
   The heaven of loving thee alone.

4 Enlarge my heart to make thee room;
   Enter, and in me ever stay;
The crooked then shall strait become,
   The darkness shall be lost in day.

HYMN LXXIV

2 For thee my thirsty soul does pant,
    While in this desart land I live:
And hungry as I am, and faint,
    Thy love alone can comfort give.

3 In a dry land behold I place
    My whole desire on thee, O Lord,
And more I joy to gain thy grace,
    Than all earth's treasures can afford.

4 In holiness within thy gates
    Of old oft I have sought for thee;
Again my longing spirit waits,
    That fulness of delight to see.

5 More dear than life itself, Thy love
    My heart and tongue shall still employ;
And to declare thy praise will prove
    My peace, my glory, and my joy.

6 In blessing thee with grateful songs,
    My happy life shall glide away;
The praise that to thy name belongs
    Hourly with lifted hands I'll pay.

7 Abundant sweetness while I sing,
    Thy love my ravish'd soul o'erflows,
Secure in thee, my God and King,
    Of glory that no period knows.

8 Thy name, O Lord, upon my bed
    Dwells on my lips, and fires my thought,
With trembling awe in midnight shade,
    I muse on all thine hands have wrought.

9 In all I do I feel thine aid,
    Therefore thy greatness will I sing,
O God, who bidst my heart be glad
    Beneath the shadow of thy wing.

10 My soul draws nigh and cleaves to thee;
    Then let or earth or hell assail,
Thy mighty hand shall set me free,
    For whom thou sav'st, he ne'er shall fail.

HYMN LXXV.

172

2 Regard our pray'rs for Sion's peace,
   Shed in our hearts thy love abroad;
Thy gifts abundantly increase,
   Enlarge and fill us all with God.

3 Before thy sheep, great Shepherd, go,
   And guide into thy perfect will;
Cause us thy hallow'd name to know,
   The work of faith with pow'r fulfil.

4 Help us to make our calling sure,
   O! let us all be saints indeed,
And pure as God himself is pure,
   Conform'd in all things to our head.

5 Take the dear purchase of thy blood;
    Thy blood shall wash us white as snow;
Present us sanctify'd to God,
    And perfected in love below.

6 That blood which cleanses from all sin.
    That efficacious blood apply,
And wash and make us throughly clean,
    And change and wholly sanctify.

7 From all iniquity redeem,
    Cleanse by the water and the word,
And free from ev'ry touch of blame,
    And make the servants as their Lord.

8 Wash out the deep orig'nal stain,
    And make us glorious all within:
No wrinkle on our souls remain,
    No smallest spot of inbred sin.

9 Then when the perfect life of love,
    The bride and all her children live,
Come down, and take us up above,
    And to thy heaven of heavens receive.

HYMN LXXVI.

175

Welcome, welcome, welcome, welcome, welcome to the faithful soul!

2 From heav'n angelic voices found,
See the almighty Jesus crown'd,
Girt with omnipotence and grace,
And glory decks the Saviour's face.

3 Descending on his azure throne,
He claims the kingdoms for his own;
The kingdoms all obey his word,
And hail him their triumphant Lord.

4 Shout all the people of the sky,
And all the saints of the Most High;
Our Lord, who now his right obtains,
For ever, and for ever reigns.

The God of Abraham

HYMN LXXVII.

ARM of the Lord, a-wake, a-wake. Thine own im-mortal strength put on; With terror cloth'd, the nations shake, And cast thy foes with fu-ry down. A-

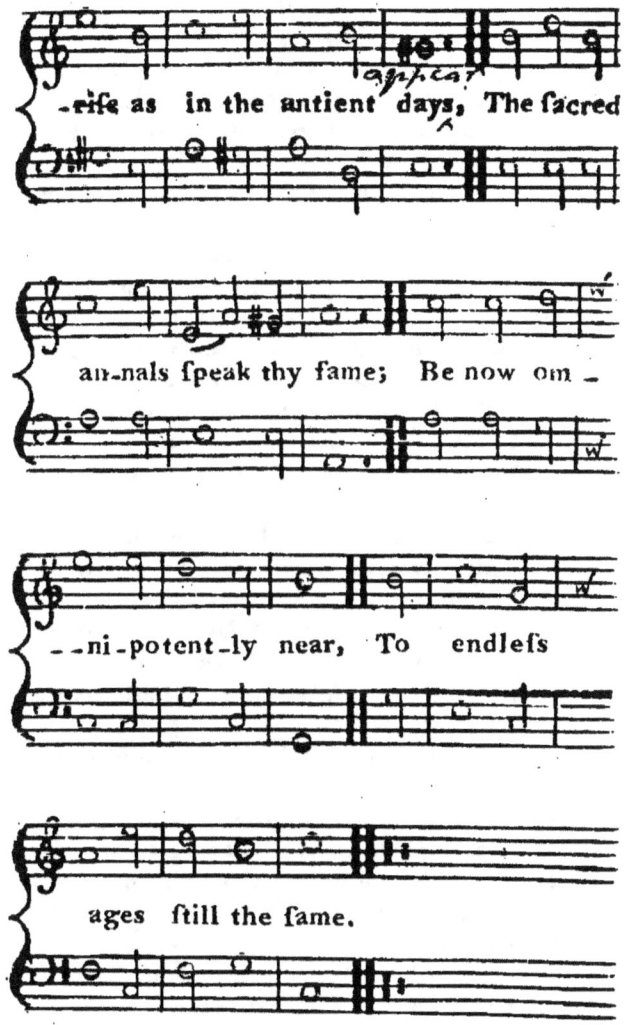

2 Thy tenfold vengeance knew to quell,
 And humble haughty Rahab's pride,
Groan'd her pale sons thy stroke to feel,
 The first-born victims groan'd and dy'd.
The wounded dragon rag'd in vain,
 While bold thine utmost plague to brave,
Madly he dar'd the parted main,
 And sunk beneath th'o'rwhelming wave.

3 He sunk; while Israel's chosen race
 Triumphant urge their wond'rous way;
Divinely led, the fav'rites pass;
 Th'unwatry deep and emptied sea,
At distance heap'd on either hand,
 Yielded a strange unbeaten road,
In chrystal walls the waters stand,
 And own the arm of Israel's God.

4 That arm which is not shorten'd now,
 Which wants not now the pow'r to save;
Still present with thy people, thou
 Bear'st them through life's disparted wave:
By earth and hell pursu'd in vain,
 To thee the ransom'd seed shall come,
Shouting their heav'nly Sion gain,
 And pass through death triumphant home.

5 The pain of life shall there be o'er,
 The anguish and distracting care,
There sighs and griefs shall be no more,
 And sin shall never enter there.
Where pure essential joy is found,
 The Lord's redeem'd their head shall raise,
With everlasting gladness crown'd,
 And fill'd with love, and lost in praise.

HYMN LXXVIII

Dresden

HE dies! the heav'nly lover dies,

The tidings strike a doleful sound

On my poor heart—strings; deep he

lies In the cold caverns of the ground.

2 Here's love and grief beyond degree,
    The Lord of glory dies for men!
But lo, what sudden joys I see!
    Jesus the dead revives again.
The rising God forsakes the tomb,
    Up to his Father's court he flies;
Cherubic legions guard him home,
    And shout him welcome to the skies.

3 Break off your tears, ye saints, and tell
    How high our great Deliv'rer reigns;
Sing how he spoil'd the hosts of hell,
    And led the monster Death in chains.
Say, Live for ever, wond'rous King!
    Born to redeem, and strong to save!
Then ask the monster, Where's thy sting?
    And where's thy vict'ry boasting grave?

2 Hark! how thy saints unite their cries,
 And pray and wait the gen'ral doom;
Come, thou! the soul of all our joys;
 Thou, the desire of nations, come!
Our heart-strings groan with deep complaint,
 Our flesh lies panting, Lord, for thee;
And ev'ry limb and ev'ry joint,
 Stretches for immortality.

3 Now let our chearful eyes survey
 The blazing earth and melting hills,
And smile to see the lightnings play,
 And flash along before thy wheels.
Hark! what a shout of vi'lent joys,
 Joins with the mighty trumpet's sound!
The angel herald shakes the skies,
 Awake the graves, and tears the ground.

4 Ye slumb'ring saints! a heav'nly host
 Stands waiting at your gaping tombs;
Let ev'ry sacred, sleeping dust
 Leap into life; for Jesus comes.
Jesus, the God of might and love,
 New moulds our limbs of cumbrous clay,
Quick as seraphic flames we move,
 To reign with him in endless day.

HYMN LXXX.

Ye e--ver-lasting doors, give way.

2 Loose all your bars of massy light,
    And wide unfold th' ethereal scene;
He claims these mansions as his right,
    Receive the King of Glory in.
Who is this King of Glory, who?
    The Lord that all his foes o'ercame,
The world, sin, death, and hell o'erthrew;
    And Jesus is the Conq'ror's name.

3 Lo! his triumphal chariot waits,
    And angels chaunt the solemn lay,
Lift up your heads, ye heavenly gates;
    Ye everlasting doors give way!
Who is the King of Glory, who?
    The Lord of glorious pow'r possest,
The King of saints and angels too,
    God over all, for ever blest.

London

HYMN LXXXI.

Thou Shepherd of Israel

THOU Shepherd of Israel, and mine, The joy and desire of my heart, For closer communion I pine, I long to reside where thou art; The

2 Ah shew me that happiest place,
    That place of thy people's abode,
Where saints in an extacy gaze,
    And hang on a crucified God:
Thy love for a sinner declare,
    Thy passion and death on the tree,
My spirit to Calvary bear,
    To suffer and triumph with thee.

3 Tis there with the lambs of thy flock,
    There only I covet to rest,
To lie at the foot of the rock,
    Or rise to be hid in thy breast;
Tis there I would always abide,
    And never a moment depart,
Conceal'd in the clift of thy side,
    Eternally held in thy heart.

2 How blest is our brother, bereft
    Of all that could burthen his mind!
How easy the soul that has left
    This wearisome body behind!
Of evil incapable thou,
    Whose relics with envy I see,
No longer in misery now,
    No longer a sinner like me.

3 This earth is affected no more
   With ficknefs, or fhaken with pain,
The war in the members is o'er,
   And never fhall vex him again;
No anger henceforward or fhame
   Shall redden this innocent clay,
Extinct is the animal flame,
   And paffion is vanifh'd away.

4 The languifhing head is at reft,
   Its thinking and aching are o'er,
The quiet, immoveable breaft
   Is heav'd by affliction no more:
The heart is no longer the feat
   Of trouble, and torturing pain,
It ceafes to flutter and beat,
   It never fhall flutter again.

5 The lids he fo feldom could clofe,
   By forrow forbidden to fleep,
Seal'd up in eternal repofe,
   Have ftrangely forgotten to weep:
The fountains can yield no fupplies,
   Thefe hollows from water are free,
The tears are all wip'd from thefe eyes,
   And evil they never fhall fee.

6 To mourn and to fuffer is mine,
   While bound in a prifon I breathe
And ftill for deliverance pine,
   And prefs to the iffues of death:
What now with my tears I bedew,
   O might I this moment become!
My fpirit created anew,
   My flefh be confign'd to the tomb.

2 Our mourning is all at an end,
    When rais'd by the life-giving Word,
  We fee the new city defcend,
    Adorn'd as a bride for her Lord:
  The city fo holy and clean,
    No forrow can breathe in the air,
  No gloom of affliction or fin,
    No fhadow of evil is there.

3 By faith we already behold
    That lovely Jerufalem here!
  Her walls are of jafper and gold,
    As chryftal her buildings are clear:
  Immoveably founded in grace,
    She ftands as fhe ever hath ftood,
  And brightly her builder difplays,
    And flames with the glory of God.

4 No need of the fun in that day,
    Which never is follow'd by night,
  Where Jefus's beauties difplay
    A pure and a permanent light:
  The Lamb is their light and their fun,
    And lo! by reflexion they fhine,
  With Jefus ineffably one,
    And bright in effulgence divine.

5 The faints in his prefence receive
    Their great and eternal reward,
  In Jefus, in heav'n they live,
    They reign in the fmile of their Lord:
  The flame of angelical love,
    Is kindled at Jefus's face,
  And all the enjoyment above,
    Confifts in the rapturous gaze.

an al-mighty hand.

2 Soon as the ev'ning fhades prevail,
The moon takes up the wond'rous tale,
And nightly to the lift'ning earth,
Repeats the ftory of her birth:
Whilft all the ftars that round her burn,
And all the planets in their turn,
Confirm the tidings as they roll,
And fpread the truth from pole to pole.

3 What though in folemn filence all?
Move round the dark terreftrial ball,
What though no real voice nor found
Amid their radiant orbs be found?
In reafon's ear they all rejoice,
And utter forth a glorious voice,
For ever finging as they fhine,
"The hand that made us is divine."

HYMN LXXXV.

201

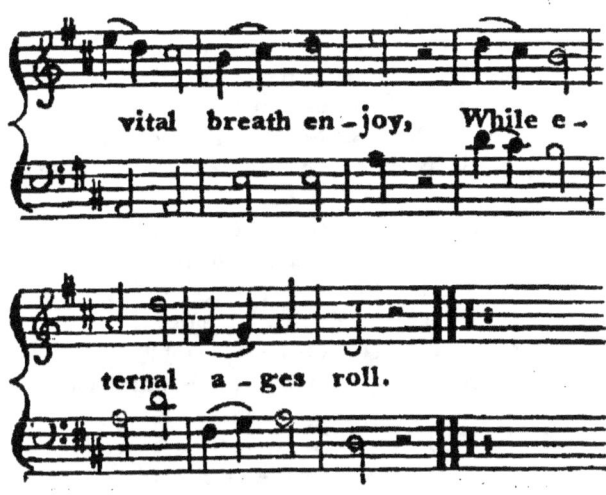

2   Thou art th'eternal Light,
     Thou shin'st in deepest night:
  Wond'ring gaz'd th'angelic train,
     While thou bowd'st the heav'ns beneath,
  God with God, wert man with man,
     Man to save from endless death.

3   Thou for our pain didst mourn,
     Thou hast our sickness borne:
  All our sins on thee were laid,
     Thou with unexampled grace
  All the mighty debt hast paid,
     Due from Adam's helpless race.

Madan's

4   Enthron'd above yon sky,
      Thou reign'st with God most high,
    Prostrate at thy feet we fall:
      Pow'r supreme to thee is given;
    Thee, the righteous judge of all,
      Sons of earth and hosts of heaven.

5   Cherubs with Seraphs join,
      And in thy praise combine,
    All their choirs thy glories sing,
      Who shall dare with thee to vie?
    Mighty Lord, eternal King,
      Sov'reign both of earth and sky!

6   Wide earth's remotest bound,
      Full of thy praise is found:
    And all heav'n's eternal day
      With thy streaming glory flames:
    All thy foes shall melt away
      From th' insufferable beams.

7   O Lord, O God of love!
      Let us thy mercy prove!
    King of all, with pitying eye
      Mark the toil, the pain we feel,
    'Midst the snares of death we lie,
      'Midst the banded powers of hell.

8   Arise, stir up thy power,
      Thou deathless Conqueror!
    Help us to obtain the prize,
      Help us well to close our race,
    That with thee above the skies
      Endless joy we may possess.

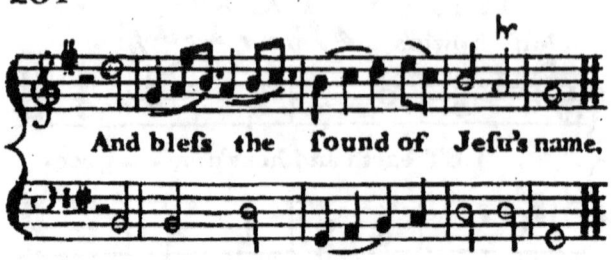

And bless the sound of Jesu's name.

2   Jesus, transporting sound!
        The joy of earth and heav'n!
    No other help is found,
        No other name is giv'n,
By which we can salvation have!
But Jesus came the world to save.

3   Jesus, harmonious name!
        It charms the hosts above!
    They evermore proclaim,
        And wonder at his love!
'Tis all their happiness to gaze;
'Tis heav'n to see our Jesu's face.

4   His name the sinner hears,
        And is from sin set free;
    'Tis music in his ears,
        'Tis life and victory:
New songs do now his lips employ,
And dances his glad heart for joy.

5   Stung by the scorpion sin,
        My poor expiring soul
    The balmy sound drinks in,
        And is at once made whole;
See there! my Lord upon the tree!
I hear, I feel he died for me.

6   For me and all mankind,
       The Lamb of God was slain;
    My Lamb his life resign'd
       For every soul of man:
    Loving to all, he none pass'd by,
    He would not have one sinner die.

7   O unexampled love!
       O all-redeeming grace!
    How swiftly didst thou move
       To save a fallen race!
    What shall I do to make it known,
    What thou for all mankind hast done!

8   For this alone I breathe,
       To spread the gospel-sound,
    Glad tidings of thy death
       To all the nations round.
    Who all may feel thy blood apply'd,
    Since all are freely justify'd

9   O for a trumpet-voice,
       On all the world to call!
    To bid their hearts rejoice
       In him who dy'd for all.
    For all my Lord was crucify'd;
    For all, for all my Saviour dy'd.

10 To serve thy blessed will,
       Thy dying love to praise,
    Thy counsel to fulfil,
       And minister thy grace;
    Freely what I receive to give,
    The life of heav'n on earth to live.

2 Equal with God most High,
He laid his glory by:
He th' Eternal God was born,
Man with men he deign'd t' appear,
Object of his creature's scorn,
Pleas'd a servant's form to wear.

3 Hail, everlasting Lord,
  Divine, incarnate Word!
Thee let all my pow'rs confess,
 Thee my latest breath proclaim;
Help, ye angels choirs, to bless,
 Shout the lov'd Immanuel's name.

4 Fruit of a virgin's womb,
  The promis'd blessing's come;
Christ, the fathers hope of old;
 Christ, the Woman's conq'ring seed;
Christ, the Saviour, long foretold,
 Born to bruise the serpent's head.

5 Refulgent from afar,
  See the bright Morning star!
See the Day-spring from on high,
 Late in deepest darkness rise!
Night recedes, the shadows fly,
 Flame with day the op'ning skies!

6 Our eyes on earth survey,
  The dazzling Shechinah!
Bright, in endless glory bright,
 Now in flesh he stoops to dwell,
God of God, and Light of Light,
 Image of th' Invisible.

7 He shines on earth ador'd,
  The Presence of the Lord:
God, the mighty God and true,

  God by highest heav'ns confest,
   Stands display'd to mortal view,
  God, supreme, for ever blest.

8   Jesu, to thee I bow,
   Th' Almighty's Fellow Thou!
  Thou, the Father's only Son;
   Pleas'd he ever is in thee,
  Just and holy thou alone,
   Full of grace and truth for me.

9   High above ev'ry name,
   Jesus, the great I AM!
  Bow to Jesus ev'ry knee,
   Things in earth, in heav'n and hell;
  Saints adore him, dæmons flee,
   Fiends, and men, and angels feel.

10   He left his throne above,
   Empty'd of all but love·
  Whom the heav'ns cannot contain,
   God vouchsaf'd a worm t'appear,
  Lord of glory, Son of man,
   Poor, and vile, and abject here.

11   His own on earth he sought,
   His own receiv'd him not:
  Him, a sign by all blasphem'd,
   Outcast and despis'd of men,
  Him they all a madman deem'd,
   Bold to scoff the Nazarene!

12   Hail, Galilean King!
          Thy humble ſtate I ſing!
    Never ſhall my triumphs end,
        Hail derided majeſty!
    Jeſus, hail! the ſinners friend,
      Friend of Publicans—and me!

13   Thine eye obſerv'd my pain,
        Thou good Samaritan!
   Spoil'd I lay, and bruis'd by ſin,
      Gaſp'd my faint expiring ſoul,
   Wine and oil thy love pour'd in,
     Cloſ'd my wounds, and made me whole.

14   Hail, the life-giving Lord,
        Divine, engrafted Word,
   Thee the Life my ſoul has found,
     Thee the Reſurrection prov'd;
   Dead I heard the quick'ning ſound,
    Own'd the voice, believ'd and lov'd.

15   With thee gone up on high,
        I live, no more to die:
   Firſt and Laſt, I feel thee now,
     Witneſs of thy empty tomb,
  Alpha and Omega thou,
    Waſt, and art, and art to come!

HYMN LXXXVIII

Cardiff

THOU God of truth and love,

We seek thy perfect way,

Ready thy choice t'ap-prove,

Thy pro-vi--dence t'o-bey

En-ter in-to thy wife defign,

And fweetly lofe our will in thine

2 Why haft thou caft our lot
  In the fame age and place,
 Or why together brought
  To fee each other's face,
To join with fofteft fympathy,
And mix our friendly fouls in thee?

3 Didft thou not make us one,
  That both might one remain,
 Together travel on,
  And bear each other's pain,
Till both thine utmoft goodnefs prove,
And rife renew'd in perfect love.

4   Surely thou didst unite
       Our kindred spirits here,
    That both hereafter might
       Before thy throne appear,
    Meet at the marriage of the Lamb,
    And all thy glorious love proclaim.

5   Then let us ever bear
       The blessed end in view,
    And join with mutual care
       To fight our passage through,
    And kindly help each other on,
    Till both receive the starry crown.

6   O might the Spirit seal
       Our souls unto that day;
    With all thy fulness fill,
       And then transport away,
    Away to our eternal rest,
    Away to our Redeemer's breast.

7   There, only there we shall
       Fulfil thy great design,
    And in thy praise with all
       Our elder brethren join,
    And hymn in songs which never end,
    Our heavenly, everlasting friend.

Here insert Mrs. Palmer's

HYMN LXXXIX.

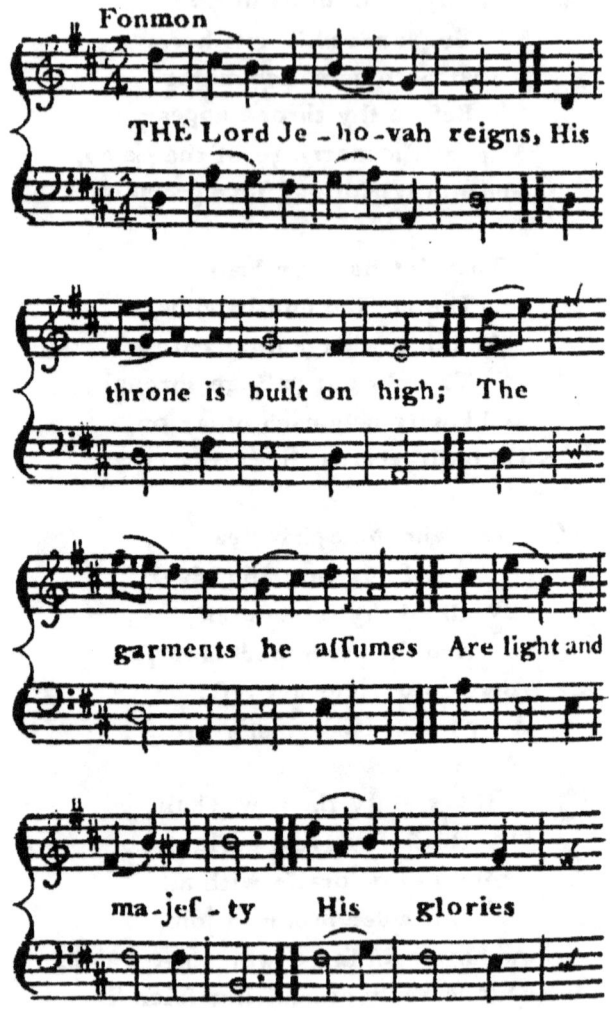

shine with beams so bright, No mortal eye - - - can bear the sight.

2   The thunders of his hand
       Keep the wide world in awe;
   His wrath and justice stand
       To guard his holy law;
   And where his love resolves to bless,
   His truth confirms and seals the grace.

3   Through all his mighty works
       Amazing wisdom shines,
   Confounds the powr's of hell
       And breaks their dark designs;
   Strong is his arm, and shall fulfil
   His great decrees and sov'reign will.

4   And can this sov'reign King,
       Of Glory condescend,
   And will he write his name,
       My Father and my Friend!
   I love his name I love his word,
   Join all my pow'rs to praise the Lord.

HYMN XC

Resurrection

REJOICE, the Lord is King! Your Lord and King a-dore; Mortals give thanks and sing, And triumph ever more: Lift up your heart;

217

2 Jesus the Saviour reigns,
    The God of truth and love,
  When he had purg'd our stains,
    He took his seat above:
Lift up your heart; lift up your voice;
Rejoice, again, I say, Rejoice.

3   His kingdom cannot fail,
      He rules o'er earth and heaven;
   The keys of death and hell
      Are to our Jefu giv'n:
Lift up your heart; lift up your voice;
Rejoice, again, I fay, Rejoice.

4   He fits at God's right hand,
      Till all his foes fubmit,
   And bow at his command,
      And fall beneath his feet:
Lift up your heart; lift up your voice,
Rejoice, again, I fay, Rejoice.

5   He all his foes fhall quell,
      Shall all our fins deftroy;
   And ev'ry bofom fwell
      With pure feraphic joy:
Lift up your heart; lift up your voice;
Rejoice, again, I fay, Rejoice.

6   Rejoice in glorious hope,
      Jefus the Judge fhall come;
   And take his fervants up
      To their eternal home:
We foon fhall hear th' archangel's voice;
The trump of God fhall found, Rejoice.

HYMN XCI.

2 Jesus, our great High priest,
   Hath full atonement made:
Ye weary spirits rest,
   Ye mornful souls be glad,
The year of jubilee is come:
Return, ye ransom'd sinners, home.

3 Extol the Lamb of God,
   The all-atoning Lamb;
Redemption in his blood
   Throughout the world proclaim,
The year of jubilee is come,
Return, ye ransom'd sinners, home.

4 Ye slaves of sin, and hell
   Your liberty receive,
And safe in Jesus dwell,
   And blest in Jesus live:
The year of jubilee is come:
Return, ye ransom'd sinners, home.

5 Ye who have sold for nought
   Your heritage above,
Shall have it back unbought,
   The gift of Jesu's love:
The year of jubilee is come:
Return, ye ransom'd sinners, home.

6 The gospel-trumpet hear,
   The news of heavenly grace,
And sav'd from earth appear
   Before your Saviour's face:
The year of jubilee is come:
Return to your eternal home.

HYMN XCII.

Dedication

FATHER, Son, and Ho-ly Ghoſt,

One in Three, and Three in One,

As by the ce-leſ-tial hoſt,

Let thy will on earth be done;

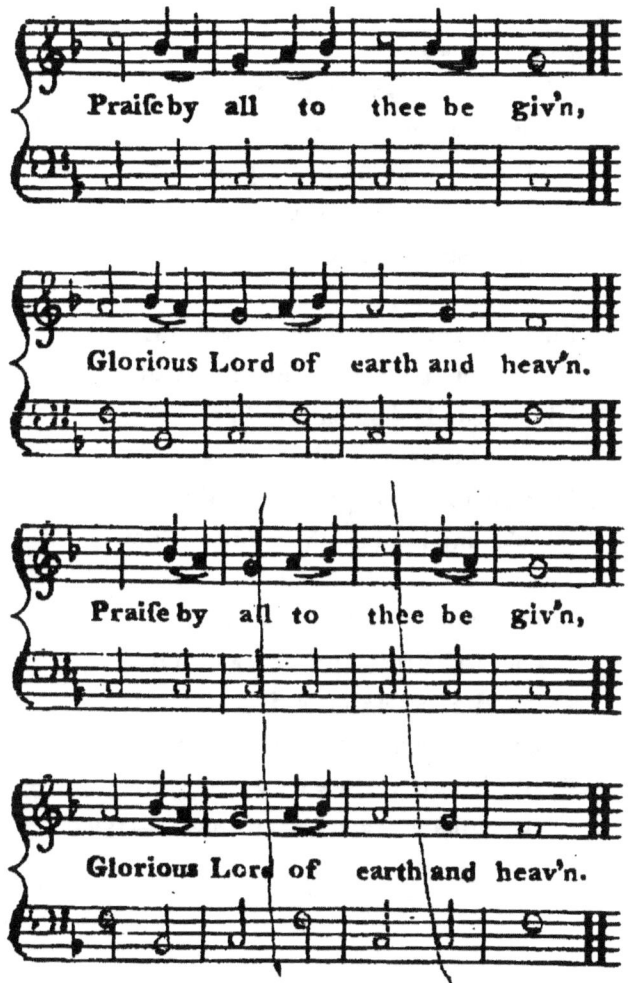

2 If fo poor worm as I
   May to thy great glory live,
All my actions fanctify,
   All my words and thoughts receive;
Claim me for thy fervice, claim
   All I have and all I am.

3 Take my foul and body's powers,
   Take my mem'ry mind and will,
All my goods and all my hours,
   All I know and all I feel,
All I think and fpeak and do;
   Take my heart — but make it new.

4 Father, Son, and Holy Ghoft,
   One in Three, and Three in One,
As by the celeftial hoft,
   Let thy will on earth be done;
Praife by all to thee be giv'n,
   Glorious Lord of earth and heaven.

HYMN XCIII

COME let us ascend, My companion & friend, To a taste of the banquet above: If thy heart be as mine, If for Jesus it pine, Come up into the chariot of love.

If thy heart be as mine, If for Jesus it pine, Come up into the chariot of love. Come up into the chariot of love.

2   Who in Jesus confide,
    We are bold to outride
 The storms of affliction beneath;
    With the prophet we soar
    To that heavenly shore,
 And outfly all the arrows of death.

3   By faith we are come
    To our permanent home,
 By hope we the rapture improve;
    By love we still rise,

   And look down on the skies;
  For the heaven of heavens is love.

4 Who on earth can conceive
   How happy we live
  In the city of God, the great King.
   What a concert of praise,
   When our Jesus's grace
  The whole heavenly company sing.

5 What a rapturous song,
   When the glorify'd throng
  In the spirit of harmony join!
   Join all the glad quires,
   Hearts, voices and lyres,
  And the burthen is mercy divine!

6 Hallelujah, they cry,
   To the King of the Sky,
  To the great everlasting I AM:
   To the Lamb that was slain,
   And liveth again,
  Hallelujah to God and the Lamb!

7 The Lamb on the throne,
   Lo! he dwells with his own,
  And to rivers of pleasure he leads:
   With his mercy's full blaze,
   With the sight of his face,
  Our beatify'd spirits he feeds.

8 Our foreheads proclaim
   His ineffable Name,
  Our bodies his glory display,
   A day without night,
   We feast in his sight,
  And eternity seems as a day.

    yond the vale of tears To that ce-
leſtial hill.

2 Beyond the bounds of time and ſpace,
    Look forward to that happy place,
      The ſaint's ſecure abode,
    On faith's ſtrong eagle pinions riſe,
    And force your paſſage to the ſkies,
      And ſcale the mount of God.

3 See where the Lamb in glory ſtands,
    Incircled with his radiant bands,
      And join th' angelic pow'rs;
    For all that height of glorious bliſs,
    Our everlaſting portion is,
      And all that heaven is ours.

4 Who suffer for our Master here,
　　We shall before his face appear,
　　　And by his side sit down;
　　To patient faith the prize is sure,
　　And all that to the end endure
　　　The cross, shall wear the crown.

5 Thrice blessed bliss inspiring hope;
　　It lifts the fainting spirit up!
　　　It brings to life the dead!
　　Our conflicts here shall soon be past,
　　And you and I ascend at last,
　　　Triumphant with our head.

6 That great mysterious Deity
　　We soon with open face shall see—
　　　The beatific sight
　　Shall fill the heav'nly courts with praise,
　　And wide diffuse the golden blaze
　　　Of everlasting light!

7 The Father shining on his throne,
　　The glorious co-eternal Son,
　　　The Spirit one and seven,
　　Conspire our rapture to compleat,
　　And lo! we fall before his feet,
　　　And silence heightens heaven.

8 In hope of that extatic pause,
　　Jesus, we now sustain thy cross,
　　　And at thy footstool fall,
　　Till thou our hidden life reveal,
　　Till thou our ravish'd spirits fill,
　　　And God is all in all.

Here insert Snowfields from p. 238

HYMN XCV.

O Love divine how sweet thou art! When shall I find my longing heart All taken up with thee! I thirst, I faint, and die to prove The greatnefs

2 Stronger his love than death or hell;
  Its riches are unsearchable,
    The first born sons of light
  Desire in vain its depth to see;
  They cannot reach the mystery,
    The length, and breadth, and height.

3 God only knows the love of God:
  O that it now was shed abroad
    In this poor stony heart!
  For love I sigh, for love I pine:
  This only portion, Lord, be mine,
    Be mine this better part.

4 O that I could for ever sit,
   With Mary at the Master's feet!
      Be this my happy choice:
   My only care, delight, and bliss,
   My joy, my heaven on earth be this,
      To hear the bridegroom's voice.

5 O that, with humble Peter, I
   Could weep, believe, and thrice reply,
      My faithfulness to prove,
   Thou know'st (for all to thee is known)
   Thou know'st, O Lord, and thou alone,
      Thou know'st that thee I love.

6 O that I could with favour'd John,
   Recline my weary head upon
      The dear Redeemer's breast!
   From care, and sin, and sorrow free,
   Give me, O Lord to find in thee
      My everlasting rest.

7 Thy only love do I require,
   Nothing in earth beneath desire,
      Nothing in heaven above;
   Let earth, and heaven and all things go,
   Give me thy only love to know,
      Give me thy only love.

HYMN XCVI.

2 If well I know the tuneful art
   To captivate an human heart,
      The glory, Lord, be Thine:
A fervant of thy bleſſed will,
I here devote my utmoſt ſkill
      To found the praiſe divine.

3 With Tubal's wretched sons no more
   I proftitute my facred power,
      To pleafe the fiends beneath,
   Or modulate the wanton lay,
   Or fmooth with mufic's hand the way
      To everlafting death.

4 Suffice for this the feafon paft:
   I come, great God, to learn at laft
      The leffon of thy grace.
   Teach me the new, the gofpel fong,
   And let my hand, my heart, my tongue
      Move only to thy praife.

5 Thine own mufician, Lord, infpire,
   And let my confecrated lyre
      Repeat the Pfalmift's part:
   His fon and thine reveal in me,
   And fill with facred melody
      The fibres of my heart.

6 So fhall I charm the lift'ning throng,
   And draw the living ftones along,
      By Jefu's tuneful name:
   The living ftones fhall dance, fhall rife,
   And form a city in the fkies
      The New Jerufalem!

7 O might I with thy faints afpire,
   The meaneft of that dazzling choir,
      Who chaunt thy praife above,
   Mixt with the bright mufician band,
   May I an heavenly harper ftand,
      And fing the fong of love.

8 What extacy of blifs is there,
   While all th'angelic concert fhare
      And drink the floating joys!
   What more than extacy, when all
   Struck to the golden pavement fall
      At Jefu's glorious voice.

9 Jefus! the heaven of heavens he is,
   The foul of harmony and blifs;
      And while on him we gaze,
   And while his glorious voice we hear,
   Our fpirits are all eye, all ear,
      And filence fpeaks his praife.

10 O might I die that awe to prove,
   That proftrate awe which dares not move
      Before the great Three One!
   To fhout by turns the burfting joy,
   And all eternity employ
      In fongs around the throne.

With faith's ſtrong arm on thee lay hold, Thee, my, Thee, my e - ternal life.

2 Tell me, O Lord if thine I am,
   Tell me thy new, myſterious name,
      Or thou ſhalt never move:
   No, never will I let thee go,
   Till I thy name thy nature know,
      And feel that God is love.

3 I feel that I have power with God,
   Thou only haſt the pow'r beſtow'd,
      And arm'd me for the fight:
   A prince through thee invincible,
   I pray, and wreſtle, and prevail,
      And conquer in thy might.

4 Thy heart, I know, thy tender heart
   Doth in my forrows feel its part,
      And at my tears relent;
   My pow'rful fighs thou canft not bear,
   Nor ftand the violence of my pray'r,
      My prayer omnipotent.

5 Give me the grace, the love I claim,
   Thy Spirit now demands thy name;
      Thou know'ft the Spirit's will;
   He helps my foul's infirmity,
   And ftrongly intercedes for me
      With groans unfpeakable.

6 Anfwer, dear Lord, thy Spirit's groan,
   O make to me thy nature known,
      Thy hidden name impart;
   (Thy title is with thee the fame)
   Tell me thy nature and thy name,
      And write it on my heart.

7 Pris'ner of hope to thee I turn,
   And calmy confident I mourn,
      And pray and weep for thee:
   Tell me thy love, thy fecret tell,
   Thy myftic name in me reveal,
      Reveal thyfelf in me.

8 Descend, pass by me, and proclaim,
O Lord of hosts, thy glorious name,
 O Lord, the gracious Lord,
Long suff'ring, merciful and kind,
The God who always bears in mind
 His everlasting word.

9 Plenteous he is in truth and grace,
He wills that all the fallen race
 Should turn, repent and live;
His pard'ning grace for all is free,
Transgression, sin, iniquity,
 He freely doth forgive.

10 Mercy he doth for thousands keep,
He goes, and seeks the one lost sheep,
 And brings his wand'rer home;
And ev'ry soul that sheep might be:
Come then, dear Lord, and gather me,
 My Jesus, quickly come.

11 Take me into thy people's rest,
O come and with my sole request,
 My one desire comply:
Make me partaker of my hope,
Then bid me get me quickly up
 And on thy bosom die.

HYMN XCVIII.

THOU God of glorious majesty, To thee, against myself, to thee, A worm of earth I cry, A worm of earth I cry, An half a-waken'd child of man An

243

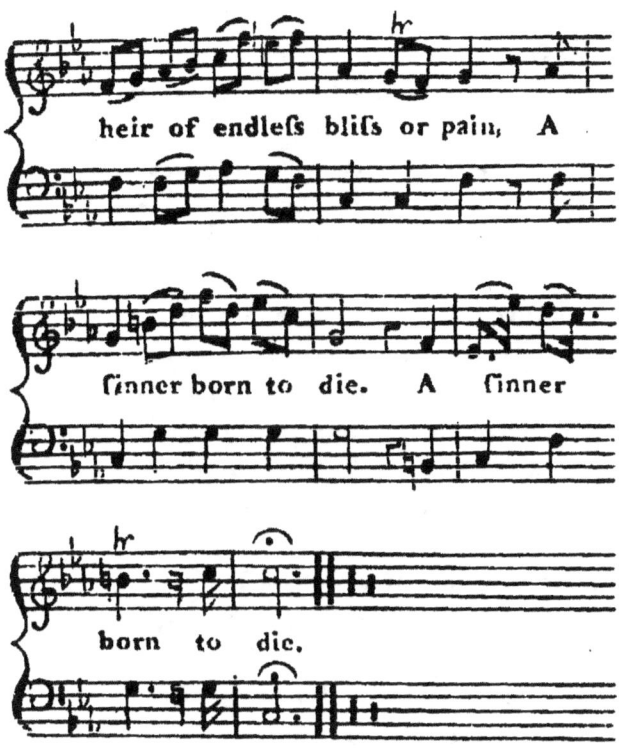

heir of endless bliss or pain, A sinner born to die. A sinner born to die.

2 Lo! on a narrow neck of land,
  'Twixt two unbounded seas I stand,
    Secure, insensible:
  A point of time, a moment's space,
  Removes me to that heav'nly place,
    Or shuts me up in hell.

3 O God, mine inmost soul convert,
   And deeply on my thoughtful heart
      Eternal things imprefs;
   Give me to feel their folemn weight,
   And tremble on the brink of fate,
      And wake to righteoufnefs.

4 Before me place in dread array
   The pomp of that tremendous day,
      When thou with clouds fhalt come
   To judge the nations at thy bar,
   And tell me, Lord, fhall I be there
      To meet a joyful doom.

5 Be this my one great bufinefs here,
   With ferious induftry and fear,
      My future blifs t' enfure,
   Thine utmoft counfel to fulfil,
   And fuffer all thy righteous will,
      And to the end endure.

6 Then, Saviour, then my foul receive,
   Tranfported from this vale, to live
      And reign with thee above,
   Where faith is fweetly loft in fight,
   And hope in full fupreme delight,
      And everlafting love.

HYMN XCIX.

2 Lo, God is here! Him day and night
    Th' united choirs of angels fing:
To him, enthron'd above all height,
    Heaven's hoft their nobleft praifes bring:
Difdain not, Lord, our meaner fong,
Who praife thee with a ftramm'ring tongue.

3 Gladly the toys of earth we leave,
    Wealth, pleasure, fame, for thee alone;
To thee our will, soul, flesh, we give:
    O take, O seal them for thine own!
Thou art the God: thou art the Lord:
Be Thou by all thy works ador'd!

4 Being of beings, may our praise
    Thy courts with grateful fragrance fill:
Still may we stand before thy face,
    Still hear and do thy sov'reign will:
To thee may all our thoughts arise,
Ceaseless, accepted sacrifice.

5 In thee we move; all things of thee
    Are full, thou source and life of all!
Thou vast, unfathomable sea!
    Fall prostrate, lost in wonder fall
Ye sons of men; for God is man!
All may we lose, so Thee we gain.

6 As flow'rs their op'ning leaves display,
    And gladly drink the solar fire,
So may we catch thy ev'ry ray,
    So may thy influence us inspire,
Thou beam of the eternal beam!
Thou purging fire, thou quickning flame.

HYMN C.

FATHER of lights, from whom proceeds
What e'er thy ev'ry creature needs, Whose
goodness providently nigh, Feeds
the young ravens when they cry: To

thee I look; my heart prepare, Sug-
geſt and hearken to my pray'r.

2 Since by thy light myſelf I ſee
Naked, and poor, and void of thee;
Thine eyes muſt all my thoughts ſurvey,
Preventing what my lips would ſay:
Thou ſeeſt my wants, for help they call,
And ere I ſpeak, thou know'ſt them all.

3 Thou know'ſt the baſeneſs of my mind,
Wayward, and impotent and blind,
Thou know'ſt how unſubdu'd my will,
Averſe to good, and prone to ill:
Thou know'ſt how wide my paſſions rove,
Nor check'd by fear, nor charm'd by love.

4 Fain would I know, as known by thee,
   And feel the indigence I fee:
   Fain would I all my vilenefs own,
   And deep beneath the burden groan,
   Abhor the pride that lurks within,
   Deteſt, and loath myſelf and ſin.

5 Ah, give me Lord, myſelf to feel,
   My total miſery reveal:
   Ah, give me Lord (I ſtill would ſay)
   An heart to mourn, an heart to pray;
   My buſi'neſs this, my only care,
   My life, my ev'ry breath be pray'r,

6 Scarce I begin my ſad complaint,
   When all my warmeſt wiſhes faint;
   Hardly I lift my weeping eye,
   When all my kindling ardors die;
   Nor hopes, nor fears my boſom move,
   For ſtill I cannot, cannot love.

7 Father, I want a thankful heart,
   I want to taſte how good thou art,
   To plunge me in thy mercy's ſea,
   And comprehend thy love to me;
   The breath, and length, and depth, and height,
   Of love divinely infinite.

8 Father, I long my ſoul to raiſe,
   And dwell for ever on thy praiſe,
   Thy praiſe with glorious joy to tell,
   In extacy unſpeakable:
   While the full power of faith I know,
   And reign triumphant here below.

HYMN CI.

Thine wholly, thine alone I am; Be thou alone my constant flame.

2 O Grant that nothing in my soul
   May dwell, but thy pure love alone:
O may thy love possess me whole,
   My joy, my treasure, and my crown:
Strange fires far from my soul remove,
My ev'ry act, word, thought, be love.

3 O love, how chearing is thy ray?
   All pain before thy presence flies!
Care, anguish, sorrow melt away,
   Where'er thy healing streams arise:
O Jesu, nothing may I see,
Nothing hear, feel, or think but thee!

4 Unwearied may I this pursue,
    Dauntless to the high prize aspire,
  Hourly within my breast renew
    This holy flame, this heavenly fire:
  And day and night be all my care
  To guard this sacred treasure there.

5 My Saviour, thou thy love to me
    In want, in pain, in shame hast show'd;
  For me on the accursed tree
    Thou poured'st forth thy guiltless blood,
  Thy wounds upon my heart impress,
  Nor aught shall the lov'd stamp efface.

6 More hard than marble is my heart,
    And foul with sins of deepest stain;
  But thou the mighty Saviour art,
    Nor flow'd thy cleansing blood in vain:
  Ah! soften, melt this rock, and may
  Thy blood wash all these stains away.

7 O that my heart, which open stands,
    May catch each drop that tort'ring pain,
  Arm'd by my sins, wrung from thy hands,
    Thy feet, thy head, thy every vein:
  That still my breast may heave with sighs,
  Still tears of love o'erflow my eyes.

8 O that I as a little child
    May follow thee nor ever rest,

Till sweetly thou hast pour'd thy mild
  And lowly mind into my breast:
Nor ever may we parted be,
Till I become one spirit with thee.

9 O draw me Saviour, after thee,
  So shall I run and never tire;
With gracious words still comfort me,
  Be thou my hope, my sole desire:
Free me from ev'ry weight, nor fear
Nor sin can come, if thou art here.

10 My health, my light, my life, my crown,
  My portion and my treasure thou!
O take me, seal me for thine own;
  To thee alone my soul I bow;
Without thee all is pain, my mind
Repose in nought but thee can find.

11 Howe'er I rove, where'er I turn,
  In thee alone is all my rest,
Be thou my flame, within me burn,
  Jesu, and I in thee am blest:
Thou art the balm of life: my soul
Is faint, O save, O make it whole!

12 What in thy love possess I not?
  My star by night, my sun by day,
My spring of life when parch'd with drought,
  My wine to chear, my bread to stay,
My strength, my shield, my safe abode,
My robe before the throne of God.

13 Ah love! thy influence withdrawn,
    What profits me that I am born?
All my delight, my joy is gone,
    Nor know I peace till thou return:
Thee may I seek till I attain,
And never may we part again.

14 From all eternity with love
    Unchangeable thou haft me view'd;
E're knew this beating heart to move,
    Thy tender mercies me purfu'd:
Ever with me may they abide,
And clofe me in on ev'ry fide.

15 Still let thy love point out my way,
    (How wondrous things thy love hath wrought)
Still lead me left I go aftray,
    Direct my work, infpire my thought:
And if I fall foon may I hear
Thy voice, and know that love is near.

16 In fuff'rings be thy love my peace,
    In weaknefs be thy love my power
And when the ftorms of life fhall ceafe,
    Jefu, in that important hour,
In death as life be thou my guide,
And fave me who for me haft dy'd!

HYMN CII.

noon-day walks he shall at-tend, And all my midnight hours defend.

2 When in the sultry glebe I faint,
Or on the thirsty mountain pant,
To fertile vales and dewy meads
My weary wand'ring steps he leads,
Where peaceful rivers soft and slow,
Amid the verdant landskip flow.

3 Though in the paths of death I tread,
With gloomy horrors overspread,
My steadfast heart shall fear no ill,
For thou, O Lord, art with me still;
Thy friendly crook shall give me aid,
And guide me thro' the dreadful shade.

4 Though in a bare and rugged way,
Through devious, lonely wilds I stray,
Thy bounty shall my pains beguile,
The barren wilderness shall smile,
With sudden greens and herbage crown'd,
And streams shall murmur all around.

HYMN CIII.

Thee will I love till the pure fire
Fill my whole soul with chaste de—sire.

2 Ah! why did I so late thee know,
    Thee lovelier than the sons of men?
Ah! why did I no sooner go
    To thee, the only ease in pain?
Asham'd I sigh, and inly mourn,
That I so late to thee did turn.

3 In darkness willingly I stray'd;
    I sought thee, yet from thee I rov'd:
Far wide my wand'ring thoughts were spread,
    Thy creatures more than thee I lov'd:
And now if more at length I see,
'Tis through thy light, and comes from thee.

4 I thank thee, uncreated sun,
    That thy bright beams on me have shin'd;
I thank thee who hast overthrown
    My foes, and heal'd my wounded mind:
I thank thee, whose enliv'ning voice
Bids my freed heart in thee rejoice.

5 Uphold me in the doubtful race,
    Nor suffer me again to stray;
Strengthen my feet, with steady pace
    Still to press forward in thy way;
My soul and flesh, O Lord of might,
Fill satiate with thy heav'nly light.

6 Give to my eyes refreshing tears,
    Give to my heart chaste, hallow'd fires,
Give to my soul, with filial fears,
    The love that all heav'ns host inspires,
That all my pow'rs, with all their might,
In thy sole glory may unite.

7 Thee will I love, my joy, my crown;
    Thee will I love, my Lord, my God;
Thee will I love beneath thy frown,
    Or smile thy sceptre or thy rod:
What though my flesh and heart decay,
Thee shall I love in endless day.

HYMN CIV.

Old 112.th Psalm Tune

THOU hidden love of God whose height

Whose depth unfathom'd no man knows,

I see from far thy beauteous light,

In-ly I sigh for thy repose;

262

My heart is pain'd, nor can it be At rest, till it finds rest in thee.

2 Thy secret voice invites me still
    The sweetness of thy yoke to prove:
And fain I would, but though my will
    Seems fix'd, yet wide my passions rove;
Yet hindrances strew all the way;
I aim at thee, yet from thee stray.

3 'Tis mercy all, that thou hast brought
    My mind to seek her peace in thee!
Yet while I seek, but find thee not,
    No peace my wand'ring soul shall see;
O when shall all my wand'rings end,
And all my steps to thee ward tend?

4 Is there a thing beneath the sun
    That strives with Thee my heart to share?

Ah! tear it thence, and reign alone,
  The Lord of ev'ry motion there:
Then shall my heart from earth be free,
When it has found repose in thee.

5 O hide this self from me, that I
  No more, but Christ in me may live!
My vile affections crucify,
  Nor let one darling lust survive:
In all things nothing may I see,
Nothing desire or seek but thee.

6 O love, thy sov'reign aid impart,
  To save me from low thoughted care:
Chase this self will through all my heart,
  Through all its latent mazes there:
Make me thy duteous child, that I
Ceaseless, may Abba Father cry.

7 Ah no! ne'er will I backward turn:
  Thine only, thine alone I am!
Thrice happy he who views with scorn
  Earth's toys, for thee his constant flame:
O help, that I may never move
From the blest footsteps of thy love!

8 Each moment draw from earth away
  My heart that lowly waits thy call!
Speak to my inmost soul, and say,
  I am thy love, thy God thy all!
To feel thy power, to hear thy voice,
To taste thy love be all my choice.

HYMN CV.

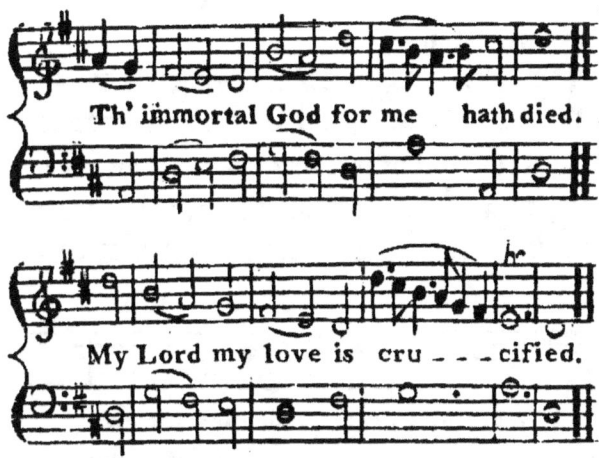

2 Behold him all ye that pafs by,
  The bleeding prince of life and peace;
Come fee, ye worms, your Maker die,
  And fay, Was ever grief like his.
Come feel with me his blood applied:
My Lord, my love is crucified.

3 Is crucified for me and you,
  To bring us rebels near to God:
Believe, believe the record true;
  We all are bought with Jefu's blood:
Pardon for all flows from his fide;
My Lord my love is crucified.

4 Then let us fit beneath his crofs,
  And gladly catch the healing ftream,
All things for him account but lofs,
  And give up all our hearts to him:
Of nothing fpeak or thing befide:
My Lord my love is crucified.

HYMN CVI

Norwich

O God of our forefathers hear, And make thy faithful mercies known,

To thee thro' Jesus I draw near,

Thy suff'ring well be lov--ed Son,

2 With solemn faith we offer up,
    And spread before thy glorious eyes,
That only ground of all our hope,
    That precious, bleeding sacrifice,
Which brings thy grace on sinners down,
And perfects all our souls in one.

3 Acceptance through his only name,
    Forgiveness in his blood we have;
But more abundant life we claim,
    Through him who dy'd our souls to save,
To sanctify us by his blood,
And fill with all the life of God.

4 Father, behold thy dying Son,
    And hear his blood that speaks above,
On us let all thy grace be shown,
    Peace, righteousness, and joy, and love;
Thy kingdom come to ev'ry heart,
And all thou hast, and all thou art.

HYMN CVII.

269

Birmingham

THOU hidden source of calm re-
THOU hidden source of calm re-
-pose, Thou all suffi- -cient love divine,
-pose, Thou all-suffi- -cient love divine,
My help and refuge from my foes, Se-
My help and refuge from my foes, Se-

2 Thy mighty name falvation is,
　And keeps my happy foul above,
Comfort it brings, and pow'r, and peace,
　And joy and everlafting love:
To me with thy dear name are given
Pardon, and holinefs, and heaven.

3 Jefu, my all in all thou art,
　My reft in toil, my eafe in pain,
The med'cine of my broken heart,
　In war my peace, in lofs my gain,
My fmile beneath the tyrant's frown,
In fhame my glory and my crown.

4 In want my plentiful fupply,
　In weaknefs my almighty power,
In bonds my perfect liberty,
　My light in Satan's darkeft hour,
In grief my joy unfpeakable,
My life in death, my heaven in hell!

2 Angels rejoice in Jesu's grace,
   And vie with man's more favour'd race,
   The blood that did for us atone,
   Confer'd on you some gifts unknown;
   Your joy through Jesu's pain abounds,
   Ye triumph by his glorious wounds.

3 Him ye beheld, our conq'ring God,
   Return with garments roll'd in blood;
   Ye saw, and kindled at the sight,
   And fill'd with shouts the realms of light,
   With loudest hallelujahs meet,
   And fell and kiss'd his bleeding feet.

4 Nor angel-tongue can e'er express
   Th' unutterable happiness,
   Nor human hearts can e'er conceive,
   The bliss wherein through Christ they live;
   But all your heav'n, ye glorious pow'rs
   And all your God is doubly ours.

HYMN CIX

277

up to thee.

2 Canst thou with-hold thy healing grace?
   So kindly lavish of thy blood;
When swiftly trickling down thy face,
   For me the purple current flow'd!
Come, Lord, &c.

3 When man was lost, love look'd about,
   To see what help in earth or sky;
In vain: for none appear'd without;
   The help did in thy bosom lie!
Come, Lord, &c.

4 There lay thy Son: but left his rest,
   Thraldom and mis'ry to remove
From those who glory once possest,
   But wantonly abus'd thy love:
Come, Lord, &c.

5 He came—O my Redeemer dear!
   And canst thou after this be strange,
Nor yet within my heart appear?
   Can love like thine, or fail or change?
Come, Lord, &c.

6 But if thou tarriest, why must I?
   My God, what is this world to me?
This world of woe—hence let them fly,
   The clouds that part my soul and thee:
Come, Lord, &c.

7 Why should this weary world delight,
   Or sense th'immortal spirit bind?
Why should frail beauty's charms invite,
   The triffling charms of woman-kind?
Come, Lord, &c.

8 A sigh thou breath'st into my heart,
   And earthly joys I view with scorn:
Far from my soul, ye dreams depart,
   Nor mock me with your vain return?
Come, Lord, &c.

9 Sorrow, and sin, and loss, and pain,
   Are all that here on earth we see;

Restless, we pant for ease in vain,
   In vain—till ease we find in thee:
Come, Lord, &c.

10 Idly we talk of harvest here,
   Eternity our harvest is:
Grace brings the great sabbatic year,
   When ripen'd into glorious bliss:
Come, Lord, &c.

11 O loose this frame, life's knot untie,
   That my free soul may use her wing;
Now pinion'd with mortality,
   A weak, entangled, wretched thing!
Come, Lord, &c.

12 Why should I longer stay and groan!
   The most of me to heaven is fled:
My thoughts and joys are thither gone;
   To all below I now am dead:
Come, Lord, &c

13 Come, dearest Lord, my soul's desire
   With eager pantings gasps for home:
Thee, thee my restless hopes require:
   My flesh and spirit bid thee come:
Come, Lord, &c.

HYMN CX.

Tally's

O What shall I do My Saviour to praise? So faithful and true, So plenteous in grace; So strong to deliver, So good to redeem The weakest be-

liver, That hangs up-on him.

2 How happy the man Whose heart is set free,
The people that can Be joyful in thee!
Their joy is to walk in The light of thy face,
And still they are talking Of Jesus's his grace.

3 Their daily delight Shall be in thy name,
They shall as their right Thy righteousness claim,
Thy righteousness wearing, and cleans'd by thy blood,
Bold shall they appear in The presence of God.

4 For thou art their boast, Their glory and pow'r,
And I also trust To see the glad hour;
My soul's new creation, A life from the dead,
The day of salvation, That lifts up my head.

5 For Jesus my Lord, Is now my defence,
I trust in his word, None plucks me from thence;
Since I have found favour, He all things will do,
My King and my Saviour, Shall make me anew.

6 Yes, Lord, I shall see The bliss of thine own,
Thy secret to me Shall soon be made known;
For sorrow and sadness I joy shall receive,
And share in the gladness Of all that believe.

2 In him we have peace, In him we have pow'r,
  Preserv'd by his grace, Throughout the dark hour
  In all our temptation He keeps us to prove
  His utmost salvation, His fulness of love.

3 Through pride and desire Unhurt we have gone,
  Through water and fire With us he went on;
  The world and the devil By him we o'ercame,
  Our Jesus from evil, For ever the same.

4 When we would have spurn'd His mercy and grace,
  To Egypt return'd, And fled from his face,
  He hinder'd out flying (His goodness to show)
  And stopt us by crying, "Will ye also go?"

5 O what shall we do Our Saviour to love?
  To make us anew, Come, Lord, from above!
  The fruit of thy passion, Thy holiness give,
  Give us the salvation Of all that believe.

6 Come, Jesus, and loose The stammerer's tongue,
  And teach even us The spiritual song:
  Let us without ceasing Give thanks for thy grace,
  And glory, and blessing, And honour, and praise.

7 Pronounce the glad word, And bid us be free:
  Ah, hast thou not Lord, A blessing for me?
  The peace thou hast given, This moment impart,
  And open thy heaven Of love in my heart.

284

HYMN CXII.

The Triumph

TIS finifh'd! tis done! The fpirit is fled; The prifoner is gone, The Chriftian is dead, The Chriftian is living, Thro' Je-fus his love, And

2 All honour and praife
   Are Jefus's due,
Supported by grace
   He fought his way through;
Triumphantly glorious,
   Through Jefus's zeal,
And more than victorious
   O'er fin, death, and hell.

3 Then let us record
    The conquering name;
Our captain and Lord
    With shoutings proclaim;
Who trust in his passion,
    And follow our head,
To certain salvation
    We all shall be led.

4 O Jesus, lead on
    Thy militant care,
And give us the crown
    Of righteousness there;
Where dazzled with glory
    The seraphim gaze,
Or prostrate adore thee,
    In silence of praise.

5 Come, Lord, and display
    Thy sign in the sky,
And bear us away
    To mansions on high;
The kingdom be given,
    The purchase divine,
And crown us in heaven
    Eternally thine.

287

HYMN CXIII.

2 The waves of the sea
    Have lift up their voice,
Sore troubled that we
    In Jesus rejoice:
The floods they are roaring,
    But Jesus is here,
While we are adoring,
    He always is near.

3 Men, devils engage,
    The billows arise,
And horribly rage,
    And threaten the skies:

Their fury fhall never
 Our ftedfaftnefs fhock,
The weakeft believer
 Is built on a rock.

4 God ruleth on high,
 Almighty to fave,
And ftill he is nigh,
 His prefence we have;
The great congregation
 His triumphs fhall fing,
Afcribing falvation
 To Jefus our King.

5 Salvation to God
 Who fits on the throne!
Let all cry aloud,
 And honour the Son!
Our Jefus's praifes
 The angels proclaim,
Fall down on their faces,
 And worfhip the Lamb.

5 Then let us adore,
 And give him his right,
All glory and pow'r,
 And wifdom and might,
All honour, and bleffing
 With angels above,
And thanks never ceafing
 And infinite love!

HYMN CXIV.

GOD of unex-ampled grace, Re-deemer of mankind, Matter of e-ternal praise We in thy passion find; Still our choicest strains we bring, Still our joyful

theme pursue, Thee the friend of sinners sing, Whose love is e-ver new.

2 Endless scenes of wonder rise
   With that mysterious tree,
Crucify'd before our eyes,
   Where we our Maker see;
Jesus, Lord, what hast thou done!
   Publish we the death divine,
Stop, and gaze, and fall, and own
   Was never love like thine!

3 Never love nor sorrow was
   Like that my Jesus show'd:
See him stretch'd on yonder cross,
   And crush'd beneath our load!
Now discern the Deity,
   Now his heavenly birth declare!
Faith cries out, 'Tis he, tis he,
   My God that suffers there!

HYMN CXV.

Kingswood *after Hamilton's*

WRETCHED, helpless, and distrest, Ah! whither shall I fly! Ever gasping after rest, I cannot find thee nigh, Naked, sick, and poor, and blind, Fast

2 Who my mis'ry can relate,
    My depth of woe reveal?
I have left my first estate,
    In hapless Adam fell.
Driven out of my abode,
I now have lost my perfect bliss,
Fallen, fallen out of God,
    And banish'd paradise.

3 I am all unclean, unclean,
    Thy purity I want,
My whole heart is sick of sin,
    And my whole head is faint:
Full of putrifying sores,
Of bruises and of wounds, my soul
    Looks to Jesus, help implores,
    And gasps to be made whole.

4 In the wilderness I stray,
    My foolish heart is blind,
Nothing do I know, the way
    Of peace I cannot find:
Jesu, Lord, restore my sight,
And take, O take the veil away,
Turn my darkness into light,
    My midnight into day.

5 Naked of thine image, Lord,
    Forsaken and alone,
Unrenew'd and unrestor'd,
    I have not thee put on:

Over me thy mantle spread,
Send down thy likeness from above,
Let thy goodness be display'd,
And wrap me in thy love.

6 Poor, alas! thou know'st I am,
And would be poorer still,
See my nakedness and shame,
And all my vileness feel:
No good thing in me resides,
My soul is all an aching void,
'Till thy Spirit here abides,
And I am fill'd with God.

7 Jesu, full of truth and grace,
In thee is all I want:
Be the wand'rer's resting place,
A cordial to the faint;
Make me rich, for I am poor,
In thee may I my Eden find,
To the dying health restore,
And eyesight to the blind.

8 Cloath me with thy holiness,
Thy meek humility;
Put on me thy glorious dress,
Endue my soul with thee;
Let thine image be restor'd,
Thy name and nature let me prove,
With thy fulness fill me, Lord,
And perfect me in love.

HYMN CXVI

Hamilton's

297

heav'n he shakes; Nature in convulsions lies, Earth's profoundest cen—ter quakes, The great Je—ho—vah dies.

2 Dies the glorious cause of all,
   The true eternal Pan,
Falls to raise us from our fall,
   To ransom sinful man:
Well may Sol withdraw his light,
   With the suff'rer sympathize,
Leave the world in sudden night,
   While his Creator dies.

3 Well may heaven be cloath'd with black,
   And solemn sackcloth wear,
Jesu's agony partake,
   The hour of darkness share:
Mourn th' astonish'd hosts above,
   Silence saddens all the skies,
Kindler of seraphic love,
   The God of angels dies.

4 O my God, he dies for me,
   I feel the mortal smart!
See him hanging on the tree —
   A sight that breaks my heart!
O that all to thee might turn!
   Sinners, ye may love him too,
Look on him ye pierc'd, and mourn
   For one who bled for you.

5 Weep o'er your desire and hope
   With tears of humblest love;
Sing, for Jesus is gone up,
   And reigns enthron'd above!
Lives our head to die no more,
   Power is all to Jesus given,
Worshipp'd as he was before,
   Th' immortal king of heaven.

6 Lord, we bless thee for thy grace
   And truth which never fail,
Hast'ning to behold thy face
   Without a dimming veil:
We shall see our heavenly King,
   All thy glorious love proclaim,
Help the angel choirs to sing
   Our dear triumphant Lamb.

HYMN CXVII.

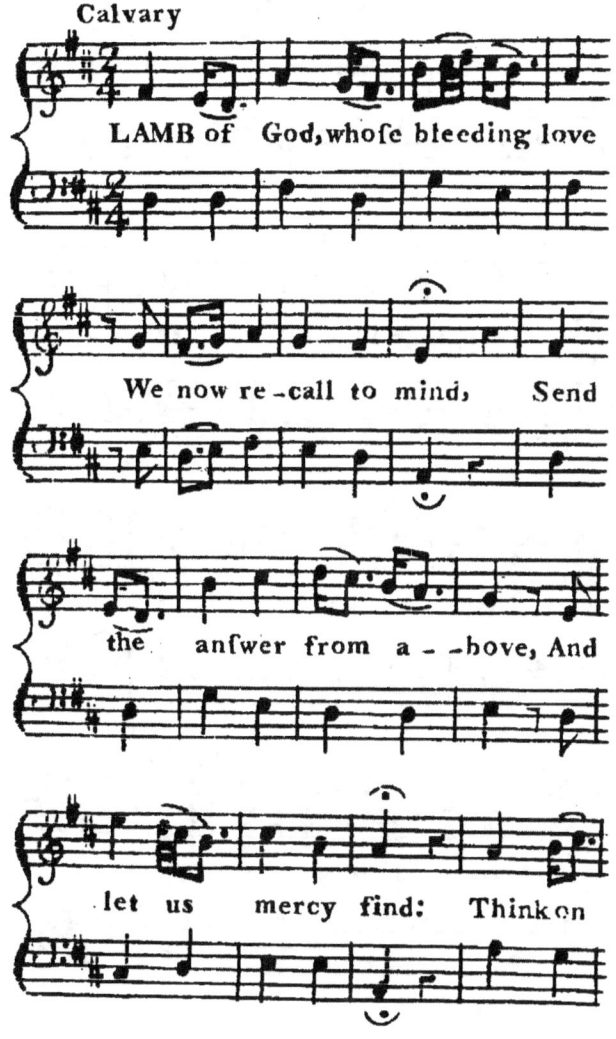

2 By thine agonizing pain,
  And bloody sweat we pray,
By thy dying love to man,
  Take all our sins away;
Burst our bonds and set us free,
From all iniquity release:
  O remember Calvary,
    And bids us go in peace.

3 Let thy blood by faith applied,
  The sinner's pardon seal,
Speak us freely justified,
  And all our sickness heal:
By thy passion on the tree,
Let all our griefs and troubles cease:
  O remember Calvary,
    And bids us go in peace.

4 Never will we hence depart,
  Till thou our wants relieve,
Write forgiveness on our heart,
  And all thine image give:
Still our souls shall cry to thee,
Till perfected in holiness:
  O remember Calvary;
    And bid us go in peace.

HYMN CXVIII.

Westminster

LOVE divine, all loves excelling,

Joy of heav'n to earth come down;

Fix in us thy humble dwelling,

All thy faithful mercies crown;

2 Breathe, O breathe thy loving Spirit
　　Into ev'ry troubled breast;
Let us all in thee inherit,
　　Let us find that second rest:
Take away our pow'r of sinning,
　　Alpha and Omega be,
End of faith as its beginning,
　　Set our hearts at liberty.

3 Come almighty to deliver,
　　Let us all thy life receive,
Suddenly return, and never,
　　Nevermore thy temples leave:
Thee we would be always blessing,
　　Serve thee as thy hosts above,
Pray, and praise thee without ceasing,
　　Glory in thy perfect love.

4 Finish then thy new creation,
　　Pure and spotless let us be:
Let us see thy great salvation,
　　Perfectly restor'd in thee:
Chang'd from glory into glory,
　　Till in heaven we take our place,
Till we cast our crowns before thee:
　　Lost in wonder, love and praise.

HYMN CXIX.

305

True Elijah

ALL hail the true E—li-jah, The Lord our God and Saviour! Who leaves be-hind, For all mankind, The tokens of his favour: The never dying prophet,

2 Come see the rising triumph,
And prostrate fall before him;
   He mounts, he flies
   Above the skies,
Where all his hosts adore him.

Borne on his fiery chariot,
With joyful acclamation
   Pursue the Lord,
   To heaven restor'd,
The God of our salvation.

3 Who see their Lord at parting,
They shall on earth inherit
  A double power,
  A larger shower
Of his descending spirit.

The spirit of our master
Shall rest on each beliver,
  And surely we
  Our master see,
Who lives and reigns for ever.

4 Yes, our exalted Jesus,
By faith we now adore thee,
  And still we sit
  Before thy feet,
And triumph in thy glory.

In vain the flaming chariot
Hath parted us asunder;
  We still thro' grace
  Behold thy face,
And shout our loving wonder.

5 By faith we catch thy mantle,
The cov'ring of thy spirit
  By faith we wear,
  And gladly share
Thine all involving merit.

We rest beneath thy shadow,
Till by the whirlwind driven,
  From earth we rise,
  And mount the skies,
And grasp our Lord in heaven.

HYMN CXX.

Dying Stephen

HEAD of thy church tri-umphant, We joyful-ly a-dore thee, Till thou appear, Thy members here, Shall sing like those in glo-ry; We lift our hearts and voices, With bleſt an-ti-ci--pa--tion, And cry a--loud, And give to God, The praiſe of our ſal--va--tion.

2 While in affliction's furnace,
   And paſſing through the fire,
     Thy love we praiſe,
     Which knows no days,
   And ever brings us nigher:
   We clap our hands exulting
   In thine almighty favour:
     The love divine
     Which made us thine,
   Shall keep us thine for ever.

3 Thou doſt conduct thy people
   Through torrents of temptation;
     Nor will we fear,
     While thou art near,
   The fire of tribulation:
   The world, with ſin and Satan,
   In vain our march oppoſes;
     By thee we ſhall
     Break through them all,
   And ſing the ſong of Moſes.

4 By faith we ſee the glory
   To which thou ſhalt reſtore us,
     The croſs deſpiſe,
     For that high prize,
   Which thou haſt ſet before us:
   And if thou count us worthy,
   We each, as dying Stephen,
     Shall ſee thee ſtand
     At God's right-hand,
   To take us up to heaven.

311

HYMN CXXI.
Canterbury

O Jesu, source of calm repose, Thy like nor man, nor angel knows, Fairest among ten thousand fair,

2 Effulgence of the light divine,
 E'er rolling planets knew to fhine,
  E'er time its ceafelefs courfe began;
 Thou when th' appointed time was come,
 Didft not abhor the virgin's womb,
  But God with God — wert man with man

3 The world, fin, death oppofe in vain,
 Thou by thy dying death haft flain,
  My great Deliv'rer and my God;
 In vain does the old dragon rage,
 In vain all hell its pow'rs engage;
  None can withftand thy conq'ring blood.

4 Lord over all, fent to fulfil
 Thy gracious Father's fov'reign will,
  To thy dread fcepter will I bow;
 With duteous rev'rence at thy feet,
 Like humble Mary, lo! I fit,
  Speak, Lord, thy fervant heareth now

5 Renew thine image, Lord, in me,
 Lowly and gentle may I be,
  No charms but thefe to thee are dear;
 No anger mayft thou ever find,
 No pride in my unruffled mind,
  But faith and heaven-born peace be there.

6 A patient, a victorious mind,
 Which life and all things caft behind,
  Springs forth obedient to thy call:
 An heart which no defire can move,
 But ftill t' adore believe and love
  Give me, my Lord, my life, my all.

HYMN CXXII.

Old 113.th Psalm Tune

I'LL praise my Maker while I've breath, And when my voice is lost in death, Praise shall em-ploy my nobler pow'rs; My days of praise

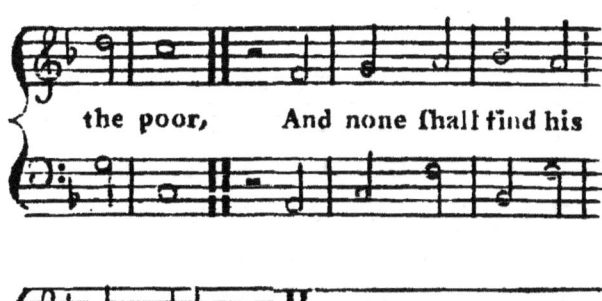

the poor, And none shall find his

promise vain.

2 The Lord pours eye-sight on the blind,
　The Lord supports the fainting mind;
　　He sends the lab'ring conscience peace:
　He helps the stranger in distress,
　The widow and the fatherless,
　　And grants the pris'ner sweet release.

3 I'll praise him while he lends me breath,
　And when my voice is lost in death,
　　Praise shall employ my nobler pow'rs;
　My days of praise shall ne'er be past,
　While life, and thought, and being last,
　　Or immortality endures.

HYMN CXXIII.

works, thy mercy's beams Diffusive as thy sun's a-rise.

2 Aftonish'd at thy frowning brow,
  Earth, hell, and heav'n's ftrong pillars bow,
    Terrible majefty is thine!
  Who then can that vaft love exprefs,
  Which bows thee down to me, who lefs
    Than nothing am, till thou art mine!

3 High thron'd on heav'n's eternal hill,
  In number, weight, and meafure ftill
    Thou fweetly order'ft all that is:
  And yet thou deign'ft to come to me,
  And guide my fteps, that I with thee
    Enthron'd, may reign in endlefs blifs.

4 Fountain of good, all blessing flows
From thee; no want thy fulness knows:
   What but thyself canst thou desire?
Yes: self-sufficient as thou art,
Thou dost desire my worthless heart;
   This, only this thou dost require.

5 Primeval beauty! in thy sight
The first-born fairest sons of light
   See all their brightest glories fade:
What then to me thine eyes could turn?
In sin conceiv'd, of woman born,
   A worm, a leaf, a blast, a shade!

6 Hell's armies tremble at thy nod,
And trembling own th' almighty God,
   Sov'reign of earth, hell, air, and sky;
But who is this that comes from far,
Whose garments roll'd in blood appear?
   'Tis God made man, for man to die.

7 O God, of good th' unfathom'd sea,
Who would not give his heart to thee?
   Who would not love thee with his might?
O Jesu, lover of mankind,
Who would not his whole soul and mind,
   With all his strength to thee unite?

HYMN CXXIV.

SOLDIERS of Christ arise, And put your armour on, Strong in the strength which God supplies, Thro' his eternal Son; Strong in the Lord of hosts, And

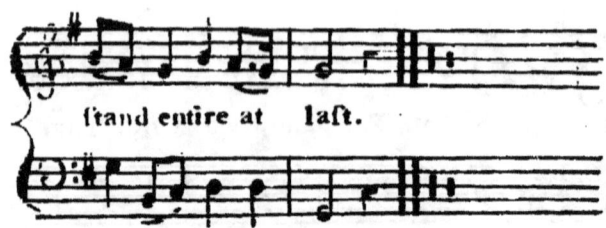

stand entire at last.

2 Stand then against your foes
In close and firm array,
Legions of wily fiends oppose
Throughout the evil day;
But meet the sons of night,
But mock their vain design,
Arm'd in the arms of heavenly light,
Of righteousness divine.

3 Leave no unguarded place,
No weakness of the soul,
Take ev'ry virtue, ev'ry grace,
And fortify the whole;
Indissolubly join'd,
To battle all proceed:
But arm yourselves with all the mind
That was in Christ your head.

4 Let truth the girdle be,
That binds your armour on,
In faithful, firm sincerity,
To Jesus cleave alone;
Let faith and love combine
To gaurd your valiant breast:
The plate be righteousness divine,
Imputed and imprest.

5   Still let your feet be shod,
      Ready his will to do,
Ready in all the ways of God
      His glory to pursue;
      Ruin is spread beneath,
      The gospel-greaves put on,
And safe through all the snares of death,
      To life eternal run.

6   But above all, lay hold
      On faith's victorious shield,
Arm'd with that adamant and gold,
      Be sure to win the field;
      If faith surround your heart,
      Satan shall be subdued;
Repell'd his every fiery dart,
      And quench'd with Jesu's blood.

7   Jesus hath died for you!
      What can his love withstand?
Believe, hold fast your shield, and who
      Shall pluck you from his hand.
      Believe that Jesus reigns,
      All pow'r to him is given:
Believe, till freed from sin's remains
      Believe yourselves to heaven.

8   Your rock can never shake;
      Hither he saith, come up!
The helmet of salvation take,
      The confidence of hope;
      Hope for his perfect love,
      Hope for his people's rest,
Hope to sit down with Christ above,
      And share the marriage feast.

9   Brandiſh in faith till then
        The Spirit's two-edg'd ſword,
Hew all the ſnares of feinds and men
        In peices with the Word:
    "'Tis written,"—This apply'd,
        Baffles their ſtength and art,
Spirit and ſoul with this divide,
        And joints and marrow part.

10   To keep your armour bright,
        Attend with conſtant care,
Still walking in your captain's ſight,
        And watching unto prayer,
    Ready for all alarms,
        Steadfaſtly ſet your face,
And always exerciſe your arms,
        And uſe your ev'ry grace.

11   Pray, without ceaſing pray,
        (Your captain gives the word)
His ſummons chearfully obey,
        And call upon the Lord:
    To God your ev'ry want
        In inſtant prayer diſplay,
Pray always, pray and never faint,
        Pray without ceaſing, pray.

12   In fellowſhip alone,
        To God with faith draw near,
Approach his courts, beſiege his throne
        With all the pow'rs of prayer;

  Go to his temple, go,
   Nor from his alter move,
 Let ev'ry houfe his worſhip know,
   And ev'ry heart his love.

13 To God your fpirits dart,
   Your fouls in words declare,
 Or groan to him who reads the heart,
   Th' unutterable prayer:
   His mercy now implore,
   And now ſhew forth his praiſe,
 In ſhouts, or filent awe adore
   His miracles of grace.

14 Pour out your fouls to God,
   And bow them with your knees,
 And fpread your hearts and hands abroad,
   And pray for Sion peace;
   Your guides and brethren bear
   For ever on your mind:
 Extend the arms of mighty prayer,
   In grafping all mankind.

15 From ſtrength to ſtrength go on,
   Wreſtle, and fight, and pray,
 Tread all the pow'rs of darkneſs down,
   And win the well-fought day;
   Still let the Spirit cry
   In all his foldiers, "Come,"
 Till Chriſt the Lord defcends from high,
   And takes the conq'rors home.

333

race, Yet will I triumph in the Lord, The God of my sal-vation praife.

2 Barren although my foul remain,
    And no one bud of grace appear;
No fruit of all my toil and pain,
    But fin, and only fin is here;
Although my gifts and comforts loft,
    My blooming hopes cut off I fee,
Yet will I in my Saviour truft,
    And glory that he dy'd for me.

3 In hope believing againft hope,
    Jefus my Lord and God I claim;
Jefus, my ftrength, fhall lift me up,
    Salvation is in Jefu's name:
To me he foon fhall bring it nigh,
    My foul fhall then outftrip the wind,
On wings of love mount up on high,
    And leave the world and fin behind.

HYMN CXXVI.

Chesunt

THE voice of my be-lov-ed

THE voice of my be-lov-ed

sounds, While o'er the moun-tain-tops

sounds, While o'er the moun-tain-tops

he bounds, He flies ex-ulting

he bounds, He flies ex-ulting

2 The scatter'd clouds are fled at last,
The rain is gone, the winter's past
The lovely vernal flow'rs appear,
The warbling choir enchant our ear;
   Now with sweetly pensive moan,
   Cooes the turtle dove alone.

3 The voice of my beloved sounds,
While o'er the mountain tops he bounds,
He flies exulting o'er the hills,
And all my soul with transport fills.
   Gently doth he chide my stay,
   Rise my love and come away."

HYMN CXXVII.

JESUS, my love, my life, my peace,
Jesus is mine, and I am his,
His bride, his dear bought property,
Who lov'd, and gave himself for me:
   Joy and glory of my soul,
   While eternal ages roll!

HYMN CXXVIII.
The 100 Psalm

BEFORE Je-hovah's awful throne, Ye nations bow with sacred joy; Know that the Lord is God a- -lone,

343

2 The scatter'd clouds are fled at last,
The rain is gone, the winter's past
The lovely vernal flow'rs appear,
The warbling choir enchant our ear;
   Now with sweetly pensive moan,
   Cooes the turtle dove alone.

3 The voice of my beloved sounds,
While o'er the mountain tops he bounds,
He flies exulting o'er the hills,
And all my soul with transport fills.
   Gently doth he chide my stay,
   Rise my love and come away."

HYMN CXXVII.

JESUS, my love, my life, my peace,
Jesus is mine, and I am his,
His bride, his dear bought property,
Who lov'd, and gave himself for me:
   Joy and glory of my soul,
   While eternal ages roll!

HYMN CXXVIII.
The 100 Psalm

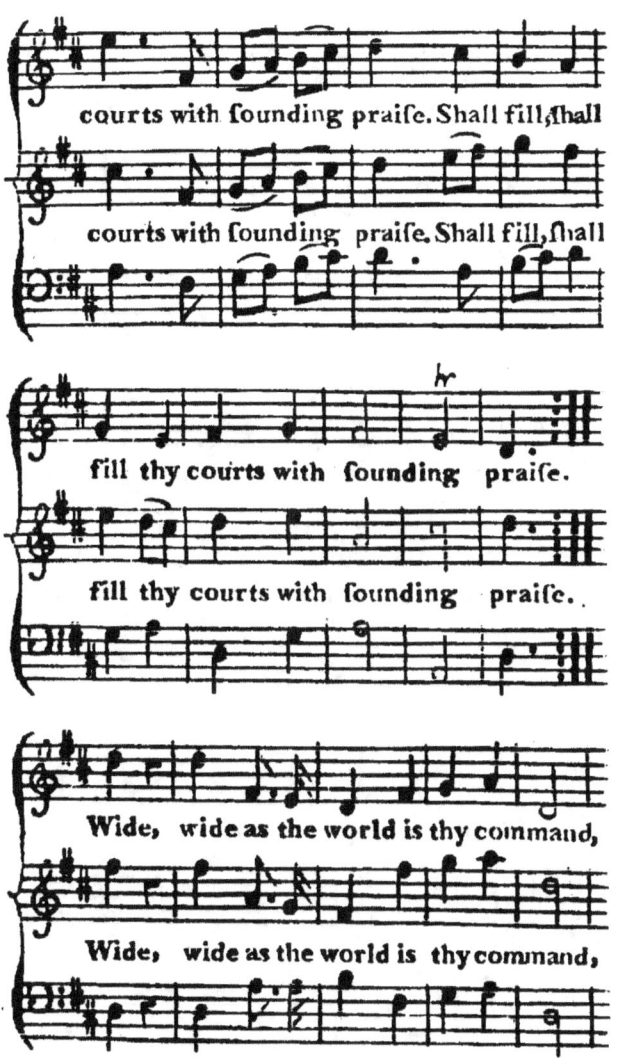

INDEX.

                                                Page Hymn

A

	Page	Hymn
All glory and Praife,	2	1
All ye that pafs by,	6	4
Ah! tell us no more,	8	5
Away with our fears,	10	6
Ah! woe is me, conftrain'd to dwell,	105	49
Arm of the Lord, awake, awake!	176	77
Ah! lovely appearance of death,	191	82
Away with our forrow and fear,	194	83
Arife, my foul arife,	206	87
All thanks to the Lamb, Who gives us to meet,	282	111
All hail the true Elijah,	305	119
Away my unbelieving fear!	330	125

B

	Page	Hymn
Being of beings, God of love,	90	43
Brother in Chrift, and well belov'd,	154	67
Blow ye the trumpet, blow,	219	91
Before Jehovah's awful throne,	342	128

C

	Page	Hymn
Come let us anew	12	7
Come ye that love the Lord,	17	11
Come defire of nations, come,	32	20
Chrift the Lord is rif'n to day,	34	21
Clap your hands ye people all,	41	23
Come thou high and lofty Lord,	48	26
Come, and let us fweetly join,	53	27
Chrift our head gone up on high,	59	29
Come holy Spirit heav'nly Dove,	80	38

	Page	Hymn
Come let us join our chearful songs,	98	46
Come let us ascend, — —	225	93
Come on my partners in distress,	228	94

E

	Page	Hymn
Eternal depth of love divine! —	148	64
Eternal pow'r, whose high abode	162	71

F

	Page	Hymn
From whence these dire portents around	86	41
Father how wide thy glories shine,	102	48
Father, if justly still we claim —	145	63
Father, Son, and Holy Ghost, —	222	92
Father of lights, from whom proceeds	248	100
Faint is my head, and sick my heart,	275	209

G

	Page	Hymn
Glory be to God on high, — —	38	22
God of all-redeeming grace —	46	25
God of all grace and majesty,— —	95	45
God of my life, whose gracious pow'r	166	73
God of unexampled grace, —	290	114

H

	Page	Hymn
Holy Lamb who thee receive, —	28	17
Hail the day that sees him rise, —	56	28
Happy magdalen, to whom —	60	30
Happy soul that safe from harms,	64	31
How sad our state by nature is.	70	33
Hail Father, whose creating call,	100	47
Hail, holy, holy, holy Lord, —	115	53
Happy soul, thy days are ended;	122	55
Happy the man who finds the grace,	139	61
He comes, he comes, the judge severe,	174	76
He dies! the heav'nly lover dies,	179	78

	Page	Hymn
Head of thy church triumphant,	308	120

I

	Page	Hymn
Jesus, come, thou hope of glory,	15	9
Jesu, my Lord attend,	18	12
Jesu, lover of my soul,	50	26
Infinite pow'r eternal Lord,	82	39
Jesu thou art my righteousness,	108	50
Jesu thy blood and righteousness,	127	57
I thirst, thou wounded Lamb of God,	150	65
Jesus, in whom the Godhead's rays	152	66
Jesu, thy boundless love to me	251	101
Jesus drinks the bitter cup;	296	116
I'll praise my Maker while I've breath,	314	122
Jesus, my love, my life, my peace,	341	127

L

	Page	Hymn
Lord and God of heav'nly pow'rs,	30	18
Lord, if thou the grace impart	31	19
Lord, all I am is known to thee,	74	35
Lo! he comes with clouds descending	124	56
Let earth and heav'n agree,	203	86
Lo! God is here, let us adore,	245	99
Lamb of God, whose bleeding love	299	117
Love divine, all loves excelling,	302	118

M

	Page	Hymn
My God I am thine,	3	2
My soul before thee prostrate lies,	142	62

O

	Page	Hymn
O Jesus my hope,	4	3
O thou holy Lamb divine,	27	16
O Son of Righteousness, arise	72	34
O thou who when I did complain,	76	36

	Page	Hymn
O for an heart to praife my God!	78	37
O Lord incline thy gracious ear,	84	40
O that my load of fin were gone,	158	69
O God, my God, my all thou art:	168	74
O thou, our hufband, brother, friend,	171	75
Our Lord is rifen from the dead,	185	80
O love divine how fweet thou art!	231	95
O love divine what hath thou done!	264	105
O God of our forefathers hear,	266	106
O what fhall I do My Saviour to praife,	280	110
O Jefu fource of calm repofe!	311	121
O God of good, th'unfathom'd fea!	318	123

P

	Page	Hymn
Praife be to the Father given,	14	8
Praife ye the Lord y'immortal choir,	118	54
Praife ye the Lord: 'tis good to raife	164	72

R

	Page	Hymn
Regent of all the worlds above:	134	59
Rejoice, the Lord is King!	215	90

S

	Page	Hymn
Son of God, thy bleffings grant,	26	15
Sweet is the mem'ry of thy grace,	88	42
Some Seraph, lend your heav'nly tongue,	110	51
Stand and adore! how glorious he	112	52
Sinners, obey the gofpel word,	136	60
Sinners, rejoice; your peace is made;	272	108
Soldiers of Chrift arife,	223	124

T

	Page	Hymn
Thou very pafchal Lamb,	16	10
Thee we adore Eternal Name,	68	32
The God of Abrah'm Praife,	130	58

	Page	Hymn
Thou Shepherd of Ifrael, and mine,	188	81
The fpacious firmament on high,	197	84
Thou, Jefu, art our king, — —	200	85
Thou God of truth and love, —	211	88
The Lord Jehovah reigns, —	214	89
Thou God of harmony and love,	234	96
Thee Jefu, thee the finner's friend,	283	97
Thou God of glorious majefty, —	242	98
The Lord my pafture fhall prepare,	256	102
Thee will I love, my ftrength my tow'r,	258	103
Thou hidden love of God whofe height,	261	104
Thou hidden fource of calm repofe,	269	107
'Tis finifh'd! 'tis done! — —	284	112
The voice of my beloved founds,	334	126

W

	Page	Hymn
Who in the Lord confide, —	20	13
When all the mercies of my God —	92	44
When gracious Lord, when fhall it be	156	68
With glory clad, with ftrength array'd,	160	70
When fhall thy lovely face be feen?	182	79
Wretched, helplefs, and diftreft, —	292	115

Y

	Page	Hymn
Ye fimple fouls that ftray —	22	14
Ye who dwell above the fkies, —	44	24
Ye fervants of God, — —	287	113

Appendix A
Flyleaf with John Wesley's Autograph and Date

Appendix B
John Wesley's Notes on Hymn and Tunes in *SH* 1780

John Wesley's notes below were transcribed by S T Kimbrough, Jr. from the copy of *SH* 1780, for which this volume provides a facsimile reprint. The volume is inscribed on the fly-leaf with John Wesley's autograph and dated Janu 10, 1780. Throughout the volume there are notes in Wesley's handwriting. They have primarily to do with the order of the hymns and the choice of appropriate tunes. The tune names have been put in capital letters by the editors.

Page	Hymn	John Wesley's Comments
16	X	Tune: BRENTFORD, JW writes TENNANT
34	XXI	Tune: MACCABEES, JW strikes through tune name and writes EASTER. The hymn is "Christ the Lord is risen today."
78	XXXVII	Tune: YORKSHIRE, JW strikes through tune name.
84	XL	Tune: MANCHESTER, JW notes delete.
90	XLIII	Tune: BRISTOL, JW strikes through tune name.
102	XLVIII	Note: "place this first"? St. Paul's.
108	L	Note: "immediately" St. Paul's.
112	LII	Note: Smith's, insert this p. 162 after Palmis.
122	LV	Note: EPWORTH, JW strikes through tune name.
129	LVII	At the end of the hymn, "Jesu thy blood and righteousness" JW writes ROCKFORD.
139	LXI	Note: JW strikes through the hymn number LXI. The hymn is "Happy the man who finds the grace."
148	LXIV	Tune: ANGLESEA, JW notes delete.
171	LXXV	Tune: EVESHAM, JW strikes tune name and writes "Purcell's."
174	LXXVI	The hymn is "He comes, he comes, the judge severe." At the end of it JW writes "The God of Abraham."
197	LXXXV	The hymn is "Thou Jesu, art our king." At the end of it JW writes "Madan's."
203	LXXXVI	Tune: MISS EDWIN'S, JW notes "after Cardiff."
213	LXXXVIII	Tune: CARDIFF, at the end of the hymn JW writes, "Here insert MISS EDWIN'S."
228	XCIV	Tune: TRAVELLER, at the end of the hymn on p. 230, JW notes, "Here insert SNOWFIELD'S from p. 238."
231		Hymn "Jesu, thy boundless love," JW notes, "p. 255 'Welch'."
238	XCVII	Tune: SNOWFIELD'S, JW notes "after TRAVELLER'S."

433

248	C		Tune: FRANKFORT, hymn is "Father of lights from whom proceeds"; at the end JW notes "CANTERBURY" (note on p. 250)
264	CV		Tune: WELCH, JW notes "after BRADFORD" (p. 255). The hymn is "O love divine, what hast thou done."
292	CXV		Tune: KINGSWOOD, JW notes "after HAMILTON'S." The hymn is "Wretched, helpless, and distressed."
311	CXXI		Tune: CANTEBURY, JW notes "after FRANKFORT". The hymn is "O, Jesu, source of calm repose."

In the tune index to the volume are the following notes:

The tune name EVESHAM is stricken through by JW and he writes DWIGHT'S (see p. 171).

At the end of MACCABEES, JW writes EASTER.

Appendix C
Index of First Lines in *SH* 1780 with Comparisons to *FC* 1742 and *SH* 1761

A check (√) indicates texts that appear in *SH* 1761 and *SH* 1780.
A bullet (•) indicates texts that appear also in *FC* 1742.
First lines marked by (†) appear *only* in *SH* 1780.
First lines in italics indicate hymns that appear only as text blocks in *SH* 1780.

First line	Hymn No.	Page No.	Author
Ah! lovely appearance of death √	82	191	Charles Wesley
Ah! tell us no more, The Spirit and pow'r √	5	8	Charles Wesley
Ah! woe is me, constrain'd to dwell √	49	36	Charles Wesley
All glory and praise, To the Ancient of days √	1	2	Charles Wesley
All hail the true Elijah †	119	305	Charles Wesley
All thanks to the Lamb, who gives us to meet √	111	282	Charles Wesley
All ye that pass by	4	6	Charles Wesley
Arise, my soul, arise √	87	206	Charles Wesley
Arm of the Lord, awake, awake √	77	176	Charles Wesley
Away my unbelieving fear √	125	330	Charles Wesley
Away with our fears, Our sorrows and tears √	6	10	Charles Wesley
Away with our sorrow and fear √	83	194	Charles Wesley
Before Jehovah's awful throne √	128	342	Isaac Watts
Being of beings, God of love •	43	90	Charles Wesley
Blow ye the trumpet, blow †	91	219	Charles Wesley
Brother in Christ, and well belov'd √ •	67	154	Charles Wesley
Christ, our head gone up on high	29	59	Charles Wesley
Christ, the Lord, is ris'n today •	21	34	Charles Wesley
Clap your hands, ye people all √	23	41	Charles Wesley
Come and let us sweetly join √ •	27	53	Charles Wesley
Come, Desire of nations, come √	20	32	Charles Wesley
Come, Holy Spirit, heav'nly Dove †	38	80	Charles Wesley
Come let us anew, our journey pursue √	7	12	Charles Wesley
Come let us ascend, My companion and friend √	93	225	Charles Wesley
Come let us join our cheerful songs √	46	98	Isaac Watts
Come on my partners in distress †	94	228	Charles Wesley
Come thou high and lofty Lord	26	48	Charles Wesley
Come ye that love the Lord	11	17	Isaac Watts
Eternal depth of love divine √	74	69	John Wesley translation
Eternal Prayer/Power, whose high abode	71	162	Isaac Watts
Faint is my head, and sick my heart √	109	275	George Herbert
Father how wide thy glories shine √	48	102	Isaac Watts

FATHER, if justly still we claim √	63	145	Henry More
FATHER of light(s), from whom proceeds √ •	100	248	Charles Wesley
FATHER, SON, and HOLY GHOST √	92	222	Charles Wesley
From whence these dire portents around √	41	85	Samuel Wesley, Jr.
Glory be to GOD on high √	22	38	Charles Wesley
GOD of all grace and majesty √	45	95	Charles Wesley
GOD of all-redeeming grace √	25	46	Charles Wesley
GOD of my life, whose gracious pow'r √	73	166	Charles Wesley
GOD of unexampled grace √	114	290	Charles Wesley
Hail, FATHER, whose creating call √	47	100	Samuel Wesley, Jr.
Hail, holy, holy, holy LORD √ •	53	40	Samuel Wesley, Jr.
Hail the day that sees him rise √	28	56	Charles Wesley
Happy Magdalene, to whom √	30	60	Charles Wesley
Happy soul, that safe from harms √	31	64	Charles Wesley
Happy soul, thy days are ended	55	122	Charles Wesley
Happy the man who finds the grace √	61	139	Charles Wesley
He comes, He comes, the Judge severe √	76	174	Charles Wesley
He dies, the heavenly Lover dies √	78	179	Isaac Watts
Head of the church triumphant √	120	308	Charles Wesley
Holy LAMB, who thee receive √ •	17	28	John Wesley translation
How sad our state by nature is √	33	70	Isaac Watts
I thirst, thou wounded LAMB of GOD •	65	150	John Wesley translation
I'll praise my MAKER while I've breath √	122	314	Isaac Watts
Infinite Pow'r, Eternal LORD √	39	82	Isaac Watts
JESU, lover of my soul †	16	50	Charles Wesley
JESU, my Lord, attend √	12	18	Charles Wesley
JESU, thou art my righteousness √ •	50	108	Charles Wesley
JESU, thy blood and righteousness √ •	56	124	John Wesley translation
Jesu, thy boundless love to me √	101	251	John Wesley translation
Jesus, come, thou hope of glory	9	15	Charles Wesley
Jesus drinks the bitter cup √	116	296	Charles Wesley
JESUS in whom the Godhead's rays √	66	152	Charles Wesley
LAMB of GOD, whose bleeding love √	117	299	Charles Wesley
Let earth and heav'n agree √ •	86	203	Charles Wesley
Lo God is here! Let us adore √	99	245	John Wesley translation
Lo! he comes with clouds descending †	56	124	Charles Wesley
LORD, all I am is known to thee √	35	74	Isaac Watts
LORD and GOD of heavenly pow'rs √	18	30	Charles Wesley
Lord if thou the grace impart	19	31	Charles Wesley
Love divine, all loves excelling √	118	302	Charles Wesley
My God I am thine	2	3	Charles Wesley
My soul before thee prostrate lies √ •	62	142	John Wesley translation

Index of First Lines of Texts in SH 1780

First Line			
O for an heart to praise my GOD	37	78	Charles Wesley
O GOD, my GOD, my all thou art √	74	168	John Wesley translation
O God of good th' unfathom'd sea †	123	18	John Wesley translation
O GOD of our forefathers, hear √	106	266	Charles Wesley
O JESU, source of calm repose †	121	311	Charles Wesley
O JESUS, my hope, For me offer'd up √	3	4	Charles Wesley
O LORD, incline thy gracious ear †	40	84	Charles Wesley
O love divine, how sweet thou art √	95	231	Charles Wesley
O love divine, what hast thou done √	105	264	Charles Wesley
O Sun of righteousness arise √	34	72	Charles Wesley
O that my load of sin were gone √	69	158	Charles Wesley
O Thou holy Lamb divine	16	27	Charles Wesley
O thou, our Husband, Brother, Friend √	75	171	Charles Wesley
O thou, who when I did complain √ •	36	76	Samuel Wesley, Sr.
O what shall I do my SAVIOUR to praise √	110	280	Charles Wesley
Our LORD is risen from the dead √	80	185	Charles Wesley
Praise be to the FATHER given √ •	8	14	Charles Wesley
Praise ye the LORD, 'tis good to raise √	72	164	Isaac Watts
Praise ye the LORD, ye immortal choir √	54	118	Isaac Watts
Regent of all the worlds above	59	134	Isaac Watts
Rejoice, the LORD is King	90	216	Charles Wesley
Sinners obey the Gospel word √	60	136	Charles Wesley
Sinners rejoice, your peace is made √	108	272	Charles Wesley
Soldiers of CHRIST, arise √	124	323	Charles Wesley
Some seraph lend your heav'nly tongue †	51	110	Isaac Watts
SON of GOD, thy blessing grant √	15	25	Charles Wesley
Stand and adore, how glorious he †	52	112	Isaac Watts
Sweet is the mem'ry of thy grace √	42	88	Isaac Watts
The GOD of Abraham praise †	58	130	Thomas Olivers paraphrase
The LORD JEHOVAH reigns √	89	214	Isaac Watts
The LORD my pasture shall prepare √	102	256	Joseph Addison
The spacious firmament on high √	84	197	Joseph Addison
The voice of my Beloved sounds †	126	334	Charles Wesley
Thee, JESU, thee, the sinner's friend √	98	238	Charles Wesley
Thee we adore, Eternal Name √	32	68	Isaac Watts
Thee will I love, my strength my tow'r √	103	258	John Wesley translation
Thou GOD of glorious majesty √	98	242	Charles Wesley
Thou GOD of harmony and love †	96	234	Charles Wesley
Thou GOD of truth and love √	88	211	Charles Wesley
Thou hidden love of GOD, whose height √	104	261	John Wesley translation
Thou hidden source of calm repose √	107	269	Charles Wesley
Thou, JESU, art our King √ •	85	200	John Wesley translation

Thou Shepherd of Israel and mine †	81	188	Charles Wesley
Thou very Paschal Lamb √	10	16	Charles Wesley
'Tis finished, 'tis done, the Spirit is fled √	113	284	Charles Wesley
When all the mercies of my God √	44	92	Joseph Addison
When, gracious Lord, when shall it be †	68	156	Charles Wesley
When shall thy lovely face be seen √	79	182	Isaac Watts
Who in the Lord confide √	13	20	Charles Wesley
With glory clad, with strength array'd √	70	160	N. Tate, N. Brady
Wretched, helpless, and distrest √	115	292	Charles Wesley
Ye servants of God, Your Master proclaim √	113	287	Charles Wesley
Ye simple souls that stray √	14	22	Charles Wesley
Ye who dwell above the skies √	24	44	George Sandys

Appendix D

These three examples show the tune SACRAMENT in a three-voice setting in *HS* 1754 [1], from which the melody, fermatas, and two of the four trills were included in *SH* 1761 [2], and the version in *SH* 1780 [3] that includes the melody, fermatas, and one trill from *HS* 1754, and a new bass without figures.

Appendix E
SH 1789 (London)

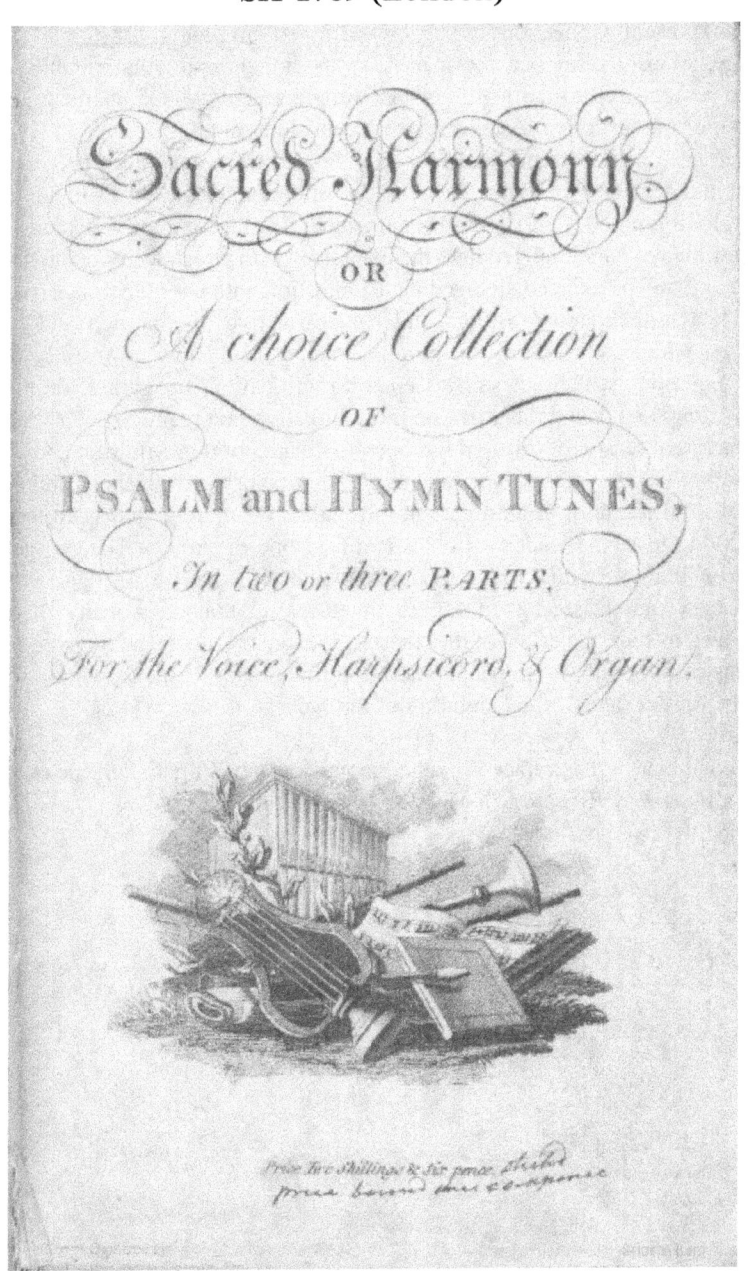

Appendix F
Excerpt from "Preface To The Present Edition," *SH* 1822.

The present Collection of Tunes, designed originally for the Methodist Congregations, having become scarce, it was thought that an acceptable service would be rendered to the lovers of that simple melody which characterized the singing of the primitive Methodists by republishing them . . . .

Certain it is, that since the airs in the "Sacred Harmony" have been suffered to fall into neglect or oblivion, the character of our congregational singing has not generally improved. . . . [I]t must be lamented, that the rage for new tunes which was for many years indulged, and the eagerness with which every collection was bought up and introduced, deluged the Connection with base, dissonant, unscientific, and tasteless compositions, utterly destructive of that rich and solemn melody, which best becomes religious services, and most powerfully excites those emotions which act subserviently to edification, by giving force to the words sung, and fixing the attention more directly upon them.

One great reason of this evil has been the inattention of Ministers themselves to this part of the service of the sanctuary; for what primitive bishops and general councils did not think it unimportant to regulate or improve, has been too often left among us to the leaders of tunes and to choirs of singers. The consequence has been, that every tune which recommended itself to a false, a vulgar, or a light taste, or which was adopted for no other reason than its novelty, has been employed to spoil the effect of the finest sacred poetry, not inspired, ever put into the lips of religious worshippers; and not unfrequently to silence whole congregations for the sake of the exhibition of the orchestra.

The remainder of the preface is a remarkable survey of Christian music excerpted from an essay by Richard Watson. See fn #19.

Appendix F
Copy of the Cover of *SH* 1822

Selected Bibliography

Adams, Nelson. "The Musical Sources for John Wesley's Tune Books: The Genealogy of 148 Tunes." Unpublished DMA Thesis. Union Theological Seminary School of Sacred Music, 1973.

Addison, Joseph. "The Lord my pasture shall prepare." No. 441. July 25, 1712. In the *Spectator*. London: Sharp & Hailes, 1711–14.

Arnold, John. *Church Music Reformed or the Art of Psalmody*. London: R. Brown, 1765.

Baker, Frank. *A Union Catalogue of the Publications of John and Charles Wesley*. Durham, NC: The Divinity School, Duke University, 1966.

———. *John Wesley and the Church of England*. London: Epworth, 1970.

Booth, Edward. Editor, *The Wesleyan Psalmist: A Collection of Psalm & Hymn Tunes, Chiefly Selected from ... the Old Masters, Together with the Most Approved Modern Tunes ... Expressly Adapted to the Various Metres in the Wesleyan Hymn Book*. London: T. Chappell, 1857.

Butts, Thomas. *Harmonia Sacra, or a Choice Collection of Psalm and Hymn Tunes*. London: Ratcliff Row Old Street, 1754.

Clarke, Marvin V. "John Wesley and Methodist Music in the Eighteenth Century: Principles and Practice." Unpublished PhD dissertation. University of Durham, UK, 2008.

Davies, Rupert E. and E. Gordon Rupp, editors. Vol. 1. *A History of the Methodist Church in Great Britain*. London, 1965.

Dolbey, George W. *The Architectural Expressions of Methodism, The First Hundred Years*. London, 1964.

Drage, Sally. "The Set Piece," in *Music and the Wesleys*, edited by Nicholas Temperley and Stephen Banfield. Urbana, Illinois, 2010.

East, William. *The Second Book of the Voice of Melody, being a Collection of ... Psalm-Tunes ... in Four Parts; with Variety of Hymns and Anthems*. London, 1750.

Green, Richard. *A Bibliography: Containing an Exact Account of all the Publications issued by the Brothers Wesley*. 2nd edition. London: Methodist Publishing House, 1906.

Heitzenrater, Richard P. *Wesley and the People Called Methodists*. Nashville: Abingdon Press, 1995.

Herbert, George. *The Temple. Sacred Poems and Private Ejaculations*. Cambridge, 1633.

Hildebrandt, Franz; Oliver A. Beckerlegge. Editors. *The Works of John Wesley. A Collection of Hymns for the Use of the People Called Methodists*. Vol. 7. Nashville: Abingdon, 1983. Originally published: Oxford: Clarendon Press: Oxford: New York: Oxford University, 1983.

Kimbrough, S T, Jr., Carlton R. Young. Editors. *John Wesley's First Tune Book: A Collection of Tunes Set to Music. As they are commonly Sung at the Foundery.* London: A. Pearson, 1742. A Facsimile Edition with Introduction and Critical Notes. Madison, NJ: The Charles Wesley Society, 2011.

———. *John Wesley's Second Tune Book: Select Hymns with Tunes Annext: Designed chiefly for the Use of the People Called Methodists.* London: n.p., 1761. A Facsimile Edition with Introduction and Critical Notes. Madison, NJ: The Charles Wesley Society, 2015.

Holcombe, Henry. *The Musical Melody, or a Collection of English Songs and Cantatas, Set to Musick by Henry Holcombe.* [London,1755]. https://books.google.com/books?id=2s_jc0BO0M8C&printsec=frontcover&source=gbs_ge_summary_r&cad=0#v=onepage&q&f=false.

Laguna, Daniel Israel Lopez. *Espejo fiel de vidas que contiene los Psalmos de David en verso obra devota.* London: Con licencia delos Señores del Mahamad, y aprovacion del Señor Haham, 1720.

Lampe, John F. *Hymns on the Great Festivals, and Other Occasions.* London: M. Cooper, 1746. Facsimile reprint, Madison, New Jersey: The Charles Wesley Society, 1996.

Leach, James. *A new set of hymns and psalm tunes: adapted for the use of churches, chapels, & Sunday schools, with accompaniments, & a thoro' bass: the whole figured for the organ, harpsichord or piano-forte.* London, 1789.

Lightwood, James T. *Methodist Music of The Eighteenth Century.* London: Epworth, 1927.

Madan, Martin. *A Collection of Psalm and Hymn Tunes Never Published Before . . . to be had at the Lock Hospital.* London, ca. 1763, 1769.

"Methodist Music," *Grove Music Online.* Accessed August 18, 2018.

Miller, Edward. *David's Harp: Consisting of about Three Hundred Tunes adapted to Mr Wesley's Selection of Hymns, One hundred of which tunes are originals composed expressly for this work by Edward Miller Doctor in Music and his son W. E. Miller with an appendix containing pieces for the practice of societies of singers, also adapted for domestic use on the pianoforte on a Sunday evening.* London. Printed for R. Lomas at the New Chapel, City Road, and may be had at Broderip and Wilkinson in the Haymarket, or of any Music or Bookseller in the Kingdom [ca. 1803].

Minutes of several Conversations between The Reverend Mr. John and Charles Wesley and Others. From the year 1741, to the Year 1780. London: J. Paramore, 1780.

More, Henry. *Divine Dialogues with Divine Hymns.* London: James Flesher, 1668.

Norris, Clive. "The Economics of Methodism in the Long Eighteenth Century." A paper presented to the Economic History Society Annual Conference. London. April 1, 2017.

Nuelsen, John. *John Wesley and the German Hymn*. Trans. by A. S. Holbrook. Calverley, Pudsey, Yorkshire, 1972.

Playford, Henry. *The Divine Companion*. London: W. Pearson, 1705.

Sandys, George. *A Paraphrase upon the Psalms of David*. London: A Roper, 1676.

Scholes, Percy A.; John Owen Ward. Editors. *The Oxford Companion to Music*. London; New York, Oxford University, 1970.

Tate, Nahum and Nicholas Brady. *A New Version of the Psalms of David*. 2nd edition. London: M. Clark for the Company of Stationers, 1698.

Temperley, Nicholas. *Hymn Tune Index* "Sacred Harmony,'" code, #SHCCPH a, http://hymntune.library.uiuc.edu/.

——. "The Lock Hospital Chapel." *Journal of the Royal Musical Association*, 44–72. Vol. 118, No. 1. [Oxford, UK, 1993]. http://www.jstor.org/stable/766542.

——. *The Music of the English Parish Church*. 2 vols. Cambridge, UK, 1979.

Toplady, Augustus. *Psalms and Hymns for Public and Private Worship*. London: Printed by E. and C. Dilly, 1776.

Watson, Richard. *Theological Institutes: or a view of the evidences, doctrines morals and institutions of Christianity*. 3rd edition. London, 1829.

Watts, Isaac. *Horae Lyricae*. London: Humfreys, 1709.

——. *Hymns and Spiritual Songs*. 2nd edition. London: John Lawrence, 1709.

——. *The Psalms of David*. London: Clark, Ford, & Cruttenden, 1719.

Wesley, Charles, Jr. *Sacred Harmony, a set of Tunes Collected by the late Rev. John Wesley, For the Congregations in his Connexion*. London: T. Blanchard, 1822. The Preface dated November 3, 1821.

Wesley, John. *A Collection of Hymns for the Use of the People Called Methodists*. London: J. Paramore, 1780.

——. *A Collection of Tunes Set to Music. As they are commonly Sung at the Foundery*. London: A. Pearson, 1742.

——. *A Pocket Hymn Book for the Use of Christians of all Denominations*. [London: Paramore], 1785.

——. *Sacred Harmony, or a choice Collection of Psalms and Hymns Set to music in two or three parts for the Voice, Harpsichord & Organ*. [London: np],1780.

——. *Select Hymns with Tunes Annext. Designed Chiefly for the Use of the People Called Methodists*. London: np, 1761.

——. *The Character of a Methodist*. Bristol: Farley, 1742.

Wesley, Samuel, Jr. "Hymn to the Trinity." *Weekly Miscellany*, 2. Vol. 89 (August 24, 1734. Reprinted with title "An Hymn to the Trinity, Three Persons and One God," 6–7. In his *Poems on Several Occasions*. London: E. Say, 1736.

Wesley, Samuel, Sr. *The Pious Communicant Rightly Prepared, or a Discourse on the Blessed Sacrament*. London, np, 1700.

Whitefield, George. *Journal of a Voyage from London to Savannah.* London: Hutton, 1738.

Wickens, Stephen B. *The Life of Rev. Richard Watson.* 2nd edition. New York: G. Lane, 1845.

Woods, Rollo G., Sally Drage, and Francis Roads "West Gallery Music," *Canterbury Dictionary of Hymnology,* https://hymnology.hymnsam.co.uk/w/west-gallerymusic?q=West+Gallery+music.

Young, Carlton R. *Music of the Heart: John Wesley and Charles Wesley on Music and Musicians.* Carol Stream, IL: Hope Publishing Company, 1995.

Zinzendorf, Nikolaus Ludwig von. *Das Gesang-Buch der Gemeine in Herrn-Huth.* [Herrnhut]: Wäysen-hause, 1735.

www.ingramcontent.com/pod-product-compliance
Lightning Source LLC
Chambersburg PA
CBHW071139300426
44113CB00009B/1014